A Story of the

Written by Dan Roberts

Illustrations by Carol Dufficy & Steve Grover

6741

CENTENNIAL STATE

EAGLE TAIL PRESS
Box 3128
Grand Junction, Colo.
242-0995

I

to

MARY

TABLE OF CONTENTS

TABLE OF ILLUSTRATIONS

V

TABLE OF ILLUSTRATIONS—Continued

Name in parenthesis denotes artist or credit.
(Div. of Comm. & Dev.)—State of Colo. Division of Commerce and Development.

TABLE OF MAPS

HON. RICHARD D. LAMM
Centennial Governor

VIII

A Forewarning

The diversity of Colorado, the Centennial State, makes it many different things; its geography is actually two geographies—one an eastern plain that gradually tilts westward and upward to address the mountainous western section that represents the other physical rampart of the state. Two histories are the product of this physical disparity, one that of the trapper and the miner who first challenged the mountains for their bounty; the other saw the cattlemen as the first arrivals and tested their mettle against the whims of Mother Nature on the trackless plains. On the footsteps and failures of their predecessors the steady, more durable farmer followed into both of these regions. With the farmer came civilization and the final taming of the land, but it was not easy.

Two histories and two geographies, the cultural development is even more confusing because there are three to contend with and with each other. The various Indian tribes were the first to come and, although their cultures were vastly different, they added a composite to the cultural picture and made more contributions than is realized. The first to interrupt the quietude of the centuries by bringing in an alien culture were the Spanish who moved northward from their southern empire. The gold rush, first to California in 1849, unleashed the horde of Anglo settlers upon the unprepared Indian nations of the Rocky Mountains and made it three. The gold rush started in Colorado in 1859 and within ten years the plains Indians were relocated in the Indian Nation; eleven years later the Utes were moved to reservations and Western Colorado phased out its Indians. Change came fast to the West. It did not take very long.

In 1900, Congressman Edward T. Taylor, from Colorado spoke these words to the National House of Representatives:

It seems to me that it is time the Western States were inquiring whether or not they are hereafter to be treated as equal members of this Union or to be relegated to the position of federal provinces and governed by federal bureaus.

This federal merchantilism remains as an item of concern in the West today. It is particularly alarming in Western Colorado where there is not only the danger of federal overbearance, but the added threat of Western Colorado becoming the domain of energy consortiums and over-zealous Eastern Slope interests. The frustrations of seeing their destiny controlled and manipulated by forces in the East are not new to Westerners.

The unusual environment of the Centennial State is its most precious asset and priceless resource. The plant and animal life that thrives in this favorable locale are a part of this heritage and picturesque setting. One of the most impressive themes in any history of the Centennial State is the one that pits people against a rugged and challenging environment on the plains, as well as in the mountains. Meeting these challenges, winning some of the struggles and losing others, probably the majority, is the story of the state and its pioneers. It is a colorful account.

A good deal of this rugged environment remains to test people in another way, to preserve their environmental heritage, rather than to conquer and destroy the very last vestige of their historical heritage. This rugged environment, beautiful "back country", "safety valve country", or "escape country", maybe this is the proper appellation; regardless, it is the precious contrast that is so often sought and so eagerly devoured by those who have had too much of the hectic pace of urbanization.

Dinosaur country. What does it matter that huge behemoths once occupied the land? It is fascinating to realize that these huge reptiles shook the ground as they foraged for their enormous food supply in Western Colorado. In these huge footsteps followed, much later, Sandia, Clovis, Folsom and Yuma, the first people to arrive. Who were these people, where did they come from and what happened to them? Next, Anasazi, Ute, Comanche, Apache, Kiowa, Cheyenne and Arapaho entered the story and added their chapters. They, and the Spanish and Anglos that followed, are all part of the story. It is quite a story, consequently, no attempt will be made to complete the volume in this effort. What follows is a pictorial summary, only a beginning, intended to merely whet the appetite of the reader, but to leave the rest up to him for his enjoyment. Getting started is not difficult, for the environment of the Centennial State can eloquently speak for itself. Also, there are relics of the past scattered here and there, remnants of the past to furnish clues to what once was. Like a virtual historical Sherlock, the observer can reconstruct the past with the evidence at hand in the greatest classroom or crime lab there is and thoroughly enjoy his effort.

Herbert E. Bolton, one of the most eminent scholars of the American West, believed a more relevant knowledge of history can be gained by visiting the sites where history took place, suggesting history is more than a musty account of the sumtotal of man's existence to be written then shelved to gather dust. The "feel" or atmosphere of history enlivens the discipline and aids those who struggle to recover their heritage and past to do so in a more profound way.

As parking lots and shopping centers blight the landscape and the frantic struggle between main street and fringe shopping centers becomes more intense, historical landmarks, agriculture areas and the environment are bulldozed into oblivion in a reckless and heedless manner. In many towns and cities in Colorado, in the monotonous pursuit of material progress, little that would even suggest the past is left standing, therefore, people are obliged to trek to the old mining and ghost towns in search of some of their heritage with which to relate. The more rapidly change occurs, the quicker bygone institutions are destroyed, and people are left stranded in a limbo of meaningless transitory horizons with nothing of significance to cling to. The mining frontier is probably one of the more visibly intact historical frontiers, nevertheless, many of these vestiges of the past have already been destroyed or have undergone a commercialization that has undermined their characters until they no longer possess the rustic authenticity of their heyday. Somewhat ironic is the part history seekers play in this destruction by encouraging tourist traps and pressures that lead to the demise of their relics of history. The threat of these bastions of history continues unabated. Cripple Creek, Ouray, Telluride, Silverton, Victor and Lake City still retain much of their rustic charm and attract every year a host of tourists, searching for historical landmarks, roots and the "aura" of history.

Hopefully, now, as more people express an interest in the past, all the remnants of days gone by will not be destroyed in the Centennial State. City fathers are beginning to realize that old landmarks and historic sites attract more tourist dollars than asphalt jungles of zombie-like parking meters. Consequently, an effort to preserve, rather than obliterate these treasures, has emerged.

The Centennial State inspired the melody, "America the Beautiful" while the composer was standing on Pikes Peak. This comes as no surprise to Colorado residents, as they are acutely aware of the beauty of their environment and are anxious to preserve this setting.

The beauty, uniqueness and diversity of Colorado make the state an ideal setting for a course of the history of Western America in microcosm, because all physical features and events in the panorama of this history reveal themselves in the Centennial State. Mountains and plains, deserts and lakes, cowboys and Indians, miners and promoters, sheepmen and sodbusters, the whole group passed into Colorado following the direction of the setting sun.

Lack of boundaries make it necessary to approach this study as a regional history. The artificial boundaries that do surround Colorado are sometimes ridiculed as an attempt to set apart the state and establish it as a unique topographical entity; however, there are real advantages to the historian and geographer, as well as others, in this arbitrary limiting and delineating, for it simplifies classification and study. At any rate, the central location and diversity of Colorado forces the regional approach, and history has a tendency to transcend limiting factors such as boundaries, even if they are natural ones. Almost any geographic, topographic, climatic, or cultural phenomenon found in the Western United States can also be located in the Centennial State. Consequently, a study of the history of the State adds a meaningful awareness and broadens the knowledge to the extent that it carries over to surrounding states and regions.

A more significant and interesting note is the role of Colorado as a cultural crossroads, a role which has superseded much of the other history or permeated its account. The Centennial State from its infancy to the present has been a predominant center of the merging Anglo, Indian, and Spanish civilizations. The dominant culture of the United States is Anglo; however, the prevailing culture, or way of life, in the Southwest is Spanish; Colorado is geographically situated in the vortex of these two cultures. Indian culture was, and is, very much present in Colorado, although, tragically, most of Colorado's Indians have been relocated in Utah, Oklahoma, or the "happy hunting grounds". The record of progress in resolving cultural conflicts has not been impressive in the past, however, current circumstances provide Coloradans with a splendid opportunity to improve the relationships of all cultures within the state and at the same time furnish to the rest of the country an example that is worthy of emulation.

The author has frequently been perplexed and disturbed by historical efforts that fail to provide adequate charts and maps for the reader who desires a perspective other than the written word; therefore, an effort has been made to furnish sufficient additional materials to enlighten and reinforce written material and, at the same time, serve as guides in the acquisition of the "feel" of history in the Centennial State.

A historiographic passion is easy to acquire, moreover, the formidable nature of the task suggests an early start, plus all the assistance possible. A good many have been studying the history and exploring the ramparts of the Centennial State for a lifetime and wish they had more time to continue this pleasant pastime.

The history of the Centennial State is a study of people, as well as a study of a geographical creation. Yuma, Folsom, Indian, Spanish, French, American or what have you, all have attempted to live within the demands of the environmental challenges offered by a varied topography and climate. Some succeeded, where others failed to meet the test. Although predecessors of modern Coloradans made more adjustments to their environment, while modern man has been more inclined to attempt to adjust the environment to his ambitious demands, an environmental balance must, nevertheless, be maintained. The passing of these previous cultures attests to the transitory nature of human existence and reveals vividly the price paid when man is unable to live harmoniously with his surroundings. The Colorado environment must now prepare for its most challenging test. As energy companies flex their bulging political muscles to browbeat the public into "going easy" on pollution and use requirements, along with contrived shortages and announcements of their unusual expenses at a time when profits are highest ever, a long, questioning look is needed into the activities of these industries and their service to and usage by the public.

The author purposely chose to use full-size pages to make the maps and charts larger and, subsequently, easier to read and use. Student artists, Steve Grover, Carol Dufficy, Jim Miller, Mike Downing, Marilyn Rottinghaus and Barry Tarter, students at Mesa College, have provided the excellent illustrations for this text. Their efforts to capture the faces and emotions of the Centennial personalities of the past have been successful and characterize the sturdy countenance of these pioneers that labored so diligently. Many of these excellent drawings would make ideal pictures for framing. In the pictures or the written word, no attempt has been made to embellish or glamorize. The topic can survive on its own; also, the simplest explanation with the minimal amount of verbage is the most useful.

It would be difficult for the author not to reveal prejudices acquired from a lifelong residency of Western Colorado, however, a sincere effort of impartiality was attempted. This historical summary can not tell the complete story, therefore, the selectivity necessary may turn to what is familiar or favored by the author. A topical approach seemed the best approach to avoid the tedium of a chronological, blow-by-blow, depiction, and the emphasis has been placed on people rather than places and politics. It would be impossible to avoid the grand design of history and the currents that shape the events and influence the history of even an isolated mining enclave of the 1860s.

The author is indebted to the efforts of those who have aided the compilation of this book. The many students of Colorado History at Mesa College, an understanding wife and family that have seen their vacations maneuvered to exploration of the Centennial State; the State Historical Museum, the Denver Public Library and other museums of the state for supplying pictures and materials. The author is deeply indebted and grateful to those who showed an interest and lent a hand with this work.

1—THE SETTING

Colorado's most precious and unique resource is its environmental setting. The diversity and grandeur of the topography of The Centennial State endows it to the extent that residents and the Chambers of Commerce of the various cities and towns do not find embellishment necessary to impressively describe their state to non-residents. It is fitting and proper and, moreover, crucial to do everything possible to continually assure the existence of this natural endowment. The "look, but do not touch" approach is no more realistic than the attitude of aggressive developers, industries or land users who disdainfully regard ecologists as hair-brained idiots. Wise use of land and resources with minimal harmful impact is possible; meanwhile, the claim that these precautions increase the cost of development to prohibitive levels does not take into consideration the long-range costs which carelessness can cause, plus the deprivation of future generations of resouces and an enjoyable environment.

Theodore Roosevelt, the first conservationist in the White House with a voice forceful enough to be heard, averred, "To disregard future generations and their rights by depriving them of their fair share of natural resources or the willful destruction of the land before they have ample opportunity to enjoy its grandeur would be the grossest neglect on the part of the present generation."

Topographically, the Centennial State is two distinct regions—the eastern two-fifths consists of a sloping, almost treeless, plain that begins on Colorado's eastern border at an elevation of about four thousand feet and gradually tilts westward and upward until it reaches an altitude of approximately seven thousand feet, where, caressing the feet of the Rockies, it joins the Front Range. These Rockies serve as a spectacular dividing rampart between Eastern and Western Colorado as they thrust skyward on their way north or south through the midsection of the Centennial State. The plains section helps to form the western perimeter of the center of America's Great Plains, consequently, making Eastern Colorado more akin geographically to the Great Plains States than to Western Colorado, which comprises the other three-fifths of Colorado.

It is helpful to the student of history and geography to designate the western edge of the plains of Colorado as the Colorado Piedmont. This fifty-mile-wide strip contains the principle cities, the political and educational centers, most of the industry, the capitol and population center.

The Rockies divide The Centennial State east and west, but, because of the mountainous nature of the western slope, the Rockies are included in Western Colorado. West of the Rockies the land gives way to mesas and plateaus that are broken by deep valleys. The rugged San Juan Mountains—the most rugged in the contiguous United States—are an obvious exception to the previously stated condition. The Centennial State has the highest average altitude of any of the connected states. The admission of Alaska to the Union in 1959 pushed aside the superlatives that the Centennial State enjoyed for seventy-three years in the altitude category. There are forty-nine peaks in Colorado with an altitude exceeding fourteen thousand feet, with the average elevation over all being sixty-eight hundred feet and the highest peak, Mt. Elbert (14,431), is located near Leadville.

Artificial boundaries that surround Colorado are superseded by these natural delineating features within the state that clearly set off one part of the state from another; therefore, as soon as a basic awareness of these ramparts is known, it is a simple matter to recognize the regions and divisions. Superimposed on the map of Western Colorado are five mountain ranges. These five principal mountain ranges of The Centennial State are the Front Range, the Park Range, the San Juans, the Sangre De Cristos and the Sawatch Range. Because of its central location, Colorado is a land-oriented state with no water transportation to speak of and no contact with oceans or other countries. In the past, many have tried to navigate the Colorado River; accordingly, an attempt was made in California to run steamships up the river from its mouth, but it ended in failure. To suggest that water is not a topic of interest in this state would be an illusion. The Continental Divide roughly follows the Park, Sawatch and the San Juan Ranges as it meanders through Colorado, frequently becoming a source of confusion because it is often regarded as a geographical barrier, rather than the separation of watersheds which it actually is, though not always being the highest point or ridge. Rivers that originate east of the divide flow into the Atlantic, and those that originate on the western side of the divide pour out into the Pacific.

More great rivers start in Colorado than in any other state. Three of these—the Platte, the Arkansas and the Rio Grande—flow into the Atlantic. The Colorado, called the Grand until the 1920's, flows

into the Pacific. These four rivers and the five mountain ranges provide helpful delineations for Colorado. The rivers all have their sources in the mountains near the center of the state and are a constant cause of strife with adjacent states. These water problems are compounded because of the arid nature of much of Colorado and other Rocky Mountain states.

Other land divisions that are useful besides the mountains, plains and the Piedmont are parks, plateaus, mesas and valleys. These features are related to mountains and are found in central and western Colorado. There are more than one thousand mountains in the Centennial State that rise over ten thousand feet; the lowest elevation is near Holly, at 3,385 feet.

The four mountain parks are easily discerned on the map and were at one time lakes; consequently, they have a smooth surface like the bottom of a lake. They all have elevations of 7,000 to 8,000 feet, too high for tended agriculture, but generally support pastoral or grazing agriculture. These parks are centrally located and follow a line from north to south between the two main mountain ranges. North Park is directly south of the Wyoming border and is about forty miles long and thirty miles wide. Walden is the park's main town and agriculture is limited to grazing because the climate is dry and cold in the winter. This park's isolated nature, its small population and scenic attractions make it an ideal vacation spot.

Inasmuch as Middle Park is small with an irregular surface, its designation as a park is questionable. It is the only park on the Pacific side of the Continental Divide; the Colorado River has its source there where Grand Lake and the surrounding mountains offer some of Colorado's most scenic attractions. Granby, Kremmling and Fraser are located in the park or nearby. During the winter months Fraser brings the Centennial State more than its share of adverse publicity when its low is the lowest in the nation, second only to Nome, Alaska or Hudson's Bay. South Park is close to the middle of the state, about seventy miles long and sixty miles wide. It is thinly populated, although it is not isolated. Several early gold-mining operations, generally the placer variety, brought people into the area in the late 1850's. The Reynolds Gang is reputed to have stashed $80,000 in loot in the north end of South Park in Handcart Gulch; supposedly, the loot has never been located. Fairplay is the area's principal city.

The San Luis Valley at one time was a great lake with an altitude of 7,000 to 8,000 feet, but here

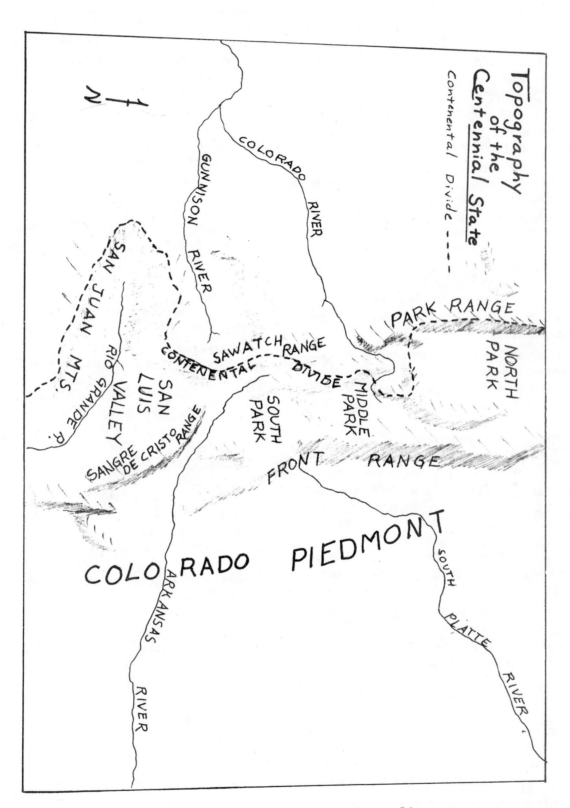

Topography of the Centennial State

Contenental Divide - - - -

COLORADO RIVER

GUNNISON RIVER

SAN JUAN MTS.

RIO GRANDE R.

SAN LUIS VALLEY

CONTENENTAL DIVIDE

SAWATCH RANGE

SANGRE DE CRISTO RANGE

SOUTH PARK

MIDDLE PARK

PARK RANGE

NORTH PARK

FRONT RANGE

COLORADO PIEDMONT

ARKANSAS RIVER

SOUTH PLATTE RIVER

N

the typical characteristics of Colorado's mountain parks no longer apply. The southern location of the valley makes tended agriculture an integral part of its industry; in addition, its size is greater than the other parks. Nevertheless, the valley does have many of the necessary features to be classified as a park. There are more people and more cities here; moreover, the first white settlers to enter Colorado came to the San Luis Valley in 1848 as a result of the Treaty of Guadalupe Hidalgo. Alamosa, Monte Vista and Conejos are some of the valley's principal cities, but their southern location does not prevent cold winters at that altitude.

These main topographical features—the Front, Park, Sawatch, San Juan and Sangre De Cristo mountain ranges; the Colorado, Platte, Arkansas and Rio Grande rivers; North, Middle and South parks and the San Luis Valley, the Continental Divide and the Colorado Piedmont can easily be located on the accompanying map. There are many other features that are significant, but the basic distinctions mentioned above will be adequate for the early history of the Centennial State; others will be mentioned later.

The Centennial State is amply blessed with a mild and diverse climate; therefore, tornadoes, cyclones, earthquakes or other major natural disasters are uncommon. The mean annual temperature is 44 degrees Farenheit, similarly, this is but slightly lower than the average temperature at the same latitude on the western seacoast. Temperature records reveal extremes of 54 degrees below zero in 1913 and a torrid 115 in 1888. The average temperature, however, is misleading; the temperature range gives a more accurate picture. The temperature differentiation between day and night, winter and summer, or between highest and lowest, is more pronounced than regions of the same latitude east or west of the Centennial State.

The Indian summers of the Centennial State are beautiful, sometimes lasting into November, and provide a lingering time for relaxation out of doors. It extends the lovely illusion of perpetual summer—perhaps making the inevitable harshness of winter a bit more bearable. Winters can be mild, or they can be equally severe. Often the warm Chinook winds sweeping down from the mountains can melt a heavy snowfall as if by magic. Changes of temperature upward at a rate of thirty degrees an hour have been recorded as a result of these Chinooks.

These temperature ranges which provide cool evenings and pleasant nights in the summer months are abetted by the dry climate and rarefied atmos-

phere. The climatic attraction of the high and dry nature of the Centennial State was the beginning of the now significant tourism industry in Colorado. Numerous early settlers, including the notorious "Doc Holliday," came to Colorado, at least partially, for reasons of health. Persons with respiratory and circulatory problems sought the change of climate for beneficent purposes, hence, adding to the number of settlers. A good number of these hopeful health seekers were fortunate enough to regain their health and many of the early settlers of Colorado were of this group. Chambers of Commerce did not hesitate to extol the virtues of Colorado's climate, sometimes making claims that the air or water possessed curative qualities, thus entreating potential settlers to come while they still had a chance to be saved.

Rainfall and humidity vary according to the topographical diversity found in the regions of the Centennial State. In some of the mountain regions, rainfall exceeds forty inches annually; nevertheless, the seventeen inch average as a whole classes Colorado as an arid state. This aridity is also noticable in the humidity, because the average relative humidity is only thirty-nine percent. There is a direct corelation between atmospheric humidity and human sensitivity to heat and cold. This explains the more acceptable tolerance of heat in the summer and how it is possible to suffer frostbite before an awareness of the extreme temperature occurs.

The fall of moisture varies as much as the temperature in location and patterns of distribution. Steady rainfall, the norm of the tropics, seldom describes Colorado, where the rain is more likely to come in the summer as thundershowers. Around Denver, seventy percent of the precipitation falls in the months from April to September; also, more rain and snow fall on the western slope of the Continental Divide, as the cooler mountains harvest the clouds before they can reach Eastern Colorado. The converse situation of more water in Western Colorado and more population in Eastern Colorado has resulted in numerous water diversion projects.

"Colorful Colorado." This title could refer to red mountains, blue skies, green lakes, black forests or awesome sunsets. The word "Colorado" is a Spanish word meaning reddish, rosy or colorful, this might also suggest the Spanish, Anglo and Indian cultural heritage of the Centennial State. The rugged and shining mountains and windswept plains call to mind a determined and colorful people that matched their wits and risked their fortunes in this demanding setting. They were a "colorful" group, indeed.

DENVER

Counties labeled on the map include:

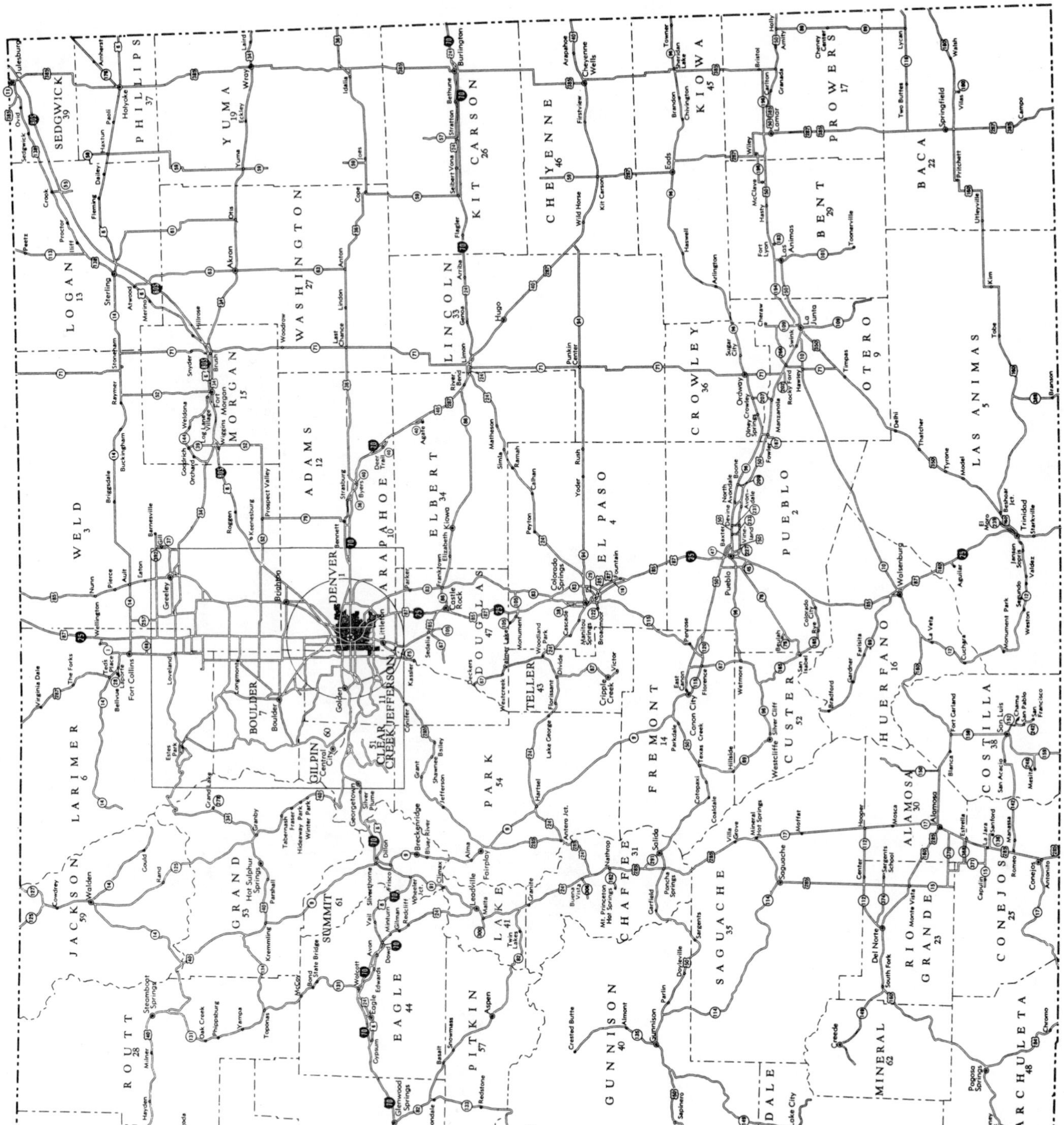

SEDGWICK 39 · PHILLIPS · YUMA 19 · LOGAN 13 · WASHINGTON 27 · MORGAN 15 · WELD 3 · LARIMER 6 · JACKSON 28 · ROUTT · MOFFAT 42 · RIO BLANCO 40 · GARFIELD 24 · GRAND 53 · BOULDER 7 · GILPIN · CLEAR CREEK 51 · JEFFERSON 11 · ADAMS 12 · ARAPAHOE 10 · ELBERT 34 · LINCOLN 33 · KIT CARSON 26 · CHEYENNE 46 · KIOWA 45 · PROWERS 17 · BACA 22 · BENT 29 · OTERO 9 · CROWLEY 36 · PUEBLO · EL PASO 4 · DOUGLAS 47 · TELLER 43 · PARK 54 · SUMMIT 61 · EAGLE 44 · PITKIN 57 · LAKE 41 · CHAFFEE 31 · FREMONT 14 · CUSTER 52 · HUERFANO 16 · LAS ANIMAS 5 · COSTILLA · ALAMOSA 30 · SAGUACHE 35 · GUNNISON 40 · DELTA 18 · MESA 8 · MONTROSE 21 · OURAY 56 · HINSDALE 63 · MINERAL 62 · RIO GRANDE 23 · CONEJOS 25 · ARCHULETA 48 · SAN JUAN 55 · SAN MIGUEL 30 · DOLORES 58 · LA PLATA 20 · MONTEZUMA 32

Mount Elbert   Elev. 14,433 ft.

2—THE FIRST NORTH AMERICANS

People evolved and developed during the ice age, then propagated their kind throughout Africa and Eurasia before the last ice age was over. The Pleistocene, or last ice age, saw the emergence and triumph of humans in North America, where they were not indigenous. It began about 50,000 years ago and ended about 10,000 B.C. The arrival of bipeds in North America, plus their route of migration, are subjects that inspire interest and conjecture. Archaeologists and anthropologists have been trying to put together the pieces of this complex puzzle for many years. It is impossible to do justice to a topic of this magnitude in this volume, however, it is too important to avoid, even if the way is foggy.

The often suggested route of mortals to America and their probable place of origin is to start in Asia with Mongoloid peoples, then bring them to America, over land or ice bridges that were only fifty to sixty miles long. These early transplanted Asians became the ancestors of the American Indians, who were also Mongoloid. The simplicity of this story may be one of the reasons it is frequently challenged and also for the appearance of many other theories that have many elements of credibility; however, all Asian people are not Mongoloid, and there is evidence that some of the early Ameri-

can Indians were mixed racially. The Caucasian Ainu aborigines of the Japanese Archipellago present some interesting possibilities; moreover, there are many other loop-holes in the Bering Strait theory, although it remains the most commonly accepted. These early inhabitants of North America have been considered inferior to modern people, because Homo Sapiens developed much later. Therefore, there was marked evolutionary improvement during the twenty or thirty thousand years of maturation. It is a natural trait of contemporaries to assume they are the ultimate apex of their culture.

North America was sufficiently hospitable to accept humans by 50,000 B.C., when people arrived sometime between then and 20,000 B.C. by crossing these land bridges. It is estimated the level of the seas fluctuated as much as 300 feet between ice ages. If the glaciers that remain even today were to melt, the seas would rise 300 feet and inundate large areas below 300 feet elevation. A lowering of 300 feet would have exposed a land bridge that was 1,000 miles wide and hardly discernible as a bridge. The land bridge probably endured, off and on, for tens of thousands of years until a sudden rise in temperature about 10,000 B.C. melted the ice, causing the water to pour back into the sea and covering the passage bridge. However, human occupancy in North America is more significant than where these people came from or how they made their long journey.

Living or fossilized remains of human inhabitants in the western hemisphere are hard to find. Those that have been found have frequently been taken from their resting places by amateurs, making it difficult to link them with the artifacts that should help to tell their story. For some reason, the chemical conditions that create good fossilized remains are not prevalent in dry regions, and so few skeletons were preserved; however, an abundant supply of artifacts have been found and dated that substantiate the existence of many groups.

One of the thought-provoking questions regarding the Bering Strait hypothesis is how to explain a migration across North America when an ice field blocked the way. However, the Wisconsin ice sheet is known to have had two advance-retreat cycles. These cycles are memorialized by terminal moraines which mark their extreme edges of advance; therefore, these rubble piles reveal boulders that have been rudely relocated hundreds of miles from their origin. The glacial retreat period most likely to have provided for a Moses-like passageway through the ice field for Asian transients ended 25,000 years ago and removed physiographic barriers. It is known that the horse and camel evolved in the Americas and migrated to Asia, while the elephant, deer, elk and moose are originally Eurasiatic, but relocated in the Americas; consequently, a broad land bridge must have been open, toll-free, at frequent intervals during the Pleistocene Epic.

How accommodating to human existence was North America in 25,000 B.C.? The answer to this question will reveal the nature and ingenuity of the first trespassers on this virgin continent. One area of agreement suggests the ice sheets, with their cold air masses as companions, pushed normal storm patterns several degrees southward in latitude. The constantly cold air mass from the ice as it mingled with the warmer air from the south, caused a perpetual cold front near the southern edge of the ice. This condition tended to provoke greater than present precipitation for hundreds of miles southward. This would account for the many fossil lakes in areas presently arid. The fauna present were mammoth, reindeer, musk-ox, bison and many smaller species—the ideal setting for hunters. It would have been attractive to the wandering bands of hunters from the old world. Most likely human inhabitation began in North America with small groups of hunters in pursuit of drifting herds of game about 25,000 B.C.

In 1926, the Denver Museum of Natural History was excavating a site close to the southern border of Colorado in New Mexico and archaeologists found twenty-three big horned bison skeletons, along with nineteen points. The big horned bison has been extinct for about 8,500 years, consequently, this find, carefully dug and studied by competent scientists from many colleges and museums, set a new course in American pre-history. Many of the spear points were found embedded in the bison bone, meanwhile, the tail bones were missing, indicating the animals had been hunted, then killed, by hunters, next skinned and the tail removed, along with the skin, in the customary manner. Here was proof beyond question of the co-existence of Pleistocene life and toolmaking hunters. The most impressive significance of this discovery was the ultimate instigation of a search for more evidence in other places. Eventually, many more were found, some more ancient than this Folsom site. Most of the sites were located on the plains east of the Rockies, suggesting the bison—disappearing 8,500 years ago, the woolly mammoth—gone 10,000 years ago, the tapir and ground sloth—which became extinct about 9,500 years ago, also foraged on the plains much like the modern bison that replaced them.

The people that inhabited these sites have been classified as Yuma, Folsom, Sandia and Clovis because of different artifacts, mostly points, that were associated with them and the dates of their existence. Sandia and Clovis lived 18,000 to 20,000 years ago and hunted the woolly mammoth; Folsom hunted the giant big horned bison from 10,000 to 12,000 years ago; and Yuma lived 6,000 to 8,000 years ago and hunted the big horned bison, along with the modern bison. Yuma seems to be the last to pass from the scene, because many Yuma sites have been found in Colorado, Wyoming, Nebraska, Montana and South Dakota. The most famous digs in Colorado are the Lindenmeier, a Folsom site located near Fort Col'ins, and the Yuma site near Yuma.

The Lindenmeier site was excavated between 1934 and 1940, with many points, stone scrapers, blades, carved bones, beads and other artifacts being unearthed. Bones of extinct bison, camel and the woolly mammoth were among the 2,000 artifacts, but no human bones were found. The biggest mystery regarding Yuma and Folsom is their physical appearance. The Lindenmeier site is dated about 20,000 B.C. and is believed to have been occupied for about a thousand years.

The Folsom point presents another interesting dilemma because of the fluted or concave sides. Many purposes are suggested for this groove—made

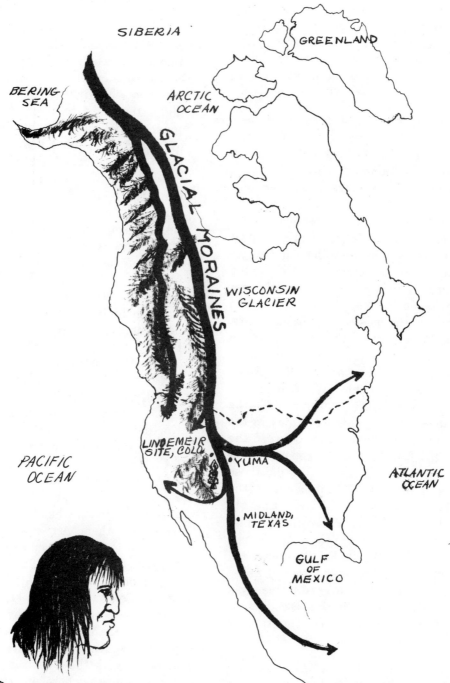

SIBERIA

GREENLAND

BERING SEA

ARCTIC OCEAN

GLACIAL MORAINES

WISCONSIN GLACIER

PACIFIC OCEAN

LINDEMEIR SITE, COLO.

YUMA

ATLANTIC OCEAN

MIDLAND, TEXAS

GULF OF MEXICO

Bering Strait Migration Route

with considerable effort—and maybe all of them are sound. Aerodynamics could be one reason, as the groove lightened the point, thus perhaps improving it, as in the case of the bayonet. The concavity improved its flight, or, possibly, the groove aided bleeding or the appearance of the point, or maybe made it easier to affix the point to the shaft. Most archaeologists favor the groove to accommodate the shaft because many Folsom points are dull near the shaft; therefore, this would prevent the thongs from being cut at this part of the point. Some Folsom points have grooves only on one side, while many have no groove at all.

The Yuma points were first recognized in a collection gathered at the Yuma site, were longer, without the groove, and the flaking was different. These points were later found at many other sites. New evidence frequently uncovers new questions. Scientists find it hard to agree on many of the riddles unearthed at the Yuma and Lindenmeier sites. Does the existence of two different points suggest two different cultures, or were they the same people using different points? Both points have been found at most Yuma and Folsom sites. Was Yuma the last of these prehistoric people? Yuma points continued to be made long after the demise of Folsom points. No pure Yuma or Folsom sites have been found; in addition, Yuma continues to the age of history at about 3,600 B.C. What is the connection between Folsom, Sandia, Clovis and Yuma? What, if any, is the connection between these cultures and the Anasazi Basketmakers that followed? How can the archaeological gap of about 3,000 years between the demise of Yuma (3,600 B.C.) and the appearance of Anasazi about 400 B.C. be explained? How did these primitive hunters hunt and kill animals like the woolly mammoth, the saber-toothed tiger, the big horned bison and many more? What finally happened to these people, and why did so many animals become extinct around 10,000 B.C.? These are questions that will occupy the imagination of many scientists for a long time. There are many fine texts that give deeper and more definitive accounts of prehistory that should be consulted for further information.

The pattern of habitation sites seems to indicate a gradual migration of these prehistoric hunters in a northerly direction as the climate warmed to invite such movement. The earlier Sandia and Clovis remains are found in Arizona, New Mexico and Southern Colorado. Folsom is not found too far north of Colorado, yet Yuma, the last of the group to appear and then disappear, leaves evidence of being in Wyoming and the Dakotas.

People have struggled with their environment for as long as they have existed; moreover, when they have been forced to do so, have made necessary adjustments for self-preservation. Culture is developed by people to protect themselves or help them adjust to their environment. Mortals came to North America when it was colder than it is now, accordingly, they had to wear clothing for warmth and found it necessary to hunt, there being an abundance of large animals for hides and meat, while plant food was scarce. Agriculture was yet unknown, so a culture was contrived to promote life in what would seem to be not the most friendly environment. A culture develops because of the need for an insulating protector between the humans and the demands of a rigorous environment. Such a culture is comprised of material objects, including tools, weapons, utensils, trinkets, clothing and shelter. Also essential, if less visibly apparent, are non-material possessions including beliefs, cults, habits and behavior patterns. These are the ingredients of a culture. People, in their self-righteousness, attempt to alter and modify their natural setting, hence, environment is a blend of natural and cultural elements. Progress in culture was necessary before a human challenge could succeed in the demanding environment of North America. The compromise between these two forces evidently occurred some time after 50,000 B.C. As this culture, or way of life, developed, it evolved and adapted to changes as they occurred. People have often struggled for a marginal existence with high stakes when the cards were already stacked against them. Any drastic change could suddenly bring an end to this marginal existence, which has happened many times in many places. Abandoned farms on the Great Plains, tumbling mine shacks in the Colorado Rockies or fading ghosts of towns that have been bypassed by the super highways are poignant examples of change. People come and people go, change is continual; either they learn to live at peace with their environment, or they must find a new one elsewhere or try to create an artificial one.

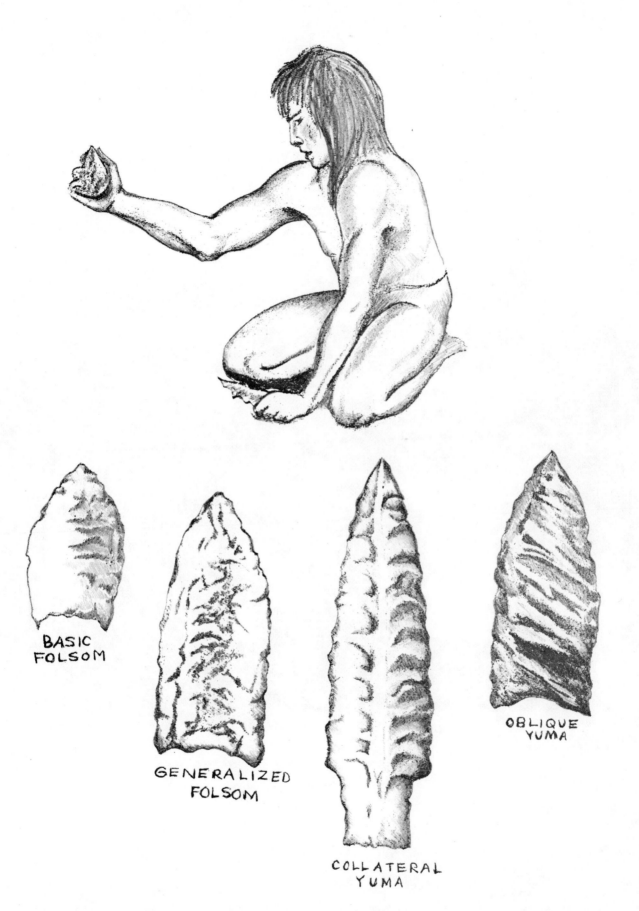

BASIC
FOLSOM

GENERALIZED
FOLSOM

COLLATERAL
YUMA

OBLIQUE
YUMA

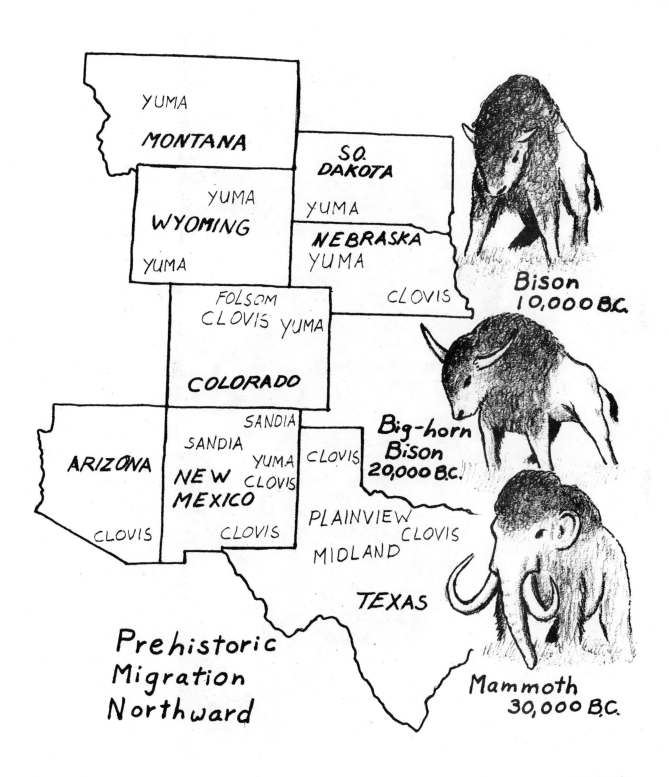

YUMA

MONTANA

S.O. DAKOTA

YUMA

WYOMING

YUMA

NEBRASKA

YUMA

YUMA

CLOVIS

FOLSOM

CLOVIS YUMA

COLORADO

Bison
10,000 B.C.

SANDIA

SANDIA

YUMA

CLOVIS

CLOVIS

ARIZONA

**NEW
MEXICO**

Big-horn
Bison
20,000 B.C.

CLOVIS

CLOVIS

PLAINVIEW

CLOVIS

MIDLAND

TEXAS

Mammoth
30,000 B.C.

Prehistoric
Migration
Northward

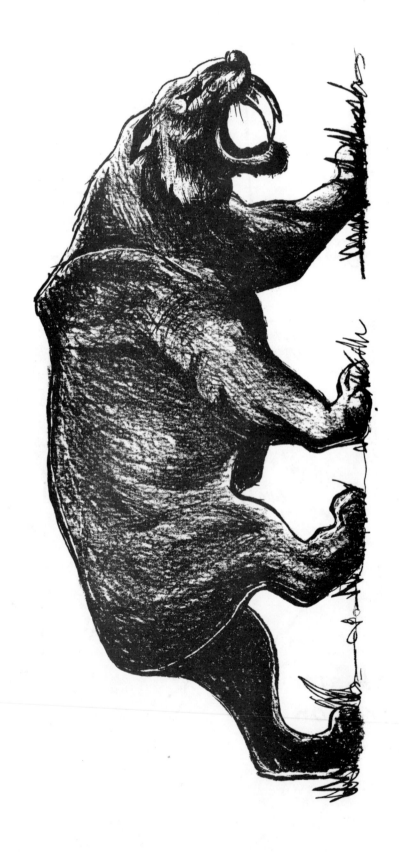

3—MESA VISTAS AND CANYON SANCTUARIES

When prehistoric people began to plant and harvest crops, they ceased to wander, became agriculturists and artisans then left a more permanent record of their existence, notwithstanding their lack of writing skills. The first agriculturists of Colorado were the Anasazi (Navajo word meaning ancient ones) people that came to the mesas of Southwestern Colorado, Northwestern New Mexico, Northeastern Arizona, and Southeastern Utah. Where these people came from is difficult to determine, but they left undisputed proof of their residency with their artifacts, moreover, unlike Folsom and Yuma man, an abundance of mummified bodies give evidence of their appearance and physical characteristics. After death, bodies were flexed, then buried or discarded in the dry soil of the Southwest where they dried and mummified, preserving hair and skin, plus revealing remote indications of facial features and color of skin. With the arrival of Anasazi, there is a continual evolution of human existence in Colorado with no apparent gaps to interrupt, as with the gap between Yuma and Anasazi.

The Anasazi appeared in what is now Southwest Colorado sometime before the birth of Christ, where their struggle began for a meager sustenance on the mesas above the canyons. To begin with, they were a poor, miserable people, living mostly on what they could gather, at the same time not even approaching the hunting capabilities of their predecessors, Folsom and Yuma man. Their standard of living did not make it possible for them to create any society, for they remained in small groups, moving about constantly, foraging for what they could find in the ground, on the ground, crawling on the ground, flying above or living on the ground. Sometimes, when they had no recourse, they ate the ground itself. They built brush wickiups, wore few, if any, clothes, were unable to protect themselves from their enemies, meanwhile, giving little indication of the strides about to be made by their descendants.

It was in this green tableland that their life began to take a turn for the better. Using the bow and arrow they had recently acquired, they became proficient hunters, stalked the deer in the mountains, set snares for rabbits and used nets to catch airborne game. This tableland, cut by steep canyons and covering 300 square feet, was to be their home for over 1,300 years. They were protected on the north and west by cliffs plunging 2,000 feet to the valleys below. They liked their new home; similarly, they appreciated the turnaround in their fortunes. They would make Mesa Verde their home, they firmly decided.

The next and most significant turning point in their lives was the beginning of the growing of corn. Historians debate the location of the first corn culture in the Americas and argue about the primacy of Mexico, Central America or Peru. Most seem to favor Mexico, where the Anasazi may have borrowed the use of corn from their neighbors to the south. Corn plants 60,000 years old have been found fossilized in rock, while other small ears of corn have been unearthed that were 3,000 years old. Europeans did not see corn until they arrived in America.

The beginning of agriculture heralded the beginning of the Basketmaker period, with the advent of a new and improved way of life for the Anasazi. The many baskets created to carry and store the corn lends the name to the people. Corn also occupied a central and sacred place in their religion, hence, altering their worship. Not a very prestigious name, "Basketmaker," but it was placed on their shoulders long after they departed, consequently, they had nothing to do with this label or no opportunity to protest. As they began to grow their multicolored Indian corn on the mesas—probably among the first people in North America to use irrigation — small communities evolved. As yields increased, the need for storage overtaxed the basket; therefore, to protect their calico corn from animals, caves were dug. They also used caves to live in, for the cyst or lined hole in the ground was the beginning of a basic structural unit that eventually evolved into a building above, or partially above the ground. Entrance was permitted by a hole in the roof, likewise, smoke exited from the same aperture.

Corn continued as the staple, with the addition of squash, beans and other food they could gather and hunt. The corn was ground on a metate, then cooked in clay-lined baskets by dropping heated rocks in a mixture of corn and water. This crude method of cooking left a lot to be desired, so it was soon improved upon. The Anasazi used nets to capture small animals and birds; darts were also used, while sometimes snares were made. The only sizable weapon was the atlatl, which was a crude, spear-throwing device that extended the length of the arm, then the safe end of the spear was placed in a slot and hurled. The weapon was a clumsy device, later abandoned in favor of the bow and arrow, or perhaps the art of using the atlatl was so difficult to master that it became a lost art.

The paucity of weapons, shields and fortresses among the Basketmakers enhances the thought that here was a peaceful, docile people who lived peacefully with reasonable prosperity, without fear of enemies. They were definitely not a warrior society, as were their successors.

They would not be the last residents of Western Colorado to feel secure in their isolated, sheltered mountain sanctuary. Their story resembles the Utes that arrived 1,200 years later, the story again of a backward and primitive people who found security and prosperity in Western Colorado, and similarly felt safe in their sanctuary, yet in a like manner were forced to move rather hurriedly.

The Anasazis were small and delicate in stature, with brown skin and black hair. Their height seldom exceeded 5 feet 8 inches, while many were much smaller. The larger Indians of America were located in the East. The Ute, like the Comanche, was much heavier built, but not markedly taller than the Anasazi. These desert farmers had little body hair, with the men wearing their hair long, the women wearing theirs short, probably because they used human hair to weave ropes and nets; therefore, characteristically, in the Indian value system, the privilege of parting with their hair was relegated to the women. The Anasazi were long headed, which gave rise to the suspicion that they were Caucasian, while there was a wide variance in the color of their skin. The use of the hard cradle board began with the Pueblo, but was soon replaced by the soft, more pliable cradle board the Basketmaker used. Maybe this is the best explanation of the difference in head shapes; likewise, it is the least complicated.

The Basketmaker skulls were distinctly different than the later appearing Pueblo. The Basketmakers' skulls were dolichocephalic—in other words, long in proportion to their width. On the other hand, Pueblo skulls, in addition to most native Americans, were brachycephalic, or simply broader headed. The backs of the Basketmakers' skulls were not flattened in the manner of the Pueblo, indicating they did not use the flat cradle board to carry their infants. It is complex to suggest two different types of people explain the discrepancy in skull shapes. The flat cradle board is easier to accept; however, if this be true, some remarkable evolutionary transition occurred.

It is time to classify the Anasazi for clarity. There were four periods in the Anasazi culture, starting with the Basketmaker I period from the time of Christ to 450; followed by the Basketmaker II period from 450 to 750; followed by the Pueblo I period from 750 to 1100; then ending with the Pueblo II period from 1100 to 1300.

The Basketmaker I period was the first, hence, also the slowest to progress. Agriculture, basket-

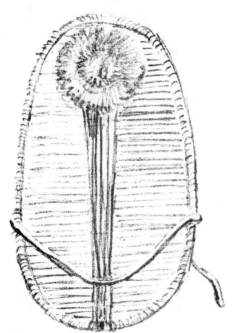

BASKET MAKER
CRADLE

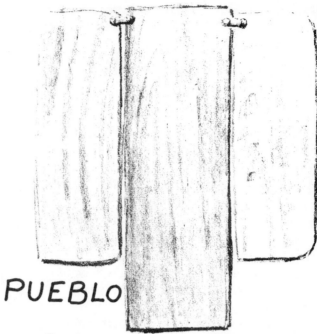

PUEBLO
CRADLE BOARD

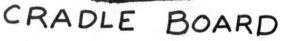

ATLATL

PIT HOUSE
CONSTRUCTION

making and improvement of dwellings were introduced; next, the Anasazi began to settle down to live a more stationary life. The cyst evolved into the pithouse, a house partially above and partly below ground.

The Basketmaker II era was one of more rapid progress, with the addition of the bow and arrow, pottery and more improvements in dwellings, along with other structural improvements. It is highly possible some of these innovations were introduced in the Basketmaker period, then gained wider usage, promotion and modification during the next stage.

The bow and arrow replaced the atlatl and gave the Basketmaker more fire power in his hunting, adding more meat to his diet. It was probably adopted from a nearby tribe. Turkey feathers began to appear in the cloth, in addition, they may have domesticated this large fowl. Many of the people of the Southwest had a fetish for jewelry, therefore, the Anasazi was no exception and were often found wearing beads, bracelets and many kinds of ornaments made from bones, stone, wood or anything available. However, the Anasazi culture did not include the ability to work with metal. The jewelry would seem to be of more importance than clothing, because most of the clothing was simple, with the men wearing little or no clothing, while the women wore small aprons. In the winter they added fur or hand-made robes.

Introduction of pottery was a great turning point, adding to the diversity of the diet, improving utensils, furthermore, giving expression in the form of art that the Anasazi had little opportunity to demonstrate before. Roaming hunters probably first saw pottery in some neighboring community, then returned to present it to their women with the blunt suggestion to duplicate the earthenware. By the process of trial and error, the pottery gradually improved. Clay is one of the most abundant materials on earth; a material to bind the clay together was sought, accordingly, a grey volcanic grit was used, giving the pots a dark grey color. The pots were made by the worm or coil method, smoothed, then left to dry in the sun. Later, dung was piled around them and ignited; eventually, crude kilns were devised. Toward the last of the Basketmaker II period, the women were making fine pots that could be used for cooking on a direct blaze; however, the Basketmaker never matched his basketmaking skill by their pottery making. Later, they were covering them with a light creamy veneer for adding designs to please the eye. They could now cook beans, along with other harder to cook foods, at the same time enjoying a more diversified diet. They could also

trade their surplus pottery for products they did not have, consequently, extending their agricultural economy by adding commerce. One of the products traded for was cotton.

The former pithouse now was built completely above the ground and ventilated with ingenious draft vents under the ground. The entrance remained in the middle of the roof, meanwhile, the houses were made of adobe bricks or stones with wood-supported roofs covered with grass.

The two Pueblo periods are noted for the improvement in masonry, while at the same time there appeared larger, more sophisticated dwellings and villages. The village pattern of life was now fully adopted, with more complex structures appearing. As masonry improved, the houses were plastered on the inside and stuccoed on the outside. Multiple buildings were fashioned by attaching several rooms or buildings together or putting one story above another. Pottery also improved with better kilns, creating smoother, lighter colored surfaces and more intricate design. Good textiles appeared, made out of a combination of cotton, yucca fiber, hair and turkey feathers put together on looms.

The Pueblo period is a separating point, because of the adoption of the unpadded cradle board that flattened the infant's head as it was carried by the mother. The purpose of this head-shaping remains a mystery; maybe it was a fad or it might have been unintentional. Revamping of the physique is nothing unusual in any age or among any people. The change in head shape is a helpful guide in determining the identity of Basketmakers and Pueblos.

The Pueblo II period, beginning in 1100, saw dramatic changes in the location of the living quarters. The villagers began to include watchtowers; the kivas were moved into the village yard. Featured were larger, better built buildings, set closer together and replacing many of the older, more scattered structures. Finally, about 1200, the Pueblos made their hasty exit from the mesas, which was followed by their incredible move to the canyon walls and recesses. The appearance or the threat of a new peril looms large as the reason for this tedious and insurmountable exodus. Marauding new tribes began to make their appearance—the Utes are the most suspect, being among the first recent Indian tribe to migrate to that region. The Comanche, Apache and Kiowa arrived a few generations later, adding to the threat. Internal strife is suggested as another possibility, but seems unlikely as a cause for such a drastic development.

The well-fortified new communities, plus the organization necessary to accomplish the task, make pressure from the outside a seemingly more credible deduction. Six to eight hundred cliff communities appeared and became the abode of the former mesa dwellers, who continued to farm the mesas, but resided in the cliffs. The amount of inconvenience that this move added to their lives is almost unimaginable. Any tourist that drives the winding highway to the Mesa Verde Park and gazes across the canyons at the elaborate and impressive structures appearing in the cliffs can only marvel at what must have transpired in those years in which these lofty apartments were occupied by such ingenious and industrious people. Whatever problems the Pueblo had before this shift were increased by their effort to gain security.

Living and moving in and about these canyon walls increased the stakes in their game of survival; therefore, narrowing that delicate line that makes it possible for man to endure in his environment. The Pueblo was now more susceptible to other threats in his monumental effort to avoid his enemies. The most sobering fact is the impermanence of the sojourn in the cliffs—the Pueblos stayed about a hundred years, then vacated the canyon walls, so their magnificent effort may have been in vain. About 1300 the Pueblos left the area, likewise, never returning to stay. This exodus is one of the most puzzling mysteries in the history of the Southwest. Why did they leave—a new threat of danger, drought, or was the life along the cliffs simply too taxing to continue? Speculating the reasons or motives of the human animal at any time, past or pres-

ent, is a risky pastime; secondly, a search for simple solutions is seldom successful. People generally take actions for a variety of reasons, rather than one or two; therefore, a combination of factors may well have been responsible for this exodus.

The appearance of the Apache and Comanche in the area at about that time made the threat of danger a popular consideration, because these renegades of the prairie were capable adversaries. A drought did occur before the evacuation, so it is a solid consideration for a cause, however, drought had occurred before without dislocating the Pueblo. Tree-ring readings by dendrochronologists also tell of the return of moisture by about 1311. When the moisture returned, why did the Pueblo remain in the south? Maybe they did return and then again abandoned the cliffs. Why did they apparently leave in such a hurry, leaving so much behind them? They are an interesting chapter in the history of the Southwest; in addition, they leave many unanswered questions to tantalize scholars of the present and future.

The first white man to view these abandoned dwellings was Escalante in 1776. In the 1880's two cowboys stumbled on the scene and, eventually, trained archaeologists began to investigate. Some of the first to climb the walls and visit the cliff communities were Finnish archaeologists, consequently, some of the best artifacts from Mesa Verde are to be found resting comfortably in the Helsinki Museum.

4—THE SKY PEOPLE

When the Spanish began to probe the vast expanse of their northern empire, they found six Indian tribes living in the area that is now Colorado. The Utes lived in most of Western Colorado, while the Apache were located in the southern part of the Western Slope; the Cheyenne and the Arapaho hunted on the plains north of the Arkansas River; the Comanche and Kiowa lived south of the Arkansas. These six modern Indian tribes of Colorado usually observed the sanctity of each others' territory, but occasionally they would trespass on their neighbor's land, which would frequently result in skirmishes or war. Some of the tribes were enemies of each other and some were allies. Some were linguistically related, but the Utes were generally the enemy of all the other Colorado tribes.

The Utes are called the "Sky People" because they lived in the Rocky Mountain valleys of Western Colorado. These indigenous Western Coloradan's called themselves the "Monts" but they were disdainfully called the "Black Indians" by other tribes. They were driven to these isolated areas by their

enemies, as no one else seemed to want these scenic valleys. Their territory overlapped into Utah, New Mexico and Wyoming, as did the other Indian lands. The boundaries the Indians used were more recognizable than the imaginary lines that became the boundaries of Colorado, because they consisted of mountain ridges and rivers.

The Utes were the first of Colorado's six major tribes to arrive and probably came from the North. Originally, they were much like the Anasazi before they became agriculturalists and began a corn culture. They were naked, dirty and miserable nomads that wandered about in small groups, foraging for what they could find, on the whole living on roots, berries, fish, grashoppers, ants, rats, and rabbits. The early Utes wore very little clothing winter or summer and had adjusted to the environment rather than developing a culture to soften its rigors. Wherever they went in their domain, they could travel light and move rapidly because they needed very little. They were the warrior tribe probably exerting some of the first pressure on the Anasazi, hence forcing their move to the cliffs.

No one seems to know for sure where the Utes came from except they came from the North. Their language resembled the Aztec's difficult and garbled tongue. The Athabascans pushed them around, especially the Navajo and the Apache. When they first came to the Western Colorado area, they lived in brush wickiups with no social structure, moreover they were a lowly tribe with very little political organization, thus scattered all over in small groups in isolated areas.

The Utes, by nature, were short, stocky and dark in appearance with round faces, therefore, were more mongoloid than the other Colorado tribes. They were members of the Shoshone branch, which included Snakes, Bannocks and Comanche as well as the Utes. The Utes were the most backward, likewise, weakest of the Shoshone group, therefore, were even despised by the other Shoshones. There was a large degree of variance in the appearance of the Utes; further some were taller, others varied in skin coloring, while others had straggly beards and generally differed in appearance. There was intermarriage among the different tribes, besides children were frequently traded, kidnapped or taken as prizes of war, consequently, blood mixing was not unusual.

Marshall Sprague ably describes the metamorphosis of the Utes in **Massacre, The Tragedy at White River.** The Utes had made some progress from their lowly beginning by 1600, moreover, they had the rudiments of tribal organization, were practicing some agriculture while, at the same time, trading deer hides with the Spanish and other Indians. The Utes were excellent butchers; amazingly, they cleaned the deer and boned it from the inside, leaving only the hide and meat to carry. When Santa Fe was established in 1609, with Taos shortly after, the buckskin economy of the Utes improved. The Utes heard of the Spanish and Santa Fe thus, naturally, were curious and anxious to visit. When they arrived in the most northern outpost in the Spanish empire, they took it all in with wide-eyed wonderment. Santa Fe was a dusty, dirty frontier town, a product of Spanish culture with the trappings of many such towns. The brown and black robes awed the Utes, later they noticed the church with its statues and processions. The blanket-clad Spanish culture with its cigarettes, peppers, onions, the gay atmosphere surrounding the cantina, next the soldiers with their muskets, were all new and amazing to the Utes. Their attention, however, was transfixed on the Spanish horses, moreover, they departed with one thought uppermost in their mind

—they had to have some of these wonderful animal for their own use. If they could add horses to thei already improving culture, it would increase thei mobility, meanwhile, adding greatly to their buck skin economy. Many historians argue whether or no the Utes were the first North American Indians t adopt the horse for their own use. The tribes of th eastern United States lived in wooded lands, hence forth, did not have the need for transportation as th tribes of the plains and mountains did. At any rate no people were more transformed by the addition o the horse to their culture than the Utes; similarly no people learned horsemanship quicker or adore horses any more than these horse-loving Utes. Th addition of the horse completely altered the natur of the Utes. The horse opened new vistas of free dom and respect, consequently, transforming th Utes from the ranks of the backward and lowly to more carefree and happy people. They discarded thei miserable past to become a happy, musical, poeti people full of dancing and mischief. Aware of thei debt to the horse for their better lives, they becam horse worshippers, accordingly, holding the horse i the same esteem as their family. They could neve reconcile themselves to eating horse flesh, as di many other tribes; at the same time the horse be came the measure of many things in the Ute valu structure. A man was judged by his horsemanship his wealth was determined by how many horses h owned; therefore, when he died he was expected t leave each of his sons ten or twelve if he was man of rank.

As the Utes acquired horses, they quickly an expertly mastered the skills of horsemanship, prob ably in a generation or two, to be matched in thi ability only by the Comanche. Gradually, all th Ute tribes added the horse to their culture, the they brought these ponies to the high mountai valleys of Colorado where they could eat the high protein grass of these picturesque mountain mead ows. The loving care, along with the new environ ment seemed to change the ponies so they becam larger, more nimble footed and stronger. This wa accomplished with very little effort on the part o the Utes, because the ponies were turned out t pasture in the high valleys in the summers and wer taken to the lower meadows in the winter.

These new, proud possessors of horses now sav their domain greatly extended, while the horse aided their buckskin economy by improving huntin in their own lands. It became easier to trespass o the land of the Cheyenne and Arapaho to hunt th buffalo, frequently enjoying a skirmish with thes proud warriors of the plains. The Utes could coun

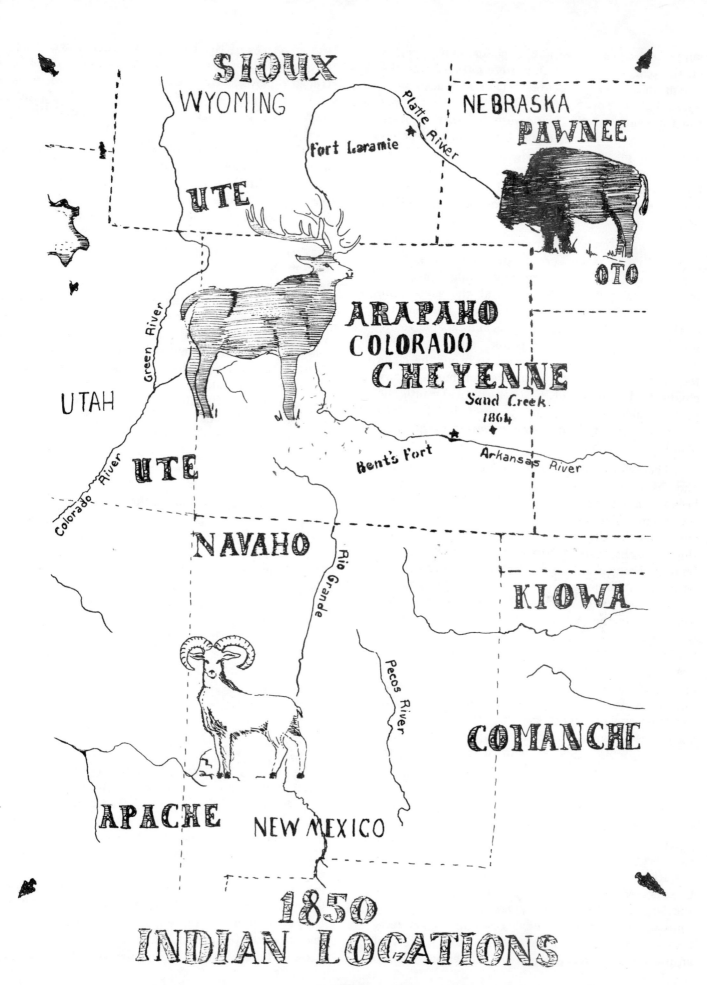

SIOUX

WYOMING

NEBRASKA

PAWNEE

Platte River

Fort Laramie

UTE

Green River

ARAPAHO

COLORADO

CHEYENNE

Sand Creek
1864

UTAH

Bent's Fort

Arkansas River

Colorado River

UTE

OTO

NAVAHO

Rio Grande

KIOWA

Pecos River

COMANCHE

APACHE

NEW MEXICO

1850
INDIAN LOCATIONS

on their horses to outdo the plains Indian ponies on the plains and, when they were pursued into the mountains, it was no contest. They expanded their buckskin trade to Santa Fe and Taos, which was the fur center of the Southwest, hence, they were no longer wandering nomads, but began to practice a vertical migration into the high valleys. They made more permanent winter camps in the low valleys or meadows, then headed into the mountains when spring came, searching for deer and other game.

As the Utes became more prosperous, they began to live in larger groups and develop political organization, with the promising young braves being given responsibilities, while at the same time being delegated to carry out the plans and policies of the elders. The more ambitious and capable young warriors maneuvered for power, and when this power was acquired, it was used to bring the clans together into bands of a hundred or more. Many chiefs tried to unite all the Utes politically into one people under leadership of one chief, but this was never accomplished among these carefree and freedom-loving people.

The "Sky People" continued to acquire horses and, as other tribes adopted the horse, the Utes became middlemen supplying the tribes surrounding them. The demand frequently exceeded the supply as the Utes bought horses from the Spanish then brought them north to the Nez Perce, Sioux, Snakes, Bannocks, Crow, Blackfeet, Cheyenne and Arapaho; it became more and more difficult to fill the demand. This horse trade and their buckskin commerce increased the contact with the Spanish, which was a significant force in the Ute way of life. Spain owned the territory of Colorado for many years, but did nothing to develop it except to send an occasional explorer to explore or look for gold. Spanish culture was carried into Colorado more by the Utes and other Indians than by the Spaniards themselves; when Spanish culture was finally brought into Colorado by whites, it came into the San Luis Valley from Mexico after Spain had lost its North American empire.

The Utes tried to remain on friendly terms with the Spanish and were generally successful, because they were the middlemen for the Spanish in the horse trade, so the Spanish were important to the Ute economy. As their economy improved, the Ute's standard of living was no longer limited to survival; the "Sky People" became aggressive capitalists, plying their trade wherever the opportunity presented itself. The horses were so expensive that an imbalance of trade occurred that seriously taxed the resources of the Utes. This problem was partially resolved by resorting to slave trade. The Utes traded captives from their enemies, or Navajo women or children, Paiutes from Utah, also Pueblo and half-breeds, but mostly Navajo, and frequently the Utes traded their own children to the Spanish. The Spanish used these captive Indians as laborers—the boys herded sheep, became vaqueros and did odd jobs around the hacienda. The women became house servants and sometimes worked in the fields herding. These servants were generally treated reasonably well by the Spanish because they wanted to convert them to Christianity, and they responded better when they were not mistreated. Some of the more articulate boys were educated in the church school and learned to read and write. Most of them learned to speak fair Spanish. This practice, more than any other, had its impact on the Utes, because when the servants grew up, they were freed and allowed to return to their own people where their training as an Indian began, or was resumed. The Ute culture had Spanish characteristics, therefore, this is probably one of the reasons the Utes were the last Indians to be forced out of Colorado. Ouray, the greatest Ute chief, spent his first seventeen years living and learning in this Spanish environment.

The transfiguration of the "Sky People" from backwardness and poverty to their new life took place in three or four generations. They now ranged widely and did not hesitate to hunt the buffalo. Their domain extended from the eastern Colorado plains to Salt Lake, and southern Wyoming to Taos. The White River Utes and the Yampa totalled about six or seven hundred; the Uncompahgres or Tabeguaches held the heartland of Western Colorado, totalling about 1,500, and were the most dominant of the Utes. In the southern reaches of the Ute land were located the Mauche, like the White River Utes—freedom loving and hard to regiment. The Mauches numbered about 500 and were located north of Taos. The Capotes were a small Navajo-like group of about 300, were peace-loving and quiet and lived near Mancos. South of the San Juans roamed the Weeminuches, who were a docile, peaceful group of about 500. There were several other small, scattered groups of Utes, some living in the mountains near Colorado Springs and Denver. The Ute population of what is now Colorado probably never exceeded 4,000 and may never have reached that number. The Utes left no written history, and information about them is sketchy. The Uncompahgres were the most advanced and best known, and Marshall Sprague, Wilson Rockwell, Al Look and a few others have endeavored to recapture

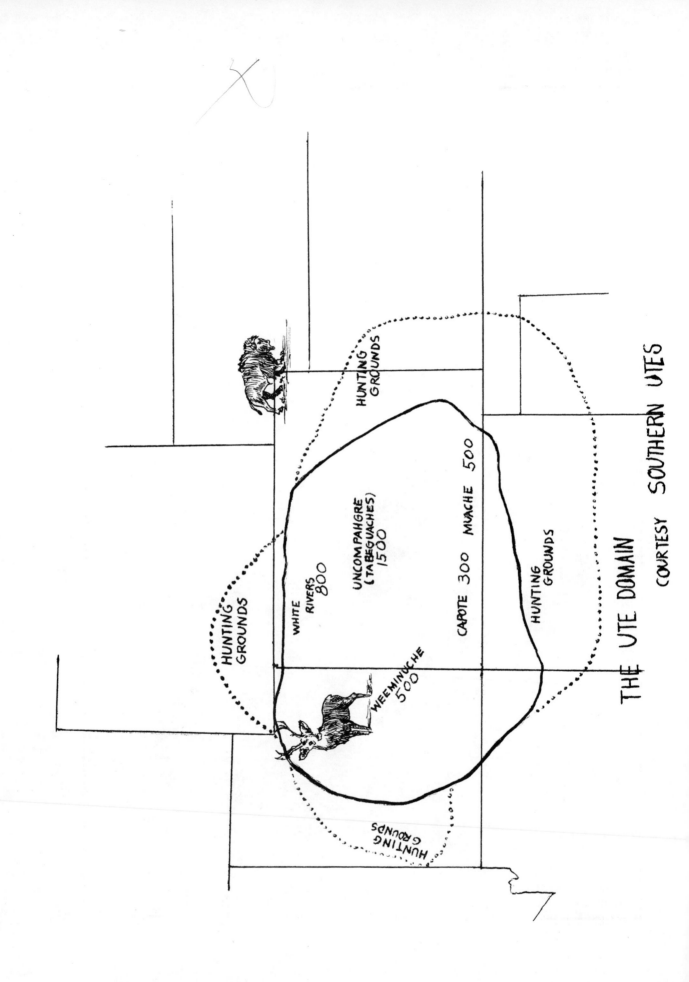

THE UTE DOMAIN

COURTESY SOUTHERN UTES

HUNTING GROUNDS

HUNTING GROUNDS

HUNTING GROUNDS

HUNTING GROUNDS

WHITE RIVERS 800

UNCOMPAHGRE (TABEGUACHES) 1500

WEEMINUCHE 500

CAPOTE 300 MUACHE 500

their past. The Memorial Museum at Montrose, Colorado has an excellent collection dealing with the Uncompahgres.

Ute Social Structure

Ute social practices varied, also little is known regarding most of them, therefore, because the ways of the Uncompahgres are better known, most of these descriptions would apply to these Gunnison River Utes. Universally, Indian children were loved and pampered until they were regarded as spoiled brats by most whites. The men were responsible for the training and rearing of the boys, while the women trained the girls in the tasks they would face in the future. The boys learned to care for weapons and horses, then became adept with both. The training of the young boys as warriors was supervised by the War Chief, who was generally a young chief who had proven himself as a warrior. The main chief was old and often referred to as the Peace Chief, and was in command except during the time of war. This is one reason the young war chiefs promoted war, because they could assume more power. The Utes had mixed emotions about corporal punishment; much like most Indian tribes, they believed the spirit of the young warrior would be damaged if he was whipped or punished physically. Their looser political and social organization prevented them from having prohibitions against such actions as other tribes, including the Cheyenne.

The Indian boy went through a puberty ritual at fourteen or fifteen, and at this time the blood of a mountain lion was rubbed on him, hopefully resulting in the assumption of the lion's traits by the boy. The Indian value system admired the stealth and cunning of the lion as well as its strength and speed. Most Indians concluded that stealth in dealing with the enemy was highly esteemed, for they had no compunctions about sneaking up on someone and doing them in. They considered it folly to expose themselves to fight out in the open; anyway, their shortage of warriors prevented them from doing so. This was another of the sources of misunderstanding between Indians and whites, although the whites soon learned guerilla warfare.

After the puberty rite the Indian became a man and was no longer a boy; he was now associated with the men and began his training as a warrior in earnest. There was no teen or "tween" age to deal with or period of doubting or experimentation; he was now an adult and was expected to act like one, as that was the main purpose of the ritual. After the ritual he was expected to sleep with an Indian girl that was pleasing to him. To the Ute beauty was measured by such things as small hands and feet (maybe another carry-over from the Orient), a well developed figure, long hair and shyness. Shyness was of exceptional importance because brashness and aggressiveness was not a trait admired by the Indian men in their women. The young brave could court his intended lover by serenading her with a hand-carved wooden flute and singing songs and riddles. He generally carried on this lamentation from the bushes near her tepee, when and if she was interested in the proposition, her assent was indicated by tossing a few pebbles in the direction of the serenade. This was an invitation to come to her tepee that night where her lover was expected to be quiet, not because it would wake her parents who were also in the tepee, but because it was considered crude to be rash and noisy about such things.

Many Indian tribes shared taboos about menstruation, therefore, the Utes were no exception. A blood tent was erected far enough from the village to avoid any ill effects, so women would go to this tent during their periods. If they rode a horse, it had to be an old, worn-out horse or it would be ruined by such use. The women at this time were cautioned not to touch weapons or hunting or fishing gear and were expected not to eat meat or fish for fear all these things would spoil the hunting and fishing of relatives. If they made love during this time, it would harm the man and generally give him a backache and cause chills. It was considered an act of bravery and sacrifice for a young brave to go to the blood tent to visit his lover.

Varied sexual experience before settling down and at a time when desire was greatest, was expected more as a matter of common sense than because of any moral considerations. Sexual problems were rare in this society that practiced almost complete sexual freedom, probably because of the lack of overtones and shame. The Ute women were relatively infertile and practiced some birth control, so this helped to avoid problems. When an unmarried girl became pregnant, she was not ostracised, so she carried her child proudly without shame or remorse. If her family would not adopt the child, which was highly unlikely, the band would. Consequently, the child would be spoiled worse under these conditions than with real parents, because children were esteemed. The Uncompahgres seldom traded their children for horses, as did some tribes.

As the Utes became more carefree, they adopted many dances from other tribes and concocted some of their own. The bear dance was a four-day affair, celebrating the end of hibernation, therefore,

generally occurring in the spring. Drums and moraches were used for rhythm and music. The morache was a notched stick, while another stick was rubbed up and down the notches to create the sound desired. The pace started slow and groggy, like a bear emerging from hibernation, then usually was increased gradually. Then men and women started out in two lines, back to back, then eventually they turned and faced one another. As the bears began to recover, romance took over and marriage frequently followed bear dances. Trappers, and other white men who have participated in bear dances, are amazed at the endurance of the Indians during this four-day hop. The Utes practiced several other dances.

Marriage was easy to arrange, but the most important step was the consent of the intended's parents. Once the marriage was agreed upon between the two families, then a quite remarkable ritual was performed. The Indian brave would dress in his best buckskin and go kill a deer, leaving it near the intended girl's tepee, preferably by a stream. The girl would dress in her best white buck, beautifully decorated with porcupine quills and beads, her hair would be parted in the middle with the part painted vermillion red, also, she would be wearing ear rings. She would take her horse to the water and squeal in feigned surprise when she saw the deer. The deer would be dressed and taken back to the lodge, then a stew was prepared of special cuts of meat and very special herbs to insure a good union. The man arrived, then ate the stew, while the girl undressed and waited on a buffado robe. From this time on they were legally married. Divorce was a simple matter for men, as all that was necessary was to leave, or throw their wife's possessions from the tent, but it was no easy matter for a woman, as it meant disgrace to her family; therefore, they would try to help her avoid it if at all possible. Plural marriage was found among the Utes, but was most prevalent with the White River Utes. Polygamy was really not common; accordingly, men were much more likely to have only one wife at a time.

The Utes prospered and found contentment in their isolated mountain retreat. All was well while they had no enemies capable of shattering their security, that is, until 1858, when the Colorado Gold Rush began.

SGrover

5—LORDS OF THE PRAIRIES

The Cheyenne and Arapaho were members of the Algonquin linguistic group, together sharing the Great Plains between the Platte and the Arkansas rivers as their hunting grounds. These two tribes lived around the Great Lakes, where they led a quiet, unassuming, farming, fishing and hunting existence until the movement westward, that began with the coming of the English, forced many of the tribes west. The Cheyenne arrived on the plains after 1700, acquired horses, completely changed their way of life, then began a culture that revolved around the buffalo. The Plains Indian's dependence on the buffalo afforded him a luxurious life for about 150 years, but when the buffalo disappeared, the Plains Indian was forced unwillingly to accept a new life.

Early accounts tell of seas of buffalo humps as far as the eye could see, with buffalo and grama grass as high as a man's head, reaching from one horizon to the other. Estimates claim a count as high as 60,000,000 buffalo, but more likely a northern herd of about 20,000,000 that ranged from Kansas to Canada, along with a southern herd of nearly 10,000,000 that roamed from Kansas to the Gulf of Mexico. The Plains Indian culture included

many tribes scattered over the Great Plains, especially the great Sioux nation, the largest Plains Indian grouping, which was related to the Cheyenne. The Plains Indian culture could not flourish until the horse was acquired; consequently, it was in a sense artificial, therefore, an assumed way of life that was new to the many Plains Indians. The brevity of duration, along with the rather abrupt development of this culture, did not prevent the evolution of elaborate and complex social structures among these proud people.

It is trite to state that the buffalo was everything to the Plains Indian, because it would be an understatement. This hairy-humped quadruped was a galloping shopping center that provided the Cheyenne with his needs. The buffalo was food, tools, needles, thread, clothing, shelter, fuel, weapons, shields, jewelry, adornments, utensils, water sacks, saddle, bridle, shoes, rugs, religion and much more. These pragmatic people were well aware of the importance of the buffalo, hence, they did everything possible to protect their livelihood. Tribal codes regulated hunting to avoid driving the buffalo out of the territory. Most of their religious rituals were an attempt to lure the buffalo or to promote the

Red Panther
A Proud Cheyenne Scout

animal's health and fertility, notwithstanding the desire to bring good fortune on the hunt. Actually, they hunted other animals, but none were as important to them as the buffalo.

The horse loomed large in the value system of the Plains Indians, as it did with the Utes, being an indication of wealth and prestige. The mobility fostered by the horse made their buffalo culture possible by aiding in the hunt, besides carrying the meat. The Cheyenne and other Plains Indians hunted the buffalo generally only once or twice a year; subsequently, a large amount of meat had to be obtained, carried to camp, dried, and made into pemmican. Small hunting parties were outlawed, hence, hunting outside of tribal designated times was a serious crime in the tightly structured Cheyenne legal system. These crimes were punished by banishment which, to the proud Cheyenne, was worse than execution, engendering some view as to the attitude of the Cheyenne when renegade Utes or others trespassed on their territory.

According to Grinnell, the Cheyenne called themselves the Tsistsista, which, roughly translated, means the "people," or us, like us, or similarly bred. As expected with oral cultures, the early history of the Cheyenne is vague, with a good deal of mythology mixed in. Their history before 1600 is practically unknown. After leaving the Great Lakes, they pushed southwestward into the Dakotas. While in the Dakotas, they intermarried with some of the Sioux, meanwhile, adopting some Sioux traits. They were pushed south of the Missouri by the Assiniboines, who possessed rifles. The Cheyenne could not match these rifles with their bows and arrows; also, the Teton Sioux became their enemies, consequently, they migrated further south. During this migration, they split into two groups: The Northern Cheyenne remained north of the North Platte; the Southern Cheyenne pushed on into the Arkansas Valley. Although this was the beginning of a physical separation, their ties remained, thus remaining allied as a people.

Information about the Cheyenne is more readily available than any other of the Colorado tribes, because many Cheyenne became educated, or made some effort to recover their history. George Bird Grinnell, Mari Sandoz, Donald Berthrong, Thomas Mails and many current writers have provided a wealth of information about the principal Colorado Plains Indian tribe.

The Cheyenne, compared to the Utes, were a tighter knit, more politically organized tribe than the "Sky People," or any other of the tribes of the Centennial State. Despite strict social codes, their political framework was highly democratic. Leaders were elected, but could be recalled if they were incompetent, even the chiefs could be unseated. They were organized into bands with a chief for every ten bands and a super chief over the tribe; however, the tribe was a very impermanent unit which was called together only to wage war or to hunt the buffalo. The tribe was not called together to wage war until the Civil War, when the provocation was war against the whites and not their Indian foes.

The Cheyenne had chiefs designated as peace chiefs, these being older and wiser men, plus war chiefs, who were younger warriors, responsible for training the young in the martial arts. This arrangement was confusing, to say the least, to the white man, because the peace chiefs would make the treaties, gladly signing in the cause of peace, then the war chiefs would refuse to honor them. In making treaties, the U.S. Government, through the Bureau of Indian Affairs, tried to negotiate with Indian tribes as they would with independent nations, as the Constitution was structured. It was expedient to designate one chief as the leader of an Indian nation, maneuver him into signing a treaty, then try to bind all the members of that tribe to the treaty. This created insurmountable misunderstandings and confusion.

To the white man, when the Indian was in a small group, out hunting or counting coup, it was a "war party;" when the Indian put on paint—as he frequently did—it was always "war paint." Most Indians were considered savages if they were of a warrior tribe and lazy good-for-nothings if they were not. These assumptions were the result of lack of understanding; likewise, pathological fear of Indians that dated back before the American Revolution, on the whole was largely responsible for the credibility gap and confusion. The insatiable thirst for Indian real estate did not lessen the difficulty.

The Cheyenne had enemies, as did other tribes. The Pawnee, their bitterest foe, were attacked on sight, with war being extremely vicious and no holds barred. Their raids were controlled by a strict code; for status, in this male-oriented society, was gained by performing exploits called "counting coup." These exploits were of a "hair-brained" nature, with most value placed on a maximum of danger or risk and a minimum of killing. Touching the enemy first, assaulting an enemy in his camp, stealing horses from the enemy camp, particularly in broad daylight, heroism in open battle, saving a comrade in battle, having a horse shot out from under you, and locating the enemy were all highly rated feats. Scalping was not highly regarded; moreover, use of long-

AFTER THE KILL

DIORAMA STATE HISTORICAL SOCIETY

range weapons was considered a form of cowardice. Teenagers went out on coup parties that were privately organized, therefore, supposedly not condoned by the tribe. These coup parties were frequently conducted at the expense of the Utes. If a young warrior claimed he had performed a coup, it was customary to take his word and not question him. Frequently, coups were recorded in paint on the horse's flank, with so many hoofprints toting up stolen horses; other signs like arrow points designating battles or something else.. Counting coup gave the younger generation an opportunity to "let off steam," thereby helping to prevent trouble at home. Rebellious youths or generation gaps were rare, but promptly dealt with if present.

The Cheyenne legal system was complicated and extensive, although not written except in the minds of the tribal elders, because the Cheyenne, unlike the Cherokee, had no written language. The elders were the statutes, dictionaries, encyclopedias and records; hence, one of the reasons elders were esteemed. There were codes for marriage, camp maintenance, civil disputes, rape, murder, illegal hunting and other crimes. They were enforced by a band council, where justice was quick. Rape was punished by being stoned to death by the women, murder by execution; while other crimes—according to their severity—were punished by the decision of the tribal council. Many words have been written regarding the apparent freedom of the Plains Indians and there is a measure of truth in this allegation; however, he was not a free man living in a free society, but subject to rigid codes with restrictions that could not be circumvented.

The social practices of the Cheyenne were also complex, hence, much different from the tolerant Utes. The Cheyenne taught sexual repression, believing that a man surrendered a portion of his manhood each time he participated in the sex act, thus, the more children, the less man. Unmarried girls were isolated, therefore, courtship was at long range and could last as long as six years. The family was courted first, with no touching privileges allowed the boy and girl until after the parents' acquiescence. Child rearing was ruled by codes requiring constant supervision—the men looking after the boys, at the same time, the women being responsible for the girls. During the hunt the women were accountable for all the children. The men entered into the play of their sons and, in addition, open displays of love and affection were not uncommon. Physical punishment was rare, requiring the approval of the tribal council. Psychological punishment was used in most cases, consisting often of some form of temporary banishment. If a baby cried, the infant was taken away from the camp and isolated, then returned when the crying ceased, thus conditioning the child that tears brought isolation. The effectiveness of this strategy in contemporary society, if applied, is an interesting question to ponder. One wonders how effective it was among the Cheyenne; however, Grinnell states that Cheyenne children were well behaved and were taken into the band with little difficulty, therefore, problem children were a rarity. Some of the Apache groups strangled loudly crying babies.

Indian tribes or primitive peoples were often a male-oriented society, with the men having the upper hand, while women performed the majority of the tedious or less colorful tasks. The Cheyenne women were a good example of this outmoded arrangement and, accordingly, worked diligently at their responsibilities. The multitude of tasks they performed seemed insurmountable. One of their most arduous tasks was the dressing of the buffalo robes. The hides were laid out on the ground and staked down; they then were vigorously scraped to remove all the meat. The hides were treated by rubbing them with a mixture of brains, fat and other waste material from the buffalo, because the Indians had no knowledge of tanning or the use of tannic acid. If they were efficient, they could cure 30 robes, which resulted in prestige plus admission into the quill or bead guild where they were taught these skills. Sometimes the hair was removed, which was as difficult as treating the hides. The women dried the meat, pounded it, also gathered berries to make it into pemmican; made the clothing; built the tepees and, in addition, put them up and took them down. They also gathered firewood, did the cooking, reared the young, meanwhile, trying to be pleasing to their men. What did the men do? They hunted game, helped in the rearing of the boys, but spent most of their time practicing and preparing for war. Their lives were dominated by this avocation; although they seldom went to war, they still spent most of their time in training, working on their weapons, ritual or the other paraphernalia of war. Although war could be a deadly game, it was mostly a game that was played for enjoyment and to pass time. Many nonproductive hours were spent by the men at this pastime, probably not without occasional comments by the women. Wasting time, energy and resources on war or its preparation seems to be the everlasting curse of society, meanwhile, the game of war continues. To suggest the Cheyenne society was male-oriented could be a mistake. Without their women it would have collapsed immediately; the society could have endured somewhat longer if deprived of the contributions of the men.

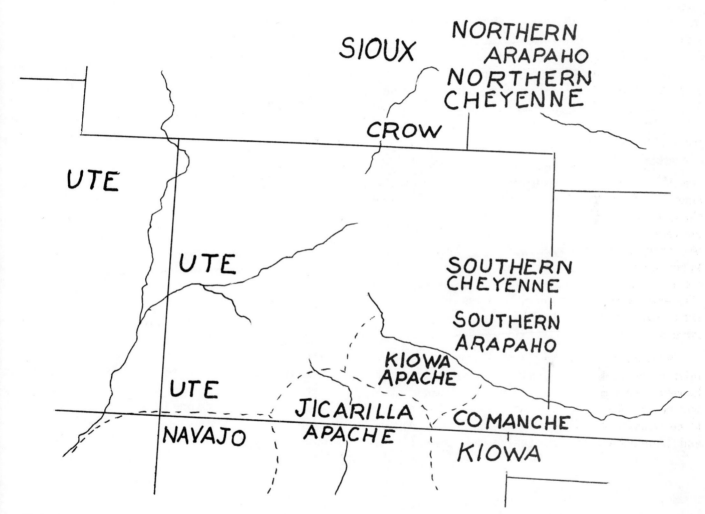

SIX NATIVE TRIBES OF THE CENTENNIAL STATE

The early history and culture of the Arapaho resembles the Cheyenne. Their origin is somewhere east of the headwaters of the Mississippi, where they lived in sedentary villages and raised corn. From the upper Mississippi they migrated to the Dakotas, where they became buffalo hunters, henceforth, dropping their former agricultural way of life. From the beginning they moved in company with the Cheyenne. When the Cheyenne split into two groups, the Southern Arapaho moved to the Arkansas River with the Southern Cheyenne and were close allies. On the other hand, the Northern Cheyenne and Northern Arapaho remained separated.

Shortly after their arrival in the Arkansas Valley in the early 1700's, the Arapaho were at war with the Navajo, Utes, Shoshone, Sioux and Pawnee. They were eventually able to make peace with these tribes, going so far as joining the Comanche and Kiowa in their raiding forays into Mexico.

When the "59ers" came to Colorado, the Southern Arapaho were camped with the Southern Cheyenne—they numbered slightly less than 2,000, while the Cheyenne were near 7,500. Although the Arapaho were known as a religious and contemplative people, they were renowned warriors. The Cheyenne knew them as the "cloud men;" to each other they were "people of our own kind." The Arapaho and Cheyenne were similar in many ways, but each had their own characteristics, including separate languages.

A resume of the six Colorado tribes would be interesting and a pertinent topic for this study, however, space will not permit this luxury. This will be the next literary effort of your author, due to be released August of 1976. The Kiowa, Apache and Comanche of Southern Colorado were raiding Indians and the subject of continual campaigns to wipe them out.

The Apache and Comanche are frequently adjudged by military historians as the greatest light cavalrymen in the history of warfare. Their reputation as warriors was deserved; however, their reputation as vicious savages was exaggerated. The Apache were related to the Navajo, who had been a more fearsome tribe before they settled down. Attempts to settle the Apache had not been completely successful, yet some of them had been Christianized. Many treaties were also negotiated with the Apache, but they were so loosely organized that many of the Apache were unaware of the treaties, consequently, they were frequently broken by both sides, then the gold rush stirred up more disputes. By the 1880's they were regarded as hopeless, so campaigns were conducted against them until they were eventually subdued. Raiding was an art to the Apache, therefore, when campaigns were sent against them, they often came out best. The stories of the Apache, plus their savagery, are legend. The Gila River Apache forced the Spanish to search for a safer, more northerly route to California, resulting in the Escalante Expedition of 1776 through the Centennial State. The Jicarillas lived around Taos, associated with the Spanish, and generally were no problem. The Apache and Comanche also called Texas their home, where they raided ranches for horses and cattle. Like Colorado, the Lone Star State had planned to remove such undesirables as Indians; therefore, the purification campaigns of the Texas Rangers were eventually successful.

Indians and their way of life make for an interesting study. More will follow in ensuing chapters. Their story is one that should be told as completely and accurately as possible; this is a considerable challenge to the historian.

6—FIRST CAME THE MOUNTAIN MEN

Vardis Fisher relates that there were a total of no fewer than a thousand mountain men of various and sundry types operating from 1820 to 1840 in the Rocky Mountains. Although Wyoming was more of a center of the fur trade than Colorado, many of these colorful introverts plied their trade, at the same time escaping civilization, in the Colorado Rockies. They have left their mark in Colorado history, as has been the case throughout the West. The difficult job of the historian is to assess their contributions along with their mutilations. With some of the lesser citizens of the forest, it is difficult to arrive at an assessment on the plus side of the ledger.

LeRoy R. Hafen has researched the mountain man era of Colorado as much as anyone. Several excellent articles can be found in **The Colorado Magazine** about the mountain man in general, or regarding particular individuals. Hafen describes them in general as consisting of several high type individuals

with Kit Carson, Jedediah Smith and Tom Fitzpatrick listed as examples of this level. He further elicits implicitly that Phil Garner was a case of the other extreme. James Beckwourth is another mountain man well known for nefarious incidents.

The available information is too sketchy on these covert enterprisers to approach fixed conclusions on them as a group; likewise, it would be unfair or incorrect to classify them as a group, then rate them as rascals or heroes accurately. Some logical assessments can be made. Many mountain men came west because of the lure of the West, along with the opportunity for profit from the rapidly growing fur trade. Other more undesirable types were fugitives from the law or civilization and made their greatest contribution to civilization by leaving it.

Regardless of their backgrounds, the trappers were molded by the life they led, plus the demands of their environment, into a life style and character

THE REALM OF THE BEAVER

that was easily recognizable. Hafen claims they were difficult to distinguish, one from another, on the whole resembling Indians in appearance and manner more than they did whites.

It seems many of these mountain wanderers were big men, considerably above the average of the time. Bill Williams, Phil Gardner, Jim Beckwourth and Dick Wooten were all well over average size. Phil Gardner was so huge in size and strange in manner, the Indians regarded him with awe and superstition.

Some trappers had college degrees, were articulate and well read. Others possessed skills in art, music or trades. Many were illiterate, with no obvious refinements. After a few years in the mountains, the gild of civilization was broken down, their language, manner and appearance revealing their occupation. The rigors, in addition to the demands of their avocation, acted as a melting pot, if they were sufficiently fortunate to survive long enough for this transition to take place.

Their role in history was a dual one. Along with the Indians, they explored and helped to name the Rocky Mountain West. On the other hand, the whiskey trade, small pox, diphtheria and cholera that came west with them lured the Indian out of their civilizations, precursors and corrupters, similar in extremes to the men responsible.

The mountain men were trappers lured west in search of the beaver. Their era was short in duration, about 1820 to 1840, then it was gone, never to return. The three categories of trappers were as follows: the free trapper, unaffiliated and unfettered, the most colorful and romantic, offering the best or the worst of the breed. Next, was the company trapper, affiliated with a company. The fur trader followed; this last specimen did not trap, but traded with the Indians. The whiskey trade was his bonanza. Jim Beckwourth describes this traffic in his biography by Bonner. Although efforts were made to limit this trade, profits were so astronomical it could not be stopped. These above three types —the free trapper, company trapper and fur trader —overlapped in their activities; however, most of the color and attention of this interesting era is given over to the free trapper. Trappers did not leave a wealth of written records; frequently, they were more concerned with hiding than revealing their activities.

A few trappers like Jim Beckwourth and John Ruxton did leave written accounts, but the stories they told were so incredible some did not believe them for many years, even though they were probably close to the truth.

Writers are inclined to make the mountain man or free fur trapper romantic and free, a noble spirit of nature, one of the pioneers of the west. The other contributions to the history of the West by these "phantoms of the Rockies" are not easy to calculate, because they were highly individualistic with no interest in settlement or civilization. They were outcasts from civilization, reduced by the environment to beasts of prey, rebels and runaways from society, often more savage than most Indians. Sometimes the trapper is called the first American "hippy," for they were Europeans who had reverted and become wild savages, who cared little for family life or the comforts that accompanied it. Once they had been mesmerized by the mountains, like the miner with his mining or the railroader when he heard the whistle of the locomotive, the mountain man became addicted to his avocation; he could not and would not have changed places with anyone.

The trapper cared not for codes or laws, except his own; henceforth, human life was taken without any regrets. The Indian had a society with codes to restrict his actions, but to the trapper, life was a bitter struggle that left little time to pity loss of life or limb; compassion for the living he could muster, but not pity. In many ways he was like an illicit businessman, often traveling in illegal territory, wary of being caught and put out of business permanently.

The mountain men were basically non-materialistic, forced to travel light with a rifle, skinning knife, horse, traps and a few utensils their only property. After the spring trapping they quickly shed any surplus they had accumulated with a whoop and a holler at the fort or rendezvous, then headed back to their beloved mountains, broke and in debt, but with high hopes of a new beaver bonanza just over the next ridge. The pelts were made into hats prized by men of fashion, but, alas, styles and fashions can be fickle.

The routine of the trapper or fur trader, who frequently traded "Taos lightning" or trinkets to the Indians, started in the spring. The free trapper usually trapped alone, stoically wading the icy streams to avoid leaving his spoor, then setting his traps and baiting them with beaver lure. The beaver would go to the bottom when he was caught in the trap; purposely, the stake holding the trap was notched to prevent the ring on the stake from sliding back up the stake; consequently, the beaver could not return to the surface for air and drowned, remaining under water and preventing coyotes or magpies from ruining the hide. The pelt was removed carefully, stretched on a green limb that encircled the oval pelt, then dried. When the pelt was dry it was cached in a safe place to await marketing. The pelts were light in weight, hence, easy to carry, with an average value of from twelve to sixteen dollars—almost as good as currency. When the beaver began to shed, the pelts were no longer of prime quality; then, the trapper would gather up his furs to head for a fort or a rendezvous. There was also a limited traffic in scalps, mostly bought by tenderfeet for a conversation piece to hang on a belt; many mountain men carried them.

The trappers were generally associated with a fur company under contract to a man like Kit Carson to trap in the Rocky Mountains. The American Fur Company was the largest fur company in the United States, but it operated in Wyoming and the Pacific Northwest. It was the first American concern to gross over a million dollars a year. John J. Astor, its founder, was the first millionaire in the United States when he founded Astoria, a fur trading post on the Pacific coast. The American Fur Company which used the fort system, however, did not build any forts in Colorado, but bought furs from Fort Bent and Fort Roubidioux occasionally.

The Rocky Mountain Fur Company was organized by William Ashley, with several associates, to operate in the Colorado Rockies. Fort Vasquez and Fort St. Vrain were used to serve the company, but the isolated mountain areas eventually resulted in the adoption of the rendezvous system, giving more flexibility. Before the trappers left for the spring trapping, a time and place were agreed upon, providing a movable exchange and increasing the company's success. Brown's Hole and Bayou Salado (South Park) were two of the most popular locations. When the trapper returned to the rendezvous or fort with his pelts, he was subject to a tight monopoly that could not be avoided. The price paid for his pelts was not competitive or subject to negotiation, but the price he paid for supplies bought from the company was high. He bought the supplies he needed before his money was spent on whiskey and squaws, then left to return to his trapping. Few mountain men made any effort to visit their homes or relatives—only once or twice in their lifetimes of trapping. Once committed to their life in the mountains, they remained.

When the beaver were through with their shedding and again prime, the trapper resumed his trap lines until winter forced him to seek the comfort of a fort or an Indian village. Some trappers continued to trap all winter in the lower mountain valleys of Southern Colorado. Many were squaw men who

found their Indian wives to be loyal and dedicated; several of the mountain men were fond of their women and loyal to them. When times were good the trapper lived well; during hard times he made the best of what he could find. In a pinch he would cut off his horse's ears or tail to make stew or tap a vein in its neck for blood. Thongs, moccasins, ants, black crickets, deer excrement soup, bark, berries or other delicacies tided him over when things were tough.

The mountain men had a culture of their own; their language was harsh, as was their character, and they were a smelly and dirty lot. They never laundered their buckskin suit or seldom removed it. When they did it usually was for the purpose of putting their adornments on an ant pile to allow the ants to forage for lice, fleas or ticks, then they would carefully shake it and put it back on. Most of the Indians were hygenic or more concerned about cleanliness; the mountain man had other more pressing interests.

As the trapper roamed the mountains in search of beaver, he gained a knowledge of his surroundings and was forced to adjust to their demands. His aggressive scramble for beaver put him out of business, because the supply was trapped out by the 1840's; moreover, beaver hats went out of style, to be replaced by the high silk topper preferred by Abe Lincoln. At first they felt the respite would be beneficial, so the beaver would be given a chance to multiply, thus renewing the bonanza but, before this happened, gold was discovered. Therefore, people began to flock to the mountains in much larger numbers in search of a new bonanza. Many of the trappers served as guides for the explorers. Kit Carson served as guide for three of the first four expeditions the "Pathfinder" made into Colorado; Fremont lost his way on the fourth expedition, hence, eleven men perished.

The trapper was not a pioneer or settler, however, and certainly was not pleased when civilization surged to the Rockies. After the trapping was gone, many of the mountain men remained near the mountains, living at Hardscrabble near present Florence. Some changed their ways, living out their twilight years in the comforts of civilization. A few scattered trappers continued to trap the isolated streams for beaver or muskrat and the forest for other furbearers. The bonanza was finished and the Indian culture was disrupted—the mountain man largely responsible for both. His trapping depleted the beaver supply, moreover, the fur trade with the Indians introduced them to smallpox, diphtheria and "fire-

JIM BECKWOURTH

COLORADO
MOUNTAIN MAN

Kit Carson

water," each taking its toll on the Indian's culture until, when civilization arrived, the red man seen by most whites was no longer the proud warrior, because his culture was now dissipated, making the settler see what he thought to be a lazy good-for-nothing.

Zebulon M. Pike

Stephen H. Long

7—EXPLORING THE WINDFALL

Thomas Jefferson was not an ordinary man, he was not even an ordinary president; therefore, when the Louisiana windfall was dropped in his lap, he quickly realized the deal could not be turned down, although it later caused him legal qualms. These misgivings were soon set aside when Lewis and Clark were commissioned to explore the new territory. Exploring land after its purchase also seems like a strange procedure, but things happened so rapidly it could not be avoided. Maybe this should have been a portent of things to come because the gold rush soon followed, so, in consequence, the West was opened, then rapidly settled, before anyone really had time to think or prepare for this vast undertaking.

The impressive travels of Lewis and Clark need not detain us, as they are well known; conversely, these two explorers did not traverse the Centennial State. Zebulon Montgomery Pike was given the opportunity to lead the first organized explorers into the valley of the Arkansas. Pike was a lieutenant in the army and an extremely ambitious man, hopeful of at least rising above major, the rank held by his father. Pike's fortunes took a turn for the better when Gen. James Wilkinson, the notorious commander of the army in the West, became his patron and promotions soon followed. During his expedi-

tion he was promoted to captain, rising by 1808 to colonel. He had been 1st Lieutenant nine years, but Wilkinson liked him and, therefore, promoted him rapidly. By the War of 1812 the young Pike was a brigadier general, when he was killed at the Battle of York.

General Wilkinson was one of the most unusual characters to appear in the history of the West. While he was assigned as commander of the army of the West, the Spanish were paying him for information regarding installations and troop movements of the United States. His friendship and frequent correspondence with Aaron Burr during Burr's ill-fated attempt to seize a personal empire somewhere in the West seems more than just a strange coincidence. Was the Pike expedition an attempt to explore the territory Burr was considering? The two events occurred simultaneously.

The Pike Expedition was a military one, organized and authorized by Wilkinson, but certainly not strong enough to seize an empire from the Spanish with only twenty-two men. The stated or alleged purpose of Pike's second expedition (the first did not come into Colorado, but went up the Missouri River) was to find the source of the Arkansas and Red Rivers to substantiate the western boundary of the Louisiana Purchase, to negotiate with the

STEPHEN H. LONG

Comanches, and, at the same time, to observe geography, check flora and fauna, and make maps and charts. It was publicized as a scientific expedition. The plan was to divide the group at the Arkansas, some going up the river to its sourse, besides, hopefully, locating the source of the Red River as well; the remainder were to follow the Arkansas to its mouth. Was this expedition connected with the Burr conspiracy? Was it an attempt to spy on the weak but land-rich Spanish, or maybe even provoke a war that would be easy to win? President Jefferson had already demonstrated his interest in the West, meanwhile, many frontiersmen and southerners were casting a covetous eye in the direction of Spanish territory. It seems strange to allege there would be interest in land to the west this soon after the Louisiana Purchase, but more puzzling occurrences than these dot the pages of history.

Gen. Wilkinson gave Pike orders to report only to him and to keep his findings secret. Pike corresponded with Wilkinson as long as possible during his trip to ask for directions in what actions should be taken by Pike if the Spanish were contacted. The Spanish, by some strange coincidence, arrived in Kansas before Pike, further, they seemed to know of his coming; maybe someone had passed this information along to them. Lt. Don Facundo Malgares had been sent by the Spanish to intercept the expedition, but could take no action unless Spanish soil was trespassed. The Spanish were expecting some kind of an expedition of a miltary nature, moreover, the Spanish archives imply this was the anticipated invasion.

The winter of 1806-1807 was spent in the area of the present location of Pueblo. The party explored the Pikes Peak region, the Royal Gorge, and the Arkansas River, but could not find its source. In January they crossed into the San Luis Valley by climbing the Sangre De Cristos, suffering from cold and exposure. Wilkinson had ordered Pike to enter Spanish territory then claim to be lost if apprehended, but it would seem incredible to assume Pike did not know he was west of the Rio Grande and in Spanish territory. When the Spanish caught up with Pike, he pleaded his innocence, then was politely asked by Lt. Malgares to accompany his troops to Santa Fe. Pike, his meager force considerably outnumbered, had little choice but to obey. Pike had become well acquainted with Lt. Malgares by the time they arrived in Santa Fe, also the Spanish lieutenant was congenial to the Americans. They were not mistreated or disarmed in Santa Fe, but were interrogated regarding their purposes. Pike's journals were confiscated by the Spanish governor, but the Americans were given ample opportunity to enjoy the Spanish culture of Santa Fe, where they visited the cantina and took in the sights. The governor was sure Pike was a spy so, therefore, had him taken to Chihuahua for further questioning, but finally, in July of 1807, almost a year to the day from his departure, he was escorted to the border and released about the time of the Burr conspiracy trial. Wilkinson, who had arrested Burr, was a witness at this remarkable trial, so Pike reported directly to President Jefferson. A few years later he published an account of his confiscated journal from memory, which was eagerly read in Europe, as well as the United States. Pike did not succeed in finding the source of the Arkansas or Red, but he brought back interesting information about the Louisiana territory and adjacent Spanish land.

Another military expedition was taken into Colorado by Major Stephen H. Long in 1819 to again make an attempt to succeed where Pike had failed. Long had already failed on an expedition up the Missouri, but was authorized to lead another party in search of the elusive sources of the Red and Arkansas. His personnel included nineteen men of varying skills, including cartographers, scientists, geographers, plus a painter. In the summer of 1820 the nineteen men rode over the Great Plains and were in the Rockies by early summer. They followed the Platte, viewed Long's Peak, then climbed Pike's Peak to prove Pike had been wrong after he had failed to climb the formidable mount, then mistakenly claimed it would never be scaled by humans. On the Arkansas the party split to begin the search for the two river sources, planning to return to Ft. Smith by separate routes. Again, the search proved unsuccessful, consequently, the two parties joined for the return to civilization, failing to accomplish their mission. They gathered new information about the mountains, because they penetrated further into them at the same time adding to knowledge of Indians, plants, and wildlife.

Major Long, strangely enough, is best remembered by historians for a mistaken assumption that endured for almost half a century. Pike was not optimistic regarding the future of the Great Plains, likewise, Long was even more unfavorable in his reports. He labelled the plains, The Great American Desert, causing the three letters, "G.A.D." to be permanent fixtures on the pages of history books used by American school children for fifty years. He claimed the area to be "not fit for man nor beast," wrongly comparing it to the Sahara Desert which, evidently, he had never seen.

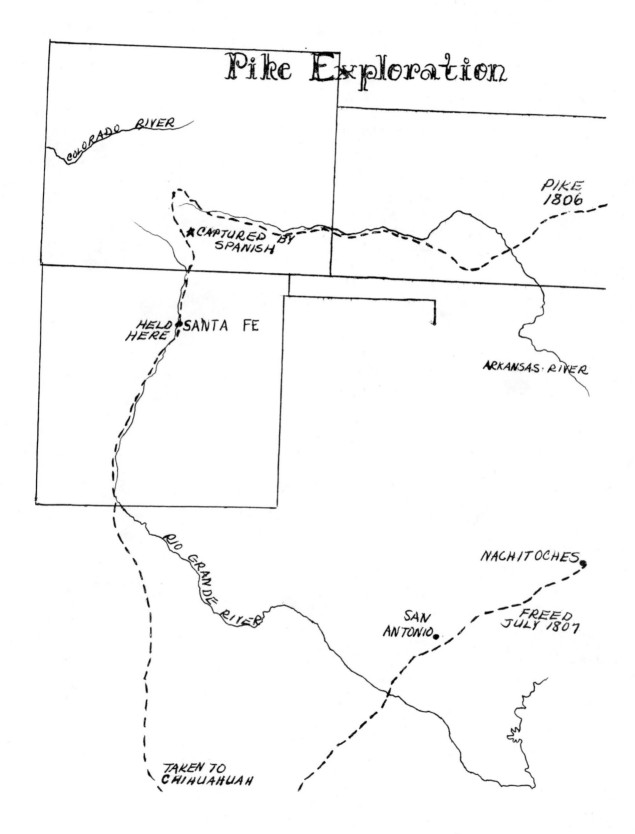

Pike Exploration

COLORADO RIVER

PIKE 1806

CAPTURED BY SPANISH

HELD HERE • SANTA FE

ARKANSAS RIVER

RIO GRANDE RIVER

NACHITOCHES •

SAN ANTONIO •

FREED JULY 1807

TAKEN TO CHIHUAHUAH

Long's error should not surprise anyone, as the Major, like most Americans and Europeans, was a creature of the forest, consequently, associating trees with well-being and security. A treeless expanse such as the Great Plains seemed alien and lifeless to them, making it necessary for them to make a considerable adjustment before accepting the plains as their home. The psychological adjustment was too much for many later settlers; some lost their minds and others packed up and left. A few of the more hardy remained, where they finally adjusted to this "dead land," as it was referred to most of the time.

Many army officers were located in the West, with little to do to keep them occupied. They saw the potential of the far-flung western frontier, moreover, made some effort to explore, later encouraging settlers. Many more military expeditions were sent westward, led by men like Col. Henry Dodge, Col. Henry Leavenworth and Col. Henry Atkinson. The mountain men did more exploring than many organized expeditions—Jedediah Smith, William Ashley, James Ohio Pattie, along with others, spent considerable time and expense exploring. More should be mentioned regarding the contributions of the mountain men and trappers in an account of exploration. Most of the explorers had mountain men or Indians as their guides so, therefore, were really not explorers at all, but gatherers and disseminators of information. This is no criticism of them, because they were able to accomplish a great deal more with a man like Kit Carson along; accordingly, when they did not have capable guides, they had problems. The first group of explorers were motivated by the newly acquired, but little known, Louisiana Purchase. By the 1840's the Iron Horse was making its appearance. The United States touched the Pacific causing men of vision to dream of transcontinental railroads and steamship routes connecting them with Asian shores. Routes through or around the Rockies would need to be found.

J.C. Fremont

8—THE PATHFINDER GETS LOST

The expeditions of Pike and Long did not diminish the interest Americans shared in newly acquired land in the direction of the setting sun; if anything, the interest in western horizons increased in intensity, to be accompanied by a thirst for more of the same. The "iron horse" had made its appearance, subsequently easterners were busily laying track to utilize this belching denizen. The 1840's was the decade of manifest destiny, with thoughts and aspirations turned toward the Pacific, with dreams of transcontinental railroads connecting steamship lines to the land of unlimited numbers of consumers. What unheard of possibilities for commerce this had to offer; also, Oregon was already practically won.

The State of Missouri was strategically located to share most of the fruits of the development of the West; the cities of St. Louis, St. Joseph and Independence would cater to the tide that was beginning to sweep westward, growing and prospering with each wave. Thomas Hart Benton, the senior senator from Missouri, was alert to all these possibilities and capable of speaking out for the interests of his native state. The ambitions of Missouri and the West were interwoven, so Benton, one of the senate's best orators, became a spokesman and messiah for the West. His prestige and influence pushed an appropriation of $30,000 through the senate, an unheard of figure at that time, for the purpose of mapping and exploring the West. Many Indian trails criss-crossed through the west, but wagons were unknown to the Red Men; consequently, the trails were insufficient, therefore, new routes that would accommodate wagons, and possibly railroads, would have to be explored and surveyed.

In 1841 John Charles Fremont eloped with Jessica Benton, the daughter of the distinguished senator from Missouri. Fremont had gained a commission in the U.S. Army in 1838 and seemed like a man with a promising future. His marriage to "Jessie" Benton did nothing to sidetrack his glowing potential; moreover, after the senator recovered from the sudden nature of this union, Fremont's prospects soared. The $30,000 appropriation from Congress was used to organize the Topographical Corps of Engineers, a special, elite group, to map and explore the West. John Fremont became the guiding light of the Corps and led them on three expeditions. Jessie was well educated, hence, probably wrote more of the accounts of these trips than Fremont, making the elopement and marriage more of a windfall; in addition, Jessie was an attractive and charming girl.

The dashing Fremont made five trips to the West, all passing through what is presently Colorado. The first three were for the Topographical Engineers, the fourth for a railroad company, ending in disaster, and the fifth was a private prospecting excursion to California. The "Pathfinder" was a good public relations man, always associating as much publicity and fanfare with his explorations as

BENT'S FORT

possible. His books were well written, also, his maps and descriptions were carefully explained and as accurate as possible. The public was kept well informed about all of Fremont's western expeditions with journals published, fully describing his trips. These journals, mostly written by Jessie, became best sellers and "musts" for all people going west in the forties, when the gold rush stirred up a considerable stampede of thousands. His journals were often thrown in the saddle bag of other explorers. The Library of Congress published 100,000 journals of his first expedition; those that followed were privately published.

The "Pathfinder" was not a trailblazer; he chose his personnel carefully for his expeditions—first in priority were mountain men that knew the mountains—naturally, his favorite was Kit Carson, his guide on his first three trips. Tom Fitzpatrick, Dick Wooten, and Parson Bill Williams also served in this capacity. Cartographers, geographers, scientists, artists along with others, were painstakingly selected to make the expeditions as successful and informative as possible.

Fremont's first western expedition was for the Topographical Corps of Engineers, setting out in 1842 to explore the territory between the Missouri River and South Pass. It was not a difficult expedition; twenty-eight men made up the entourage; Kit Carson accompanied the party west. When the journal was published, the account encouraged many to go to Oregon to settle, taking the journal along to guide the way.

The second expedition followed the route of the first, but went on to Salt Lake, then along the Humboldt into California. There was a sizeable amount of interest in California, which was isolated from its Mexican landlords; it was known as "a land of milk and honey." The party arrived at Sutter's mill in 1843 without any suspicion as to what would transpire at that location in a few years. His journal became the most popular guide for the Fortyniners that followed, many in the same tracks.

Fremont's third effort occurred in 1845, was connected with the Mexican War, included a party of sixty-two men—mostly soldiers—also, the group was equipped with a cannon. Senator Benton was now chairman of the military committee of the Senate and President James K. Polk had been elected on an expansionist ticket. Many peculiar activities are associated with this expedition, the alleged purpose again being to locate the elusive sources of the Rio Grande, Arkansas and Colorado Rivers. The official order did not mention California, but this is where the party went. The men were carefully

selected for their marksmanship and ability as soldiers, moreover, the entourage headed straight for California without stopping to map or explore. The details of Fremont's participation in the war are sketchy and need not detain us. The "Pathfinder" got involved in a dispute with Col. Stephen W. Kearney over who was in command. Fremont had a colorful exchange with Kearney, who outranked him. Fremont was returned east almost a prisoner of Kearney, to be court martialled, found guilty of mutiny, disobedience, and unbecoming conduct. President Polk approved the sentence, but pardoned Fremont, who resigned his commission in anger at the injustice.[1]

The ill-fated fourth expedition was a private venture for a group of St. Louis businessmen. The Mexican War was over, moreover, the Mexican Cession—a huge tract of land that makes up the present southwestern United States—extended the western boundary to the Pacific. The interest in a transcontinental railroad now mushroomed, therefore, many began to consider plausible routes, ever hopeful the road would favor their city by passing through. St. Louis was located on the 38th parallel, so the "Pathfinder" was hired to explore a route straight west of St. Louis on the 38th parallel that would surely give the Missouri city a terminus. To insure the establishment of the route as an all-weather route west, the "Pathfinder" decided to travel during the winter months to test the locale. The 38th parallel went through the heart of the San Juans, some of Colorado's highest mountains; of course, Fremont was not completely aware of all this, also he had a reputation to uphold.

The party arrived at Bent's Fort in October of 1848 with a thirty-three man expedition and asked for Kit Carson. Carson had severed his connections with the Bent brothers and was in Taos, depriving Fremont of his most trusted guide. Some of the mountain men at the fort warned that an expedition of the nature planned by Fremont was dangerous, but Fremont was too impetuous to listen to this sage advice. He was to regret his impetuosity. Finally, Parson Bill Williams, a great trapper, reluctantly consented to serve as guide and signed a contract; Dick Wooten also agreed to go along. One hundred and twenty mules, each carrying a bushel of corn, were brought along to carry baggage and serve as food if the situation demanded. The party of thirty-five men soon returned to the original number of thirty-three because two, including Dick Wooten, wisely decided to desert the venture. Wooten was the most capable mountain man and guide in the group.

The party spent the night of November 22nd at Fort Pueblo then arrived at Hardscrabble (Florence) the 25th. They crossed the Wet Mountains without too much difficulty, but when the party began to climb into the Sangre De Cristos it began to snow. Williams suggested it might be prudent to turn back or delay, so they paused and rested at White Oak Creek. It was here that Wooten demonstrated his wisdom by leaving the expedition. When they resumed the climb, the heavy, wet, new-fallen snow began to ball up on the mules' hooves, greatly impairing their progress. The summit was reached on the third day of December, which was crossed through a pass filled with deep snow. The next day they proceeded toward the San Luis Valley, and out of the mountains, ever hopeful of finding grass for the mules to feed on, along with a much needed respite from the snow. They were dismayed to find the valley covered with a blanket of snow four or five feet deep with cold temperatures, accompanied by near-blizzard conditions. There was nothing to do but continue on, so they began to climb into the La Garita mountains toward the Continental Divide, near the location of the present town of Del Norte, which has an altitude of 8,000 feet. The divide along the 38th parallel was almost 14,000 feet, therefore, as they climbed, the snow deepened, the weather turned colder, and Williams again suggested delay. As they continued, the mules began to die, the snow deepened, also, there were times when the high, steep mountains made the climbing treacherous. They were not too far from where a man by the name of Alferd Packer, along with five unlucky companions, camped on Lake San Cristobal about twenty-five years later. Fremont decided to continue, but the party missed Willow Creek, which would have taken them toward Cochetope Creek and out of the mountains, only to mistakenly follow Alder Creek, which led them higher into the La Garitas. There were no passes in the area, therefore, as they climbed higher, the group seemed to be in mountains that were looking down on the tops of other mountains, like the weary climber that views each ridge ahead with great anticipation, hoping it is the highest so when he crosses it he will begin to descend, ending the arduous climb. The party never reached the Continental Divide, because they soon realized the seriousness of their plight; the harsh reality of being lost in the mountains in the winter was not a pleasant prospect.

In December they reached what seemed to be the divide, but a blizzard with winds of sixty miles an hour made it impossible to continue, so they camped for a day, then moved on. The impetuous

Fremont finally gave the order to fall back, but the men were in such bad condition that many could not walk, so the stronger built fires and sat around them until Christmas. The dwindling food and supplies added to their dilemma. As they pondered their situation, rescue seemed to be their only hope. If help could be summoned from Fort Garland, the oldest fort in Colorado, they could be saved. Four of the ablest were sent to the fort with the decision that the remainder would wait sixteen days for rescue; however, Fremont committed the unpardonable sin of abandoning his command, therefore, the men strung out on their own in small parties to find Fort Garland. One of the four sent for help had died; secondly, eleven of the thirty-five men that left Fort Pueblo in December perished. Many of the others reached the San Luis Valley in deplorable condition, some with frozen feet or hands or both, others were suffering from snow blindness, while several were in such bad shape they could not even sit up. The valley was crusted over, making it extremely painful to walk with the frozen feet which were without protection. The soldiers gathered the survivors in small groups to take to Fort Garland. Parson Bill Williams was found snowblinded, with his partner missing. The good condition of Williams caused some speculation as to the fate of his partner, moreover, afterward Williams' nickname "Parson" was replaced by another more damaging, but possibly more appropriate appellation. The following spring Williams returned to the La Garita to recover the abandoned goods left behind and was killed by Indians.

Fremont's friends blamed Williams for the failure of the mission, while his enemies blamed the "Pathfinder," whose reputation as an explorer was tarnished, but the account of this expedition made interesting reading. In 1849 Fremont entered Congress as a senator from California where he had in 1850 struck gold. Fremont was the first republican candidate for the presidency, so he was able to outlive his failure enough to overcome its blemish. The failure of the expedition, along with the accompanying tragedy, cast an aura of pessimism on the future of Colorado as a transcontinental railroad link; moreover, Fremont stated that he doubted if such a route existed through Colorado.[2]

Captain John Gunnison renewed the search for the disputed route in 1853, setting out for the Topographical Corps of Engineers which had been favored by new appropriations. This expedition was better equipped and profited from Fremont's mistakes. They moved over the Santa Fe Trail, down into the San Luis Valley by way of LaVeta Pass,

FREMONT Lost in the
La Garitas

out over Cochetope Pass, into the valley of the river that bears their leader's name. The party followed the Gunnison River into the Va'ley of the Grand, where the Gunnison joined the Grand in its winding journey through the canyons and deserts into the Gulf of California.

Gunnison was equally pessimistic about routing a railroad in the Colorado mountains and alluded that better possibilities must exist. After leaving Colorado, the party was beset by a band of Paiutes; unfortunately, Gunnison and seven of his men were killed and mutilated, adding to the growing disinterest of railroads in the vicinity.

The "Pathfinder," not to be outdone, made his fifth and final trip west, following essentially the same route Gunnison had explored. He completed the survey, showing that construction of a railroad on that route was possible and again, with the help of Jessie, published a glowing account which garnered him most of the credit for finding and surveying the route. Debunkers of such railroad routes had never heard of the narrow gauge or names like William Jackson Palmer or Otto Mears. Railroads would soon be built in places that would leave these detractors speechless.

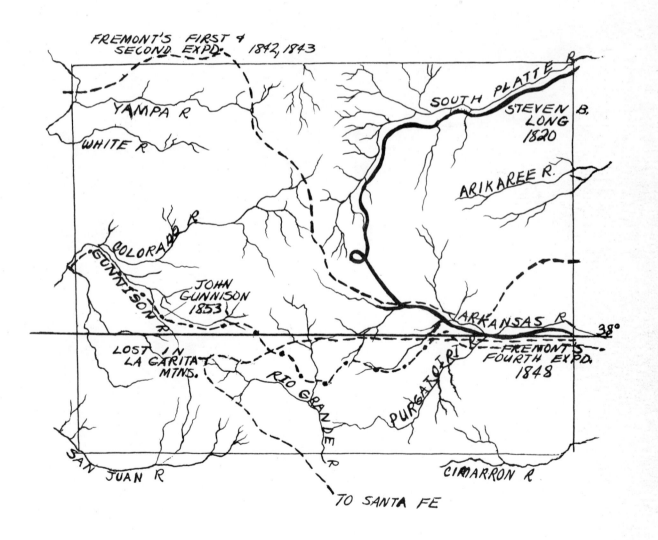

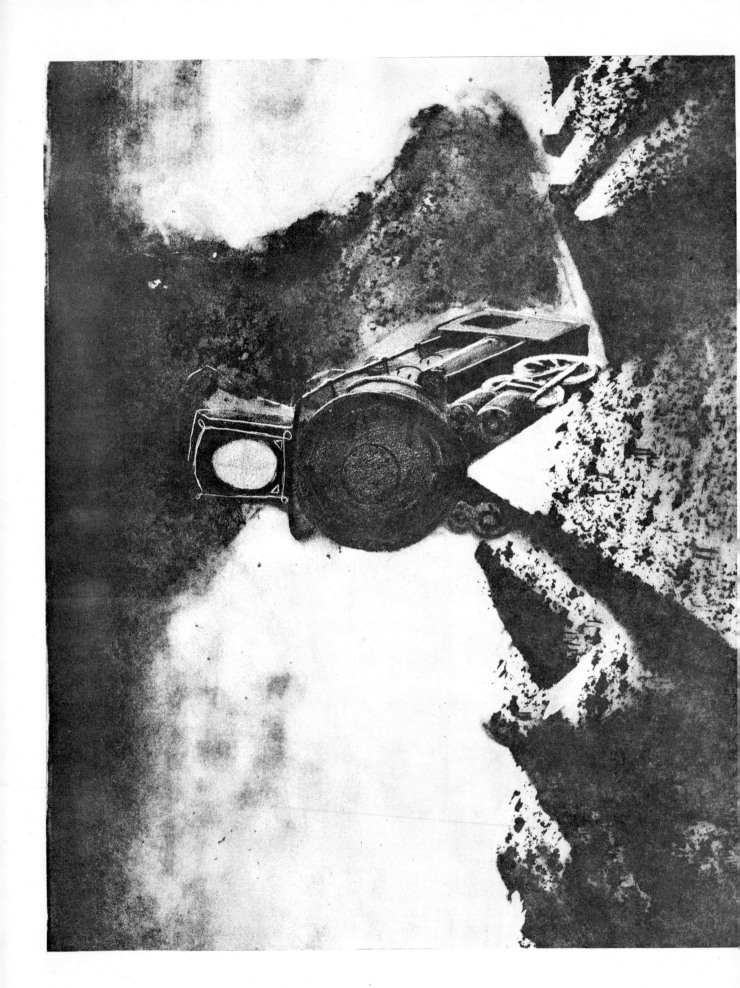

9—SPANISH CULTURE MOVES NORTH

Colorado as a culture frontier has been one of the themes your author has attempted to maintain in the development of this story. The first whites to come to the Centennial State to settle came north into the San Luis Valley, encouraged by the Treaty of Guadalupe Hidalgo of 1848. The treaty acknowledged former Spanish and Mexican land claims, similarly allowing a period of five or ten years for claimants to begin to improve their grants but, if the land was not improved within that period, it would retrocede to the United States. Mexico had made an effort to obtain a firmer grip on its northern territory—so isolated from Mexico City—after the Texas Revolt in 1835 so, therefore, had issued land grants to its own people that could finance settlements and then develop the land. The lesson learned in Texas by the granting of land to Gringos discouraged reiteration of such practice. Huge sections of the San Luis Valley and the valley of the Arkansas were granted to impresarios, but the Mexican War broke out in 1846 before the land could be claimed. The

Mexican War was ended by the Treaty of Guadalupe Hidalgo in 1848, which encouraged a small flurry of settlers to enter the San Luis Valley.

The people of Spanish extraction that migrated to Southern Colorado brought their culture and language with them, where it remains as the dominant culture of Southern Colorado to this day. The Treaty of Guadalupe also guaranteed former citizens of Mexico, who came into the United States with the Mexican Cession, status as full-fledged citizens of the United States with all rights included. In 1849 these settlers began to move in and establish the first towns and permanent residences in the Centennial State, bringing sheep, livestock, and rudimentary agricultural tools with them. San Luis was the first town founded in Colorado in 1851; soon several other Spanish speaking hamlets followed. Spanish is still spoken in the towns of the southern part of the valley as the prevailing tongue. Naturally, many firsts are associated with this indigenous portion of the state—water rights there have high priority. The first irrigation, agriculture and permanent settlements were established in the Rio Grande Valley. Ft. Massachusetts, changed later to Ft. Garland, is the oldest fort of continual operation in Colorado.

The Latin culture varies according to its location, along with the force of the culture it has been in contact with thus resulting in different manifestations and characteristics. When the culture-conscious Spanish came to the Americas, it was their plan to assimilate and Christianize the natives; realizing the complexities of their way of life and Catholicism, they made modifications and simplifications to make their task less burdensome. The various Indian cultures made new alterations as they blended the Latin culture with theirs; their folkways and practices had an impact, therefore, new interpretations resulted. The northern empire was so far-flung from the center of Mexico that much of the culture was carried north by Indians—the Utes for example, meanwhile, the isolation prevented any supervisory action by the Spanish.

The Latin culture was a by-product of Spanish Catholicism, both carried north by the black or brown-frocked friars, monks and clerics. The Jesuits organized and ruled the southern reaches of the vast northern empire of Mexico, while the Franciscans were given jurisdiction in what is now the southwestern part of the United States, excluding California. In 1598 Juan de Onate, with a contingent of troops and 300 colonists, accompanied by a few Franciscan missionaries, set out to establish themselves on the Rio Grande in what soon became known as New Mexico. Thus, two frontiers began to develop simultaneously — one under the Jesuits in northern Mexico, the other in the Franciscan-directed Rio Grande Valley. Onate ranged further to the north to explore and search for gold, and he was the first white man in the territory of the Centennial State. Thus, Spanish culture began to move north; in addition, the founding of Santa Fe and Taos soon followed.

Onate traveled through Arizona, New Mexico and Colorado, exploring the country, but more ambitiously pursuing the obsession of Spanish conquistadores, the yellow metal. This neglect of crown responsibilities caused him to be dismissed from his position, forfeit his land grant and be thrown in prison in Mexico City.

In 1765 Juan Maria de Rivera was motivated to make a trip north by more rumors of gold. His party left Santa Fe, followed the Rio Grande north, skirted the San Juan Mountains and finally reached the Gunnison River. They blazed a trail by carving crosses on cottonwood trees and returned the same

route. Their prospecting proved fruitful, but not impressive. The small amount of ore samples they located did not result in Colorado's first gold rush.

One of the more energetic expeditions north into the Centennial State from Santa Fe was the Escalante effort. The journey of Silvestre Velez de Escalante and Francisco A. Dominquez had two purposes. The Franciscan friars were fearful of the Russian and English penetration of the northwest which threatened missions in California; furthermore, Spain was aware of the political ramifications caused by the presence of these rivals. The southern land route from missions in Mexico to connect with the California missions was in difficult terrain, not to mention the problem of the Yuma, Apache and other troublesome groups. A more northerly route between Santa Fe and the California missions seemed to be the reasonable solution. Hence, it was the purpose of the two God-fearing Franciscans to blaze such a trail from Santa Fe to Monterey.

The summer of 1776 in the southwest was undoubtedly more uncomfortable than the muggy one in Philadelphia experienced by the co-signers of the Declaration of Independence. At any rate, it was while things were "hot in Philadelphia" that the padres headed north. Without arms, the band of fourteen set out northward—two padres, the Alcalde of Zuni, the military captain of Santa Fe and accompanying soldiers and Indians.

Turning northwest, the expedition followed the Rio Chama, then crossed the San Juan near the present New Mexico-Colorado line. Striking out across the Southwest corner of Colorado, they headed into the Animas Valley, reaching the Dolores. They went down this river for eleven days, then headed due north into Colorado The entourage followed the Gunnison briefly, then forded the Colorado near where the Gunnison and Colorado rivers intersect at the Ute ford. From the Grand Valley, Escalante headed westward, crossed the White, then the Green south of the Wyoming line. They then paralleled the Uintah and Wasatch Mountains into the Salt Lake Valley. By this time it was October and the surrounding mountains wore a mantle of snow.

The approach of winter caused them to abruptly end their journey and head south. It required eleven days to find a crossing over the Cosnina (Escalante's name for the Colorado) then they returned to Santa Fe January 2, 1777. The padres did not locate their route, nevertheless, had they continued westward from the Salt Lake Valley, a relatively easy route was available. The two padres were the first whites to view the remarkably spectacular scenery in the San Juan Mountains and Black Canyon of Colorado, along with the Wasatch Range and red sandstone

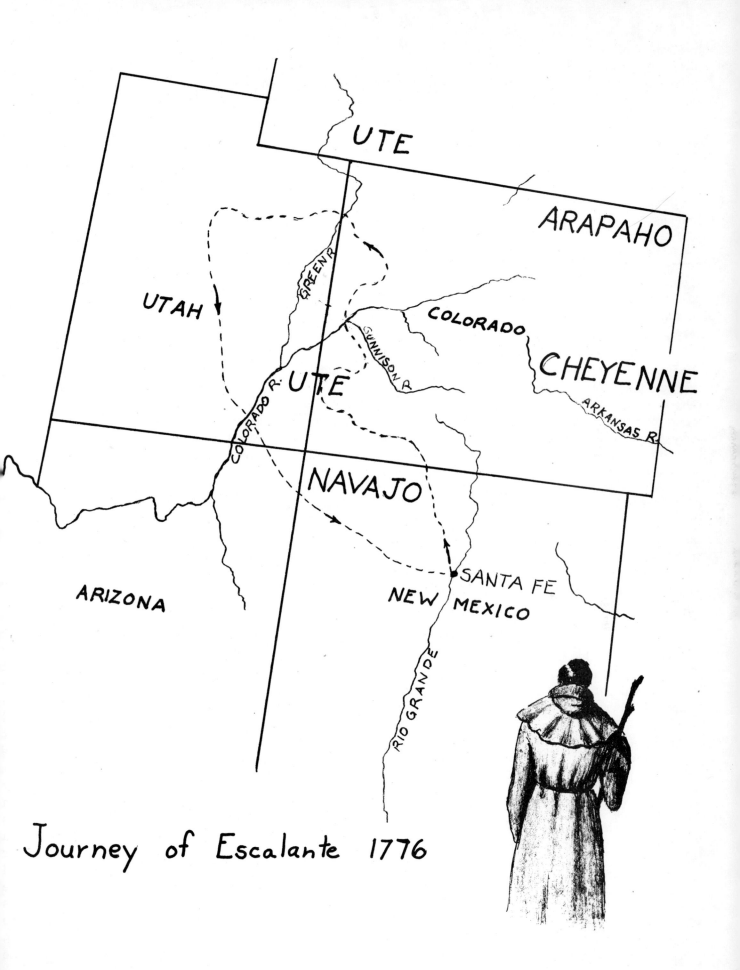

UTE

ARAPAHO

UTAH

COLORADO

CHEYENNE

GREEN R.

GUNNISON R.

ARKANSAS R.

UTE

COLORADO R.

NAVAJO

ARIZONA

SANTA FE

NEW MEXICO

RIO GRANDE

Journey of Escalante 1776

formations of Southern Utah. More Spanish adventurers would follow; however, Onate was the first white man in Colorado, while the two padres were more methodical and provided a journal to describe their impressive journey.

The dedicated order of Franciscans remained in New Mexico until after the Mexican Revolution, administering the work of the Church and establishing farms and ranches to keep the Indians busy. Their scattered domain offered them an ever-increasing challenge in carrying out the work of the Church, administering sacraments and extending the faith. As more lands were settled, the work increased, forcing the friars to rely on assistance from lay brotherhoods to perform sacraments in the more isolated and far-flung communities. These lay Catholics were responsible for adding to the alteration of Spanish culture, while the Catholic lay orders gradually assumed a larger role than was intended. Many such orders developed, each with different practices and characteristics. When the Franciscans were ordered out of New Mexico in the 1840's, these orders began to perform the work of the Church on their own where priests were not available. The town of San Luis was without a priest for over ten years, others for longer periods of time, forcing priests who could to travel, leaving much of the work of the Church to the lay brothers—visiting the sick, caring for the poor, performing baptisms, marriages, last rites, communion and whatever had to be done. Consequently, Latin Catholicism had different manifestations. After the Latin countries won their independence, the Church was frequently connected with the opposing conservative forces, losing some of its force and undergoing changes.

The best known of the lay brotherhoods of the Southwest were the Los Hermanos Penitente and the Third Order of St. Francis. The Penitentes became quite popular from 1860 to 1920, then began to decline, but are still active in many communities of Southern Colorado. Some claim the brotherhood began in Mexico about 1600, but it probably started in Spain much earlier. The Franciscans were a dedicated austere order, with many of the brothers practicing asceticism and, although such practices were banned by papal degree in 1349, they continued and were probably brought to New Mexico by the devout Franciscans. Spain was not touched by the Protestant Reformation or the industrial or scientific revolutions, therefore many medieval aspects of Catholicism endured, especially in agricultural areas such as Durango and Estremadura. The Penitente Brotherhood that developed in New Mexico was a combination of Spanish and Franciscan practices. The brotherhood became widespread and popular in the

Philippines, where it is widely accepted at present. It seems more likely that the brotherhood began in Spain, then was taken to Mexico and the Philippines.

Juan de Onate was a Penitente who often scourged himself in the presence of his troops; many of his men took up the whip and followed his rather painful example. The Penitentes, like many of the other lay brothers, performed the work of the Church, did works of charity, cared for the sick and served in many capacities; however, they are best known for their flagellation and mock crucifixion; understandably, the cross is their main symbol.

Latin culture differs regarding the concept of God, his relationship to man, and man's purpose. During the 19th century the United States was the most religious country in the world, with New England Protestantism and Bible Belt Fundamentalism, two of the more forceful sects. Consequently, many Anglos considered their God to be a wrathful and merciless deity as portrayed in the famous sermon, "Sinners in the Hands of a Wrathful God," frequently given by Jonathan Edwards, where sinners were reminded they were dangling over the pit of hell by a slender thread, to be doomed forever if they did not repent. After hearing one of these "fire and brimstone" sermons, adoration or love were superseded by fear of God.

Latins, on the other hand, were inclined to look at God as being merciful and understanding, able to forgive a sinner. All men were sinners—God understood that and did not expect purity—therefore, if man admitted he was weak or sinful and made a sincere attempt to atone, God would understand and forgive. The sacrament of penance with confession, contrition and absolution served most Latins, but some wished to be more remonstrative in their attempts to atone and gain absolution. They also believed sins were inspired or committed by the flesh, subsequently, they had to be eliminated by way of the flesh.

Latin Catholicism had assumed some characteristics native to the Southwest, and adoration of the Virgin was emphasized. The lay brothers modified the rites, then there were other differences inspired by culture, locale and language variances. After the Mexican War and the Treaty of Guadalupe Hidalgo, the Spanish and the Anglo heirarchy of Catholicism collided over rites that prevailed. The policy of universalism and consistency dominated the thinking of the Church, therefore, changes were made in the rites of churches in the Southwest. In some ways the new innovations seemed strange and alien, making the settlers of Southern Colorado seem as outsiders in their own church Many rebelled or left the Church and joined the Penitentes. The Franciscans

Morada

were banned in 1840 because of their tendency to dabble in politics, so the shortage of clerics appreciated setting into motion the increase in numbers and activities of the brotherhoods between 1860 and 1920.

Charles Lummis, in **The Land of Poco Tiempo,** described the Penitentes, showed pictures of some of their activities and rites which he labelled barbarous, therefore was responsible for much of the first publicity they received. Many Penitentes regarded this account as unfair; therefore, they have made an attempt to avoid any adverse publicity since. The brotherhood has no such reservations in the Philippines, where their rites are open to public scrutiny. Nevertheless, curious Anglos are not welcomed by most Penitentes in the Southwest.

Membership in the Penitentes is by invitation, after which follows a five-year probationary period when the novice proves his merit. A married man cannot become a member without his wife's consent. Their meetings are held in the morada, house of death, where most of their rituals and ceremonies take place. The morada consists of three rooms—one used for meetings, one for ceremonies and the other contains the death cart, sometimes a torture rack, and similar equipment, with an array of whips hanging on the walls. During the five years of probation the novice learns the canticle—the rules of the order and a profession of faith. This takes place inside the morada.

After 1840, when the Franciscans were expelled from New Mexico, the secular priests took over the duties of the Church. The priests stayed in the towns, leaving the isolated communities for the Penitentes to administer and care for. The Penitentes continued many of the Franciscan practices, using their prayers and hymns in their own rites and practices. The Franciscans had traveled over the Southwest, now the Penitentes took up the circuit, increasing in number and bringing new modifications to Catholicism.

The Penitentes have elaborite rituals, also, the organization is comprized of many complex dogmas. The novice, during his five-year probationary period, is not permitted to speak to members of the order while he proves his merit. In the past most of the prominent men in town belonged to the order, consequently, the community was sympathetic with the group to the extent that prying Anglos could be jailed during Holy Week, observed between Palm Sunday and Easter. The Penitentes have other observances held during the year and graciously respond to requests from non-Penitentes for assistance in bereavement, charity, grave digging and other needs of families unable to pay church fees for these services.

If a brother becomes seriously ill, he is often taken to the morada and cared for there until he recovers or succumbs. Frequently, the family is unaware of the illness or death until notified by the brothers, because it is not unusual for a brother to spend several days in the morada without reporting to his relatives.

Holy Week, the most important time and the highlight of the activities, includes initiation of new members, special rites with the crucifixion as a climax.

A Cristo is chosen at the beginning of Holy Week, with the honor going to the most respected and devoted brother. After he is chosen, he stands trial by being crowned with thorns, spat upon, lashed by members and himself, then carries the cross to Ca'vary where he is crucified. Not all orders practice the mock crucifixion; also, the methods used by the orders that practice this Roman innovation vary. There is a good deal of competition for the honor of representing the order in the symbolic suffering of Christ on Good Friday by carrying the heavy cross.

Initiation begins on Tuesday, as the initiates, accompanied by their sponsors, hopefully knock on the door of the morada and carefully begin to recite the canticle, which should gain them admittance if done correctly. The mayor informs the novice about what his duties as a Penitente will be; he stresses loyalty, obedience and faithfulness in carrying out the rites, explains the purpose and need for flagellation, then cautions the aspirant about the secrecy expected to be kept by members. The novice strips to the waist, kisses the hands and feet of the brothers and bends over, placing his hands on a bench or table. The Sangrador (bleeder) cuts his back with a piece of flint, stone or glass to create the Seal of Obligation, which consists of two or three horizontal and vertical gashes. The seal guarantees membership for life and, after it is cut, the initiate receives forty lashes from the brothers. Each brother chants, "for the love of Christ bestow on me," as he scourges the novice, alternating the three lashes with chanting, followed by another three lashes. If the initiate should cry out for mercy or pass out, he was deemed unworthy and not admitted. After he has received his lashes, the initiate must continue to flog himself.

During Holy Week the brothers remain in the morada and continue their rituals. There are many moradas located in Southern Colorado; in some towns where politics are more important, there is a democrat and a republican morada. No one is asked or coerced to whip himself or bear a cross or be a Cristo, all of these practices are voluntary. Somenes brothers simply carry the cross on their back th arms outstretched for special penance to atone r their sins, not being Cristos, but members with a agonizing conscience. The crosses are extremely mbersome, weighing as much as 200 pounds.

On Thursday of Holy Week the brothers file in ocession to the church, often accompanied by their milies, singing and chanting the alabados—elabo- te and complex verses that have come down from e Franciscans. These hymns represent the oldest tive music of the Southwest. They are hymns of aise, moreover, they are among the finest relig- us poems of all time. The Franciscans are noted r their beautiful hymns and prayers such as "The ayer of St. Francis."

The purpose of the order, as the name implies, penance, not only for their sins, but for the sins the world. The members also worship God and e symbolic suffering of Christ is one of their dom- ant themes. The morada is elegantly decorated ith crosses, images; moreover, bound figures of hrist—frequently life size—hang on the walls. The ull is another Penitente symbol found on the altar d sometimes embroidered on the altar cloths, sym- lizing discipline of the mind, as well as the body, us poignantly reminding brothers of the fate that vaits them. The cart of death is another reminder death which is used as a torture device. It is ade of heavy timber with wooden wheels and is led with rocks. The brother pulls the cart with a pe around his bare chest, walking barefoot, shout- g "Penitencia" until his chest and feet bleed.

The most important event of Holy Week oc- rs on Good Friday, when the Cristo carries his oss to Calvary to be crucified. During procession e brothers wear short trousers and hoods, but are herwise bare of foot and body. Hoods are not orn in the Philippines where secrecy is not main- ined. The Cristo leads the procession, followed by e new members, scourging themselves as they arch—one blow for every two steps. They are fol- wed by the brothers and their families; the alaba- os are chanted as they proceed to the chosen site. he cross is erected for the Cristo to be tied in po- tion. Sometimes the Cristo is so emotionally over-

wrought that he pleads to be nailed to make his suf- fering more meritorious. This has been done in the past in the Southwest, but is not done now. It is, however, still done in the Philippines. Crucifixion is a product of Roman imagination, the practice of which causes death by suffocation as the muscles of the diaphragm gradually contract, halting breath- ing, so if a person was left on the cross long enough, he would perish, regardless.

After thirty minutes the Cristo is removed from the cross and the procession returns to the morada, chanting as they go. The Cristo is taken to the morada and nursed back to health; if he should die, he would likely have been buried in an unmarked grave. On Saturday morning the chanting proces- sion returns to the cross, flogging has ceased, the cross is carried back to the morada and stored for the next Holy Week observance. The brothers are relieved of their uneasy conscience, therefore, the transgression slate is wiped clean. They have paid for mankind's sins, moreover, they are reasonably sure God understands their sincerity.

The Third Order of St. Francis was originally organized among the wealthy of the Southwest to perform works of charity. The greatest privilege was internment in the brown robe of a Franciscan monk. Gradually, the order grew and changed; as the need occurred, members accepted new responsi- bilities within Catholicism. Eventually, as their im- portance increased, their membership appreciated and the order became more powerful and influential, which led to political involvement. After some dif- ficult political experiences, the order began to de- cline. They were not as large in numbers as the Penitentes.

The Spanish culture brought into the Centen- nial State had undergone alteration and modification in the 300 odd years since it arrived in Mexico City. This culture which dominates the southwestern Uni- ted States had made its share of contributions. The cattle industry, the cowboy, over a hundred varieties of fruits and vegetables, place names, language, art, music, to name only a few, remain as a reminder of this heritage.

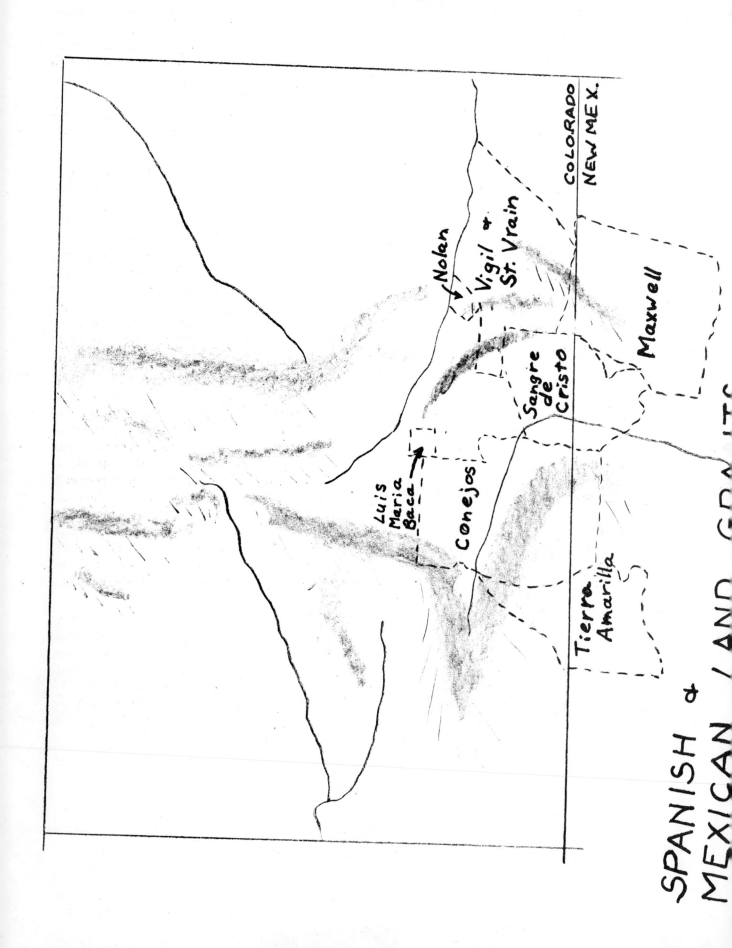

SPANISH &
MEXICAN LAND GRANTS

Nolan

Vigil &
St. Vrain

Luis
Maria
Baca

Conejos

Sangre
de
Cristo

Maxwell

Tierra
Amarilla

COLORADO
NEW MEX.

10—BENT'S FORT AND THE SANTA FE TRAIL

The clash of civilization, along with the increase in activity of Americans in what is now Colorado began in earnest in the 1820's in the southwest corner of the state. Two factors are responsible—one, the development and use of the Santa Fe trail, the other the construction of Bent's old fort on the Arkansas River. Commerce, or more specifically, profit, was inspirational in the case of both. Commerce is the by-product of the insatiable desire of the human animal to possess what he does not have, but what is possessed by another. "The grass is always greener on the other side of the fence," as the saying goes. The Santa Fe Trail was even more attractive because it brought the best—or worst—of the products of two different cultures together for exchange, henceforth, adding an exotic nature to the "trinketry" involved. The fur trade along with its colorful character was an added attraction.

The geographic expedience of tapping the commercial potential of New Mexico was a dream Missourian merchants entertained long before they were able to experience reality. The simple facts dictated such a trade. "It was destined." Missouri was much closer to Santa Fe, the northern mecca of the Spanish empire, than was Mexico City. Spain was well aware of the vulnerability of their empire north of Mexico and was only exceeded by the "gringo" in this realization. Santa Fe was on a once-a-year contact with Mexico City when times were normal. Frequently, these crown contacts occurred at intervals of two years. The journey from Mexico City to Santa Fe was long, arduous and hazardous. In miles, depending on the route, it was 1,100 to 1,200 miles from Mexico City to Santa Fe,

800 from Missouri. The official expeditions north, due to crown business, could require six months one way or a year to make the round trip. The climate, terrain and desolate nature of the territory traveled could add to time or difficulty of this trip. If Mexico had been judiciously administered, undoubtedly these problems would not have been insurmountable. The truth was, however, Spain often had more than it could handle in Mexico and Peru, therefore, the northern empire suffered times of neglect.

Santa Fe, founded in 1609, and Taos, founded in 1820, chaffed from this imperial neglect. Moreover, the merchants in both enclaves sought to improve commerce beyond the meager performance they were experiencing. Spain was unable to keep them supplied with necessities, consequently, a brisk commerce was not possible. The ambitious merchants in New Mexico were anxious to explore alternatives to improve conditions they believed to be deplorable.

Merchants of Missouri implicitly understood the geographic advantages that favored them. They had made a number of attempts to "crash" the market without success. Spain was unsympathetic to their overtures; secondly, Spain was fearful of a Yankee filibuster and expansion thrusts. Consequently, Americans were not tolerated in Santa Fe or Taos. If they entered either settlement, there was a good chance they would be thrown in prison, regardless of their purpose. The Pueblo Revolt in 1680, when Spaniards were temporarily evicted from New Mexico by the Pueblos, the mysterious Pike Expedition, French, British and Yankee intrigue, along with internal explosions, had made Spain sensitive regarding its northern satellite. The 350-mile advantage possessed by Yankee traders was of little significance if commercial barriers to New Mexico remained.

The facts were simple enough; merchants of Missouri and New Mexico were anxious to do business. The merchants of Santa Fe were as anxious as their counterparts across the Mississippi. When Spain's American empire exploded with a rebellion, followed by revolution resulting in the independence of Mexico, changes followed rapidly. The new, shaky government of Mexico was more tolerant of Yankee commerce, while at the same time too occupied to prevent its start, if it desired. Therefore, in 1821 the gates opened, the merchants of Missouri and New Mexico embraced in a profitable squeeze and, at the same time, a new era began. The past restrictions were obliterated with one grand sweep, while a new, bold future began to unfold.

The establishment of the Santa Fe Trail was a notable link in the chain to bring the products and characteristics of two cultures together. The cultural aspects of this highway cannot be ignored The precise historian would prefer to set time, founder and length of the Santa Fe Trail down explicitly and connect the terminals with the stops by a definite line; however, the caravan and cattle trails of the west were not established or maintained in a specific manner. Trails were struck by trial and error, by trying to find the best routes around obstacles available, meanwhile, changing directions when improvements were located. Water and grass were needed for the four-legged mobility, consequently, when the supply of these essentials waned, trails deviated one way or the other. In areas where grass was in short supply, the trail might well shift twenty miles right or left to converge at a stream crossing or mountain pass, when necessary. No, cattle and caravan trails of the west were not fixed as maps suggest.

As the Santa Fe Trail emerged, the New Mexico capital was already established as a hub of the southwest. It, along with Taos, were the equipping centers for American trappers on the Arkansas, Rio Grande, Gila and Colorado rivers and their tributaries. Santa Fe also served as a jumping-off point for California or other western locations. Names mentioned among those to be the first to bring wagons loaded with articles of trade were Jacob Fowler, Hugh Glenn and William Becknell. Fowler and Glenn came from Fort Smith, Arkansas, following the Arkansas River, then turning south. To their surprise and gratification, they received a warm welcome and, at the same time, were granted license to trap the region for beaver.

Shortly after the departure of the Fowler-Glenn party from Fort Smith, William Becknell came out of Missouri with a wagon over a route that eventually made up much of what became the Santa Fe Trail. Becknell and his two partners also proved a journey in a wagon to Santa Fe was possible, which may somewhat explain the reason Becknell is given the title of "father or founder" of the Santa Fe Trail. Also, Becknell facilitated a profitable exchange of goods in Santa Fe. In the early 1820's, the Santa Fe Trail was born of these circumstances.

Fowler, Glenn and Becknell were not the only pioneers to commercially probe New Mexico. The twenty years between 1820 and 1840 were the heydays of trapping and the mountain men in the Rockies, so fur trading and trapping assumed a large proportion of the attention in New Mexico, as was also the case at Fort Bent. Taos became a hangout for mountain men and the supply base or shipping point for "Taos lightning," which trickled north for trade to the Indians for beaver pelts. Taos, north of Santa Fe, was conveniently located for traders wishing to avoid the high customs of Santa Fe. If the necessary transaction could be expedited in Taos, more profits could be realized by both parties, plus a considerable depreciation in miles traveled was gained.

The Santa Fe trade was two-way in a nature that added to profit. It was not necessary for a trading company to "deadhead" or travel empty. The manufactured goods from Missouri and points east was bartered for pelts, blankets, whiskey and other products of New Mexico. The cultural barriers were pushed aside in the name of profit. Santa Fe tolerated the transient traders and their excesses in Taos and Santa Fe for the sake of commerce. The Yankee traders and trappers tolerated the irksome customs and different culture for the sake of commerce and pleasures of the palate, as well as the bed. It was not as denigrating as the "kow tow" demanded by the Chinese, besides, Santa Fe was an interesting and exotic oasis, far from the confining restrictions of home and hearth. A visit to Santa Fe or Taos was eagerly anticipated by participants in the commerce. With luck, these anticipations were not disappointing.

Much can be said about the testing of equipment and animals on this infant heavy freight highway. By the mid-1820's huge caravans stretched far and wide across the dust-clouded, wagon-wheel rutted artery. The Santa Fe Trail preceded the Oregon, Mormon, 49-er and 59-er treks west. Huge cargos were hauled west for the first time, where new demands engendered by the dry western climate gave

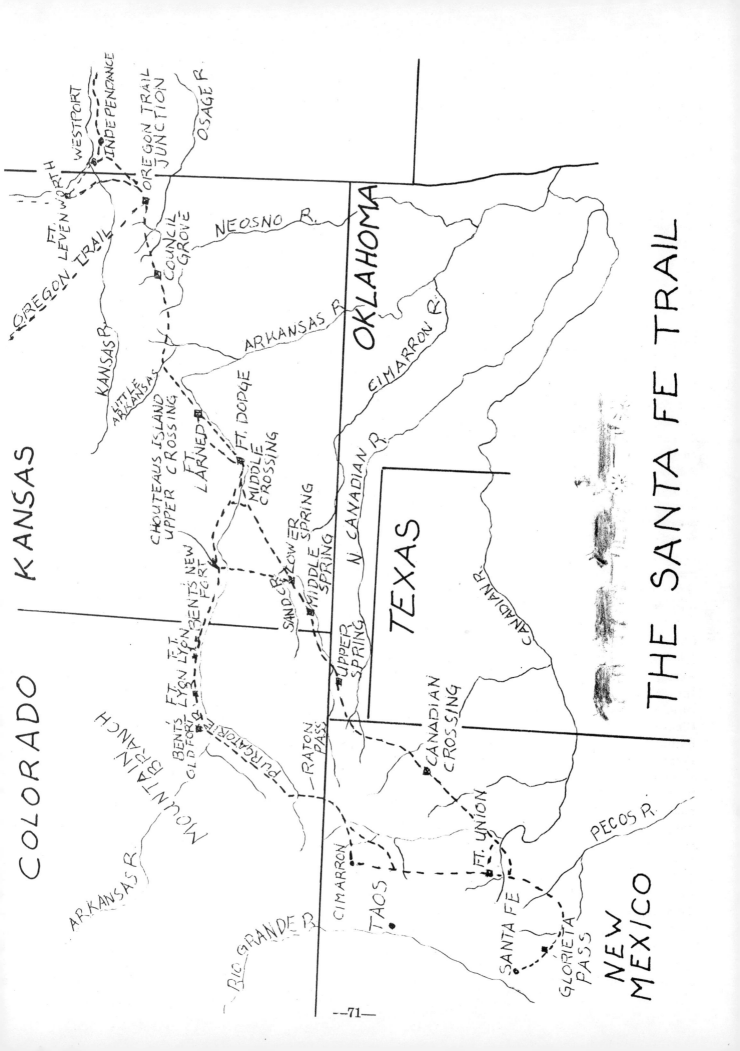

THE SANTA FE TRAIL

conventional equipment, methods and animals a severe test. The long stretches without contact with civilization or water, together with difficult stream crossings and Indian depredations, added sobering challenges. Needless to say, in the name of profit, the trade went on, the problems were dealt with, business flourished and increased.

The Mexican War of 1846 to 1848 did not slow the persistent traffic. From 1820 to 1870, before railroads pushed into the Southwest, the Santa Fe Trail and its traffic of goods and culture did not suffer seriously from interruptions. Freighters grew wiser in what equipment best filled the requirements of western climate and terrain, so, in another sense, the trail was the "daddy of them all" in the West. Now, for the story of a stockade of equal significance.

BENT'S FORT

The story of a fort and a premier pioneer western family is another chapter of Colorado History similar to the Santa Fe Trail saga that, because of literary expediency, requires arbitrary selectivity. In other words, only bits and pieces of the story can be told in this volume. This remarkable bastion of civilization, remotely situated on a treeless, trackless plain serving as a beacon of civilization and a sanctuary from danger and want on the untamed frontier, marks the beginning of white institutions in Colorado. The stockade also loomed as the challenge to the Mexican empire to the south and was the stronghold from which the effort to relieve Mexico of its northern territory was launched.

Following the footsteps of Pike and Long, Charles and William Bent headed west. They left Missouri in the spring of 1824, not sure where they were going or really what they would do. One thing they were sure of, they were going to find their future, whatever it turned out to be, in the West. Charles was twenty-five and William was fifteen, hardly an age for conquest. Charles was a West Point graduate, but had long planned to forsake the military career for the lure of the West. There were, perhaps, twenty-five men in the original party, mostly trappers, along with about fifty horses and mules. The purpose of their expedition was to enter the fur business by trapping furs and trading among the Indians for their furs. In addition to their provisions, they carried an ample supply of trinkets to facilitate this trade, plus plenty of powder and lead. This expedition probably had the blessings of, or some connections with, the American Fur Company.

Their only plans were to locate somewhere along the Arkansas where wood, water and grass were available. They had planned and prepared, so they knew how to build stockades and log cabins. In the interest of success in their venture, the Bents kept their true motives secluded for purposes of security from competition until they were successfully established. If they could become well organized and established, it would be safe to invest as long as the territory was theirs. Their first years in the West were spent scouting out the country and getting acquainted with their potential Indian customers. The Utes, Cheyenne and Arapaho were the first tribes they encountered. The good will and cooperation of the Indians were the cornerstone of success for the Bent brothers, this Charles already knew. The Indians kept their distance for several months, but gradually contacts were made. At the same time the group spent most of its time trapping.

It was at this time Charles Bent realized the necessity of proselytizing the Indians. He would have to seek them out; they were curious about his intentions, but not curious enough to make contact. They only observed from afar. Charles visited Indian camps and invited the Indians to come to his camp. Both Bent brothers were able to gain the friendship of the Indians and the friendship was mutual. The Bents frequently pursued the interests of the Indians in the future against the whites.

In 1826 Ceran St. Vrain stopped at the Bent Camp on his way from Taos to St. Louis to market his furs. The Bents were able to include their harvest of furs in St. Vrain's caravan, so this was the beginning of a mutually beneficial relationship. St. Vrain was twenty-two years old and had made a trip from St. Louis to Santa Fe with one of the Becknell caravans. While in Santa Fe, the Missourian was able to obtain trapping rights. Trapping extensively in New Mexico and Arizona, he was unfortunate enough to have his pelts confiscated, because of a change in governors. After 1826, the Bents and St. Vrain became close personal friends and a partnership was formed. The firm, Bent Brothers and St. Vrain, was born.

Meanwhile, the Bents were making progress with the Indians, who began to come into camp with their pelts to trade. The hundreds of Indian trappers in the area could supply a good deal more furs than the few trappers the Bent Brothers hired or traded with. The Indians were essential to produce the volume needed to turn a good profit. The next consideration was selection of a point of operation and construction of a fort.

In 1826 the fort site was chosen on the north bank of the Arkansas on Turkey Creek, about twelve miles above the present Las Animas. High ground was purposely chosen and the river flowed by on

CHARLES BENT

each side. The fort afforded a picturesque view in all directions when it was finished. Construction began in 1828 and a structure 135 x 180 feet was planned. The walls were five feet at the base, tapering to two feet at the top. The Spanish style of the structure may have been the suggestion of Ceran St. Vrain, because the Bents had not ventured to New Mexico. In 1829 a crew from Taos was engaged to construct the adobe bricks. Carpenters constructed frames and roofs from timber cut along the river. The structure stood complete in 1832—a sturdy, fireproof sanctuary. Originally, it was named Ft. William, but the name Ft. Bent was widest used, so it was finally adopted.

William Bent became fort superintendent and his older brother, Charles, did the traveling. The well chosen site on the Santa Fe Trail, together with the friendship of the Indians, complemented the trade at the fort, as well as trade on the Santa Fe Trail. The operation grew and expanded rapidly.

The mountain route along the Arkansas eventually became the main route of the Santa Fe Trail. Early in the inception of the trail, the short route appealed because of the saving in miles; however, the "Cimarron cut off," as it was dubbed, meant no water when the Cimarron was dry, which was frequently the case, and more chances of unwanted contacts with the Comanche. Also, the trail was 800 miles long with Missouri at one end and Santa Fe at the other, with no rest stations other than Bent's Fort between. The Cimarron cut of by-passed Bent's Fort, eliminating the only stop where supplies could be obtained. Prudence dictated the choice of the "Mountain Route" through the southeast corner of what now is the Centennial State. There were other routes intersecting the Santa Fe Trail that also omitted Bent's Fort. Routes out of southern Missouri, Arkansas and northern Texas, plus other minor routes excluded a visit with the Bent brothers.

The fort was also responsible for attracting wagons from the Cimarron cut off. It was another trading stop, reasonable accommodations were available, and a blacksmith and harness shop served caravans with equipment problems. As news of the fort spread, it became a gathering oasis for Indians, trappers and travelers—the three main types to be found within its walls or camped nearby. Charles Bent's public relations work with the Indians paid off in handsome profits. The Cheyenne, Utes, Arapaho, Comanche and Kiowa were the principle tribes that brought their pelfry into the fort to

TRADING WITH THE INDIANS

CERAN
ST. VRAIN

WILLIAM BENT

trade. The marriage of Charles to a Cheyenne woman was somewhat responsible for this cooperation. William Bent kept things running smoothly at the fort. Supplying food, water, maintaining and supervising the operation, required imagination, leadership and acumen.

In 1852 the first fort was abandoned and a new location was chosen about thirty-five miles down the Arkansas River, east of the old fort. The new fort was constructed much like the old one, 200 feet long and 100 feet wide. The new fort became more of a political force. It continued to function as a part of the Santa Fe trade, but more and more it became an outpost for policing the Indians. Troops and Indian agents replaced the more colorful trappers who preceded them. The buffalo robes supplanted the beaver, and 1859 saw onset of the gold rush. With the settlement of the plains and the demise of the buffalo, there were no longer any Indians to trade with. The Bent's Fort phase of history was 1826 to 1857 and a new tide was sweeping into the Southwest.

Other forts, hopeful of sharing the Bent brothers' success, were constructed. None of them enjoyed the attention or significance of the Bent brothers.

John Gantt and Jefferson Blackwell located further upstream in 1832 and Maurice Le Doux built a fort near Hardscrabble; however, these forts were not successful because the Platte River was fast becoming the center of the buffalo pelt business that was now replacing the beaver hide as an item of commerce. In 1838 Louis Vasquez and Andrew Sublette erected Ft. Vasquez near present Platteville; this post survived about four years. Ft. Lupton appeared in 1836 and did business with the Indians for about nine years. Ft. Jackson followed in 1837. This competition motivated the Bent, St. Vrain and Company to construct Ft. St. Vrain six miles north of Ft. Vasquez. Antoine Roubidoux operated Ft. Roubidoux on the Gunnison River, where he traded with the Utes during the thirties. However the Utes burned his fort and drove him out for double dealing. Roubidoux also had Ft. Uintah in the Uintah Basin.

The 1840's saw the peak of the buffalo hide business. With the gold rush, followed by the open range cattle industry, a new era unfolded. By 1870 the Plains Indians were relocated in Oklahoma. Another chapter in the Centennial drama came to a close.

BENT'S FORT

DIORAMA STATE HISTORICAL SOCIETY

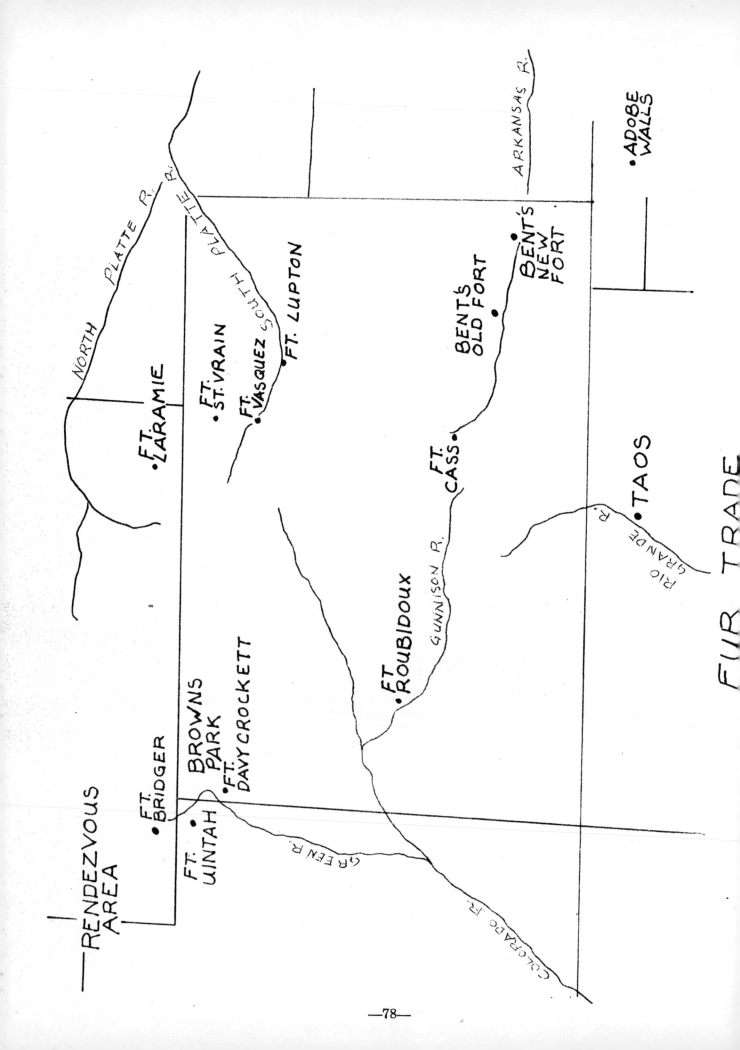

FUR TRADE

RENDEZVOUS AREA

FT. BRIDGER

BROWNS PARK

FT. DAVY CROCKETT

FT. UINTAH

GREEN R.

COLORADO R.

FT. LARAMIE

NORTH PLATTE R.

SOUTH PLATTE R.

FT. ST. VRAIN

FT. VASQUEZ

FT. LUPTON

FT. ROUBIDOUX

GUNNISON R.

FT. CASS

BENT'S OLD FORT

BENT'S NEW FORT

ARKANSAS R.

ADOBE WALLS

TAOS

RIO GRANDE R.

FORT SCENE

NATHANIEL
HILL

11—THE PIKES PEAK HOAX

The peace and serenity of the centuries was relatively undisturbed by the trappers and explorers. The six native American tribes of the Centennial State went about their hunting and trapping with little trepidation or cause for alarm. Then, abruptly, in 1859 the gold mania roughly cast aside the past and ushered in another era. Although gold mining was mainly restricted to mountainous areas of Western Colorado, it was, nevertheless, the catalyst responsible for the beginning of the cavalcade of white settlement in the Pikes Peak region.

Colorado actually experienced several mining booms from 1859, its infancy, until 1920, when decline set in. Mining, along with agriculture, was one of the top two industries of the State. The first mining boom was a bitter disappointment; this 59er gold rush did not reach expectations because of the scarcity of placers and the hard to process refractory ores. Colorado really began to prosper with the silver boom of the 1870's, which ended with the crash of 1893. The crash was lessened by a new gold rush centered in Cripple Creek, but also providential in Leadville and the San Juans. These early rushes overlapped somewhat and were responsible for bringing people and prosperity to Colorado.

It all started in California then ended several years later on the Yukon. Gold is where you find it despite geological phenomenon or metallurgical skill. Gold had been mined in Georgia before the Forty-niners trekked to the Golden Gate, but California was the strike that set off the long stampede. When the Mexican War ended in 1848 politicians speculated about the settlement of the vast newly acquired territory and the yet to be settled portion of the Louisiana Purchase. Self-appointed experts estimated it would require 200 years to tame the continent and settle the West. How wrong they were. In 1850, California had 100,000 residents and was clamoring for statehood; the vanishing frontier was nowhere to be found by 1890. Many factors were responsible for this rush to the Pacific, but none was more significant than the yellow metal that became an emotion that turned sensible and practical people into re'entless gold seekers. The gold rush made a "crash program" out of the westward movement with the Indian the pawn.

Details of the California rush need not detain us; however, there are circumstances that make some of the events significant. It is fortunate the first big strike occurred in California and also providential that it was on the Pacific coast. The location stirred up people to cross the continent, helping to acquaint the populace with new land with promising possibilities, and the fabulous nature of the California strike made gold an emotion that led to other rushes. Much of the gold first mined was placer variety, already processed by nature then deposited in loose gravel easy to process. Many sizable nuggets were picked up out of the beds of streams, making it possible for several of the argonauts to enjoy some measure of success. Most of the wild eyed Forty-niners were novices, with no prior experience or knowledge to help them in their search for pay dirt, forcing them to rely on the typical trial-by-error process of the impatient, get-rich-quick breed they were. The easy pickings in California gave them a chance to learn while they earned without too much discouragement. In an area where the going was more difficult, such crude methods would have met with failure, therefore the fervent belief that gold was easy to find in the West would not have soared to proportions that inspired the bonanzas that followed. Gold had been discovered in Georgia earlier, resulting in the relocation of the Cherokees in Oklahoma, but this strike was not of the magnitude to excite the imagination.

The Forty-niners soon learned by experience, while their crude mining methods improved until there were several gold diggers with some practical knowledge that could be put to use elsewhere when the occasion arrived. Soon there was a surplus of miners, naturally their impatience to get rich caused them to consider other possibilities, consequently the strike spread into Nevada, Arizona and Colorado. Many had passed through these areas on their way, panning a few pans as they went.

Juan Rivera and other Spanish explorers searched in Colorado for gold, but did not find it in the quantities and ease with which they did in Mexico or Peru, although many stories and rumors persisted about riches in the Rockies. James Purcell was prospecting in the mountains and is mentioned in the Pike Journal as being in the Pikes Peak region and of informing the Pike Expedition of success in finding gold. However, the California rush had not occurred to stir up the avarice in the potential gold seekers, so no rush followed.

Many of the miners passed through Colorado, some of them from various locations. The imposing distances and obstacles of Colorado set it apart from the other mining rushes; actually Colorado was more a part of the mid-west than the Pacific seaboard. William Green Russell had experience in both the Georgia and California gold fields when he stopped

in Colorado to prospect on his way home. Russell had heard the rumors of gold in the Colorado Rockies and was considering the organization of a party of prospectors to return.

Many of the Cherokee tribe, relocated in Oklahoma, had some mining experience in Georgia so they wandered into the Pikes Peak country to try their luck in a new locale. When William Russell left Colorado, he returned to Georgia by way of Oklahoma, where he visited with some of the Cherokees related to him by marriage. His Indian friends informed him of their prospecting in the Rockies with subsequent conversation resulting in plans for an expedition. The party returned to the Pikes Peak country in 1858; joining the Cherokees on the way, after arriving in north central Colorado, they began to prospect in the small streams that ran into the Platte River located there. The party camped on Cherry Creek and, with high expectations, began to work the gravel of the creeks. Their efforts proved to be only partially successful, as they did not find enough pay dirt to meet expenses. Many of the original party of over a hundred became discouraged and returned home, but William Russell, his two brothers, and about thirty others continued to look for gold. A pocket of productive gravel on Dry Creek yielded a few hundred dollars worth of gold, but no impressive finds were made; nevertheless, the meager success of the Russell party produced the Colorado Rush.

The U.S. was suffering from the Panic of 1857 therefore people, who believe what they want to believe, found it convenient to associate reality with all the rumors coming out of the Pikes Peak country. Colorado was called the Pikes Peak Country at the time of the rush, but the name was shortened to Pikes Peak. When the Fifty-niner talked of the Pikes Peak Gold Rush, he did not refer to the indomitable mountain, but the whole region. Stories of gleaming sandbars of gold, Indians shooting bullets of gold, and mountain peaks of gold filtered out of the early gold camps back to the Midwest, where they were savored by potential prospectors anxious to go anywhere but where they were.

A host of visitors came to the Russell diggings later to exaggerate the extent of productivity in the expedition. D. C. Oakes talked to the Russells, returned to the Midwest with samples of gold, and began to publish his **Guide to the Pikes Peak Gold Fields.** The pamphlet included maps and directions to Pikes Peak with information about gear, topography, and suggested mining locations. Oakes was not guilty of prevarication, because the Russells had found gold, although not an impressive amount. His

S Grover

Wm
GREEN
RUSSELL

pamphlet simply described the country and told how to get to Colorado and what to bring.

Another visitor to the Russell diggings was William Byers, a newspaperman and founder of the **Rocky Mountain News,** Colorado's first newspaper. The ambitious publisher was anxious to create interest in the Colorado gold rush to promote the region and his personal interests, so he published glowing accounts of the Russell find. Many other interested merchants in Missouri, Iowa, Kansas and other jumping off places to the Pikes Peak country added to this embellishment of actual facts. As a result, 100,000 people flocked to Colorado in 1859.

Most of the horde returned to their home states bitterly disappointed before the summer was over, irate about the "Pikes Peak Hoax." The slogan, "Hang Byers and Oakes for starting this damned Pikes Peak hoax," was chanted on the way back over the plains, Byers was hanged in effigy and a mock funeral, including a stuffed dummy and pine box, was conducted for Oakes. About 30,000 remained and continued to prospect or tried farming; many began to lay out paper cities, hopeful of mushrooming metropolises.

The search for gold continued—George Jackson, an experienced miner, made a promising strike near the junction of Chicago and Clear Creeks, but it was so late in the fall heavy snow prevented him from developing it until the next year. In January of 1860 another strike was made at Gold Hill. In April, John Gregory made the most impressive find near what soon became Central City. News of these strikes soon spread and the returning flood ceased, saving the Colorado Gold Rush. Many more towns were staked out than charters were applied for. As the country became more settled, Denver and Golden vied for the supply business of the mining towns. Most of the people that remained were repaid for their patience and confidence in the region's future.

The strike spread to South Park, over the Continental Divide to Breckenridge, Frisco, and Dillon in Utah Territory with more outfitting towns in Boulder, El Paso (Colorado Springs) and Pueblo following. To describe a gold rush and the descent of a horde of people on a defenseless mountain gulch would defy the pen of a Clemens or Harte. The excitement, chaos, uproar seem unimaginable; also, all the action was slightly illegal, because the argonauts were trespassers on lands promised to the Indians by the Treaties of Ft. Laramie and Ft. Atchison, "for as long as the rivers flow and the grasses grow." These treaties were verified by the Kansas-

DIORAMA STATE HISTORICAL SOCIETY

GOLD PANNING

GEORGE
JACKSON

GOLD SLUICE OPERATION

DIORAMA STATE HISTORICAL SOCIETY

JOHN
GREGORY

HYDRAULIC MINING

ebraska Bill of 1854, although it is highly doubt-ul this technicality bothered the Fifty-niners. They olved their own problems by making their own laws here none existed, organizing mining districts, set-ng up towns, and joining into vigilante groups hen it proved necessary. In 1866 the U.S. Congress nally pass d a law verifying their claims.

Colorado started as a poor man's mining opera-on with simple tools and crude methods, giving veryone an opportunity to try his luck. Soon the lacer gold, mostly buckshot, wire or flour gold, was one and the simple mining days were over. Lode nining replaced the placers in the streams and be-ame the more important character of the new in-ustry. A few of the veins were quartz with loose nd easy to process ores, where gold was partially reed and crushing and separation not too difficult. fter the quartz was crushed, the placer process as repeated. The old Spanish arrastre was used to rush some of the early and looser ore, but was soon eplaced by stamp mills, which were deafening in ecibles.

The years of 1864 to 1868 were poor years for olorado, therefore population continued to decline. ilpin County was the only consistent producer, also his period was marked by a buying and consolida-ing of claims with the small operations gradually elling out to larger concerns. Finally, the profes-ionals began to come in. Many of the new lodes roved difficult to process, because they contained efractory ore that was hard to crush, in addition he gold was difficult to separate. The increase in

expense of processing called for a larger operation with more volume.

Nathaniel Hill, a teacher, chemist, and metal-urgist was sent to Europe to learn the latest in hardrock mining and smeltering so the hard, refrac-tory ores of Colorado could be dealt with on a sci-entific basis. He was hired by the capitalists who had invested money in Colorado mining. When he returned, he brought trained people back with him, a smelter was built at Blackhawk and heat and chemicals were applied to the stubborn, refractory ores.[1]

Many hardrock miners also came to the Colo-rado mines later to have their names sprinkled throughout the history of Colorado mining camps. A casual stroll through many of the old cemeteries shows stones with inscriptions that read, after the name, "Cornish miner, killed in a mine cavein or dynamite explosion." The miners successfully as-saulted the stubborn ores and the smelters reduced them to residue. Telluride ores were found and these combinations of minerals interacted on each other, making the process easier. The first problems accompanying the rush were resolved, but Colorado was not growing—the population of Denver was less than 5,000 and in 1861 there were less than 30,000 residents in the territory. Colorado's isolation and mountain barriers still discouraged rapid growth. The coming of the "iron horse" would soon solve the weighty problems of supply and transportation to the isolated Pikes Peak Country.

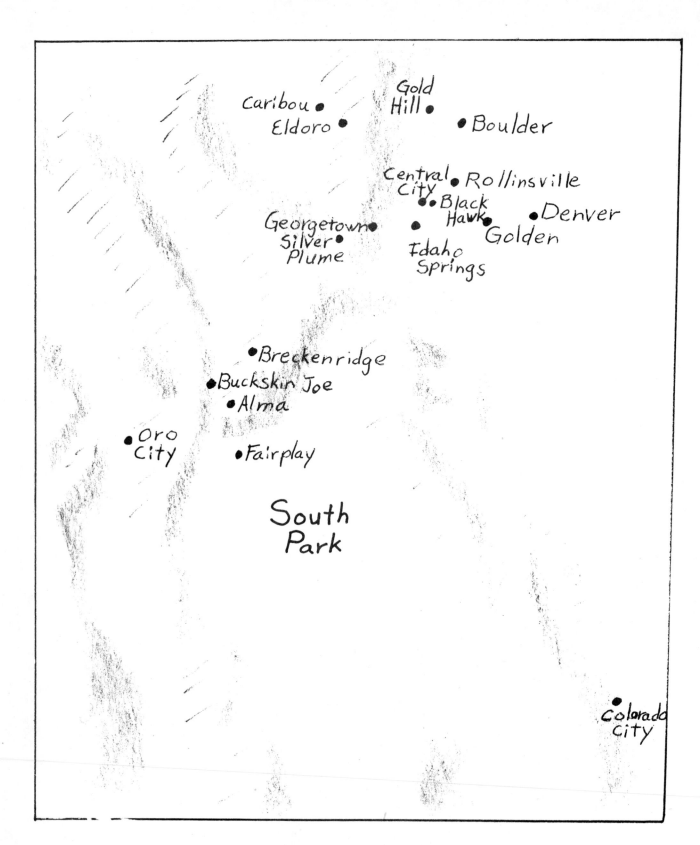

Colorado Gold Rush   1859-1863

12—COLORADO BECOMES A TERRITORY AND FIGHTS THE CIVIL WAR

The circumstances that ushered Colorado into the Union as a territory and as a state were both pragmatic and unusual. The Civil War, expected at any time, encouraged President Lincoln to organize all the western territory possible and secure it before it could become Confederate. Colorado was quickly admitted to the Union as a state in 1876 to expedite the election of a president.

There were several areas of concern for President Lincoln after he took office as the first Republican president. Many were not related to the West; however, the West was on his mind. Many historians argue that the West was not important in the Civil War, at most only a sidelight, not a determining factor. President Lincoln worried about western states seceding from the Union and many of the southwestern states did leave. Golden was a center of Confederate sentiments; furthermore, mass demonstrations occurred in Denver's rival city. Confederate raiding parties were an unpleasant and destructive reality of the war. Nathaniel Bedford Forrest and Jeb Stuart raided all through the lower sections of the North, while at the same time Colorado was plagued by some of these depredations.

A more sobering consideration was the possibility of Indian uprising. If the Indians made use of the opportunity provided by the Civil War to unite against their white antagonists, it would be more detrimental to the North, because the South had removed most of their Indians by this time. The coming war could also be viewed by Mexico as a golden opportunity to regain lost territory or prestige; secondly, the isolated ramparts of the West were almost impossible to defend. Any power willing to take the chance could cause the Union great difficulty if it showed too great an interest in California, one of the more attractive and isolated western states. Lincoln was equally concerned about a Confederate invasion of the West. Both sides needed bullion—found mostly in Colorado, California or Nevada—to back up their sagging currency and finances. These concerns prompted the move for a Colorado Territory; therefore, on February 26, 1861, Congress created the Territory of Colorado.

Governor William Gilpin and most of the other newly appointed officials arrived in Colorado in May of 1861, then promptly began to set up the government. Gilpin had been a major in the army, had served with Fremont, moreover, the new Governor had campaigned against the Utes and Apache; he seemed well fitted by experience for the task ahead. The Civil War was now beginning, also, the West was a crucial factor, with the ability to determine the outcome in a closely fought war. Gilpin's military experience plus his knowledge of the West would be helpful. He was also a loyal Union man and Republican, points not to be overlooked. There were many Confederate sympathizers in Colorado that would need surveillance. The newly appointed governor quickly appointed a military staff and began to organize a volunteer militia, with Col. John P. Slough as commander, Lt. Col. Samuel Tappan and Maj. John M. Chivington (at first chaplain), as officers.

In 1861 the census of Colorado showed a population of 20,000 males, 5,000 females, 86 slaves—72 located in Golden—while Denver's population was about 5,000, with Confederate-leaning Golden comprising about 4,000.[2] Western migration or commerce was not ended by the war. The flow of settlers west continued, especially those of conscript age, while at the same time wagons continued to move over the Oregon and Santa Fe trails with few interruptions. Events on the battlefront overshadowed the history of the frontier, meanwhile, many of the miners in the gold towns or other far-flung frontiers of the West referred to the war as, "that thar war back in the States." The winner of the war would probably gain the West, very sparsely settled in 1861, with transportation and communication practically non-existent. The Indians were still strong and, therefore, capable of making use of the war, if they decided to do so. Most of the West, when the showdown came, went with the cause of the North, as they had more family and economic ties with the North so were most sympathetic with the Union; however, there were many that were undecided or unconcerned, as well as the pro-Confederates.

In case the war did come to the Colorado Territory, the problem of defense was critical, as the people were poorly defended. The troops were not located near the population centers, but at Ft. Lyon on the Arkansas and Ft. Garland in the San Luis Valley, therefore, not near the towns of Denver or Golden or on the Colorado Piedmont where most of the people were located. The development of the frontier went ahead, despite the war, meanwhile, the population of the Colorado territory continued to increase, even with many of the young men going to battlefronts in the South. Governor Gilpin moved as fast as possible to provide a militia to protect the towns of Colorado from Indians or Confederates, accordingly, the first regiment was ready by September of 1861. The troops were housed and trained at Camp Weld (named after the secretary of the territory) in Denver, while a second regiment was added early in 1862, with an effort to recruit a third underway. The Union held that the territories should be able to provide their own protection against Indian attack, while the Union would send troops if a Confederate invasion of Colorado became a reality.

Governor Gilpin faced a monumental problem in mustering a militia, because no money had been provided by the federal government for this purpose, consequently, there was no extra money in the Colorado Territory. Gilpin solved the dilemma by writing drafts on the Treasury of the United States for a sum of about $375,000, but the Secretary of Treasury was not informed, therefore, when the drafts arrived in the capital, they bounced clear back to the Colorado Territory. Most historians do not think Gilpin had any authorization to issue the drafts, but this seems strange; the governor was well acquainted with Lincoln, accordingly, it appears highly irregular for him to issue the drafts without some authorization from Lincoln. Lincoln was not a meticulous administrator, therefore, the President may have forgotten to inform the Secretary of Treasury when he instructed Gilpin to raise a militia. The President must have been aware that some funds from the federal government would be necessary for this purpose. When the drafts bounced, it caused a slight depression in the Colorado Territory, making Gilpin far from popular with the businessmen who held the questionable drafts. Finally, Lincoln intervened and the drafts were honored; Gilpin was recalled to Washington to be replaced by John Evans. Gilpin was treated rather shabbily, besides he was a capable and experienced westerner. Gilpin might have been able to avoid some of the darkest chapters in the history of the Centennial State by resolving the Indian problems in a more humane way before the Sand Creek episode exploded.

With Governor Gilpin's quandary resolved by making him the scapegoat, training of the Colorado militia began in earnest under the "fighting parson" at Camp Weld. Maj. Chivington showed too much ability as a fighting man and leader to serve as the chaplain, so he was used in this capacity; his vocabulary was more appropriate as a soldier than a parson. Originally, the plan called for relieving the regulars at Fort Garland for duty in the South with the Colorado militia assuming the regulars' former responsibilities. Two more companies were mustered, some coming from other rural areas in Colorado. Two companies were also recruited from the Canon City and Fountain areas.

The Colorado Volunteers were a ragtag, nondescript group of soldiers. The expected equipment from the federal government seldom arrived, however, when it did, it was inferior in quality anyway. Each volunteer carried a different kind of a rifle, their uniforms were makeshift, meanwhile, there was a shortage of ammunition and other materials. The problem of transport that plagued the isolated Colorado mines was felt during time of war.

During the "lame duck period," while James Buchanan was still in office, John B. Floyd was the Secretary of War. This southerner made an effort before going out of office to abundantly stock the South with military supplies and officers before the war began, moreover, this was accomplished at the expense of the North. This incredible arrangement was applicable to Texas and New Mexico when the forts were stocked; at the same time an attempt was made to staff the Confederate army with the best officers possible. Floyd and the Confederates reasoned that good officers were scarce so they could be used to recruit troops, then eventually be-

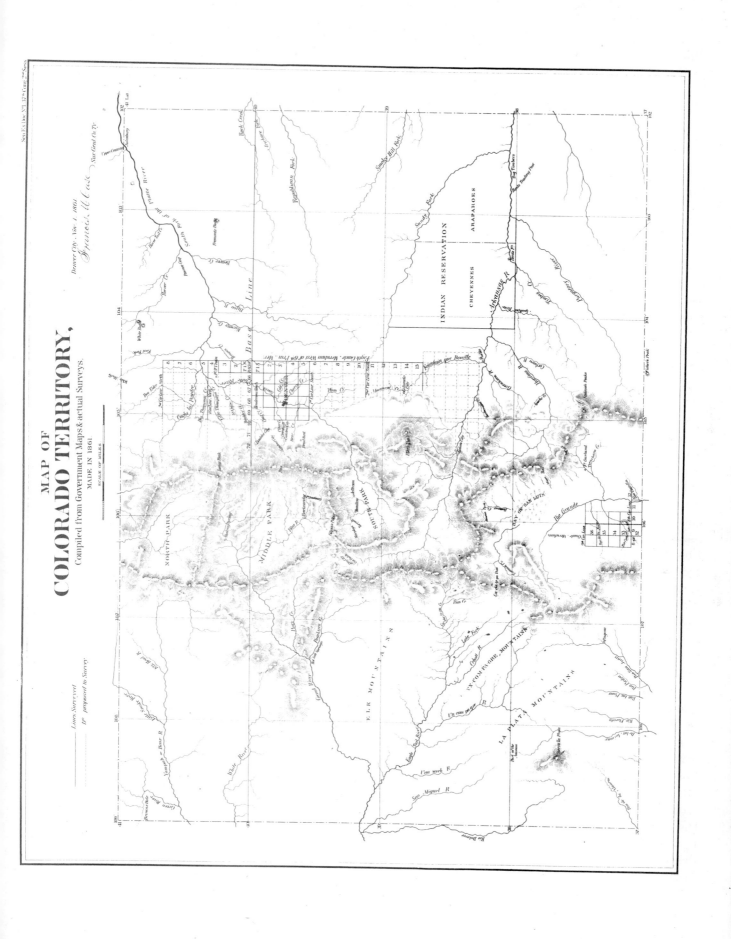

MAP OF
COLORADO TERRITORY,
Compiled from Government Maps & actual Surveys.
MADE IN 1861.

SCALE OF MILES

Denver City. Nov. 1 1861
Francis M Case Sur Genl Co Ty.

Lines Surveyed
Do proposed to Survey

came the backbone of the Confederate army of the West. Col. William Loring was unwisely placed in command of the Union troops in the West. Loring was a fine officer, but he was a loyal southerner who remained as the Union commander in the West for several months after the war had begun, presenting another untenable situation. From his headquarters at Santa Fe, Col. Loring did everything in his power to help the Confederates, later, three months after Fort Sumter, he resigned to join the Confederacy.[3]

Col. Loring was replaced by Col. Edward R. S. Canby, whose loyalty to the Union cause could not be questioned. Canby established his headquarters at Fort Craig, which was about 150 miles north of El Paso on the Rio Grande River. Canby had his hands full; he was confronted by a stronger army, and, although New Mexico was mostly loyal to the North, the South controlled Arizona. In the Confederate States Convention, held in May of 1861, Arizona and western New Mexico were represented and listed as Confederate states.

The opinion that the West would go to the winner of the Civil War, therefore, it was folly to be concerned about defending any part of the West, was widely supported. When the South began an invasion the question was dropped, hence, the war in the West began. The war in the West was vastly different from the war in the South. There were no cities to capture, no communication or transportaion centers to destroy, moreover, very little population to be defended. The South was interested in bullion and other resources they lacked; their shaky finances needed bolstering; also, conquest of the West might impress Europe enough to encourage support for the South. There were many southern sympathizers in the West who could possibly be recruited to increase the size of the outmanned Confederate forces.

To the South these reasons were adequate to justify an invasion, so they began to take over forts in Texas. February 1861, Lt. Col. John Baylor began his move into New Mexico from El Paso by way of the Rio Grande. Fort Fillmore fell to the Confederates without a fight, giving Southern New Mexico to Baylor who promptly proclaimed it a Confederate state. The menace of Baylor's success along the Rio Grande was apparent to Col. Canby who hastily began to assemble all federal troops at Fort Craig, enlarging the post, adding to its strength and fortifications to prepare for a visit from the Rebels.

The strategy of the South included a plan to push north up the Rio Grande to Colorado, gaining the gold fields of Colorado, moreover, leaving California cut off and defenseless. When this campaign began early in 1862, the Union Army was in poor shape to resist. The 19th Infantry was stationed at Santa Fe where Col. Canby had already lost several of his men, some were wounded and sick; his total strength was less than 2,500 men. His forces were isolated at Fort Craig with no reinforcements in sight, meanwhile, he was running short of supplies. Col. Canby began to look for sources of help and sent out a request for reinforcements; the closest military contingent was the Colorado Volunteers. Governor Evans responded to Col. Canby's desperate plea, therefore, two companies were hastily sent toward the Rio Grande. When the two companies arrived at Fort Garland, they were mustered into the United States Army as Company "A" and Company "D" of the Second Colorado Infantry. Efforts began to recruit more volunteers in northern New Mexico under the leadership of Kit Carson.

Col. Baylor was made governor of Confederate Arizona, so his command passed to Col. Henry H. Sibley who, with 3,700 fresh troops, resumed the assault. By a peculiar quirk of circumstances not uncommon in the Civil War, Sibley and Canby were brothers-in-law. Sibley was a capable officer with a reputable record in the Mexican War. His troops were mostly Texans; the brigade marched up the Rio Grande with little opposition. After the fall of Albuquerque Col Canby decided to make a stand at Fort Union. After a march of 175 miles in five days, the Colorado Volunteers arrived at Fort Union where they paused to rest as the effort to recruit more troops continued. Several engagements followed while, at the same time, there were many minor battles fought in the vicinity. It is impossible to describe these in total in the limits of this text; the encounters of the Colorado Volunteers are all that can be given attention.

Col. Slough and the staff of the Colorado Volunteers, fresh and not battle weary, undoubtedly commented on the conservative approach and strategy that was being used by the beleaguered Canby. They were particularly disturbed by his apparent decision to abandon Santa Fe to the Confederates. In an effort to save the city, Col. Slough left Fort Union and headed for the city. There were about 1,300 troops in the entourage of Volunteers; an advance group of 500 was sent into La Glorieta Pass in March of 1862. The pass was about twenty-five miles long and ran from east to west; it was located east of Santa Fe. In a narrow defile about seven miles long, called Apache Canyon, the Colorado Volunteers attacked a contingent of Confederates, after capturing some scouts and catching the Texans by surprise. The charge on the camp proved victorious

Gov. William Gilpin

Col. John Chivington

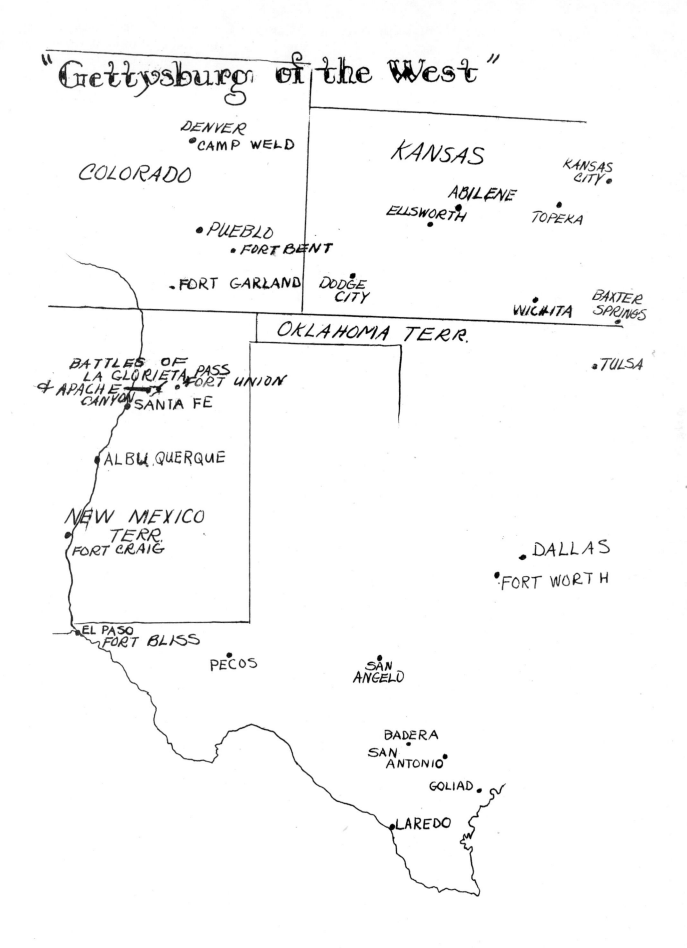

"Gettysburg of the West"

COLORADO

DENVER
• CAMP WELD

• PUEBLO
• FORT BENT

• FORT GARLAND

KANSAS

KANSAS CITY •

ABILENE
ELLSWORTH
TOPEKA

DODGE CITY

WICHITA   BAXTER SPRINGS

OKLAHOMA TERR.

BATTLES OF
LA GLORIETA PASS
& APACHE
CANYON   FORT UNION
SANTA FE

• ALBUQUERQUE

NEW MEXICO TERR.
• FORT CRAIG

• TULSA

• DALLAS
• FORT WORTH

EL PASO
FORT BLISS

PECOS

SAN ANGELO

BADERA
SAN ANTONIO •

GOLIAD •

LAREDO

—97—

for the Coloradans, although it was a bloody battle. The attack was led by Maj. John M. Chivington who returned to his superior, Col. Slough, with the news of victory in the battle of Apache Canyon.

Col. Slough was camped at the east end of La Glorieta Pass and formed a daring plan—the narrow defile would be a good place to finish the Confederates. He planned to send a group of troops to the rim of the canyon, to encircle the Confederates, then to have them attack from the rear while he made a frontal assault from the east. Maj. Chivington began to climb the ridge with about a third of the force, climbing carefully beyond the ridge to avoid alerting the Confederates. They were able to encircle the camp of the Texans then waited for the sound of battle, as ordered. When they heard the battle commence, the camp was attacked and wrecked. Seventy-three wagons were piled together and burned, 600 mules and horses were bayonetted. Next, they attacked the Confederates from the rear. Unknown to the Volunteers, reinforcements had joined the Texans, therefore, the main battle was a bitter one. After five hours of frenzied fighting, the Union troops were driven back and a truce was called to bury the dead. When the Texans saw the smoke from their camp and were attacked from the rear, they mistakenly concluded Col. Canby had arrived with the main Union forces. They were also without supplies or mounts, so they decided to withdraw. Col. Canby was severely criticized for not pursuing the fleeing army after the battle of La Glorieta Pass, often referred to as the "Gettysburg of the West." Col Slough was so distraught he resigned to join the Union Army in Virginia, where he distinguished himself. Maybe Col. Canby did not want to threaten domestic tranquility by pursuing his brother-in-law, as many claim. La Glorieta Pass was the turning point in the war in the West, as the Confederacy abandoned their plans for California and Colorado. The Colorado Volunteers covered themselves with glory in these two battles and were promptly ordered back to the territory by Governor Evans to protect the populace from Indians.

After the battles of Apache Canyon and La Glorieta Pass, 5,000 troops were dispatched from Fort Leavenworth and 5,000 more were available in California, so Col. Sibley faced a total of over 12,000 troops with 3,000. The odds were too heavily stacked against the Rebels. These circumstances did not diminish the fine efforts of the Colorado Volunteers in the campaign against the Confederates in New Mexico. The Civil War did not come to the Centennial State; also, these two battles helped to keep Colorado from becoming a Civil War battlefield. The Indian campaigns that were soon to follow turned the course of history in another direction and did more to mar the glory of Apache Pass and La Glorieta Pass than the force of numbers or statistics.

3—RAIDING BECOMES A REALITY

Raiding was one of the most effective strata-gems of the Confederacy; names like Jeb Stuart, Nathaniel Bedford Forrest and William Quantrill, who pillaged Lawrence, Kansas, were well known and feared. Most of the Confederate raiders were organized by the Confederacy, then mustered into the army to raid for the cause of the South. They raided in uniform, were outfitted by the Confeder-acy with the purpose of recruiting troops, harassing the North and gaining money, along with needed supplies. The best known of the Confederate Raid-ers was James Reynolds and his Texas Guerillas. The Reynolds gang, along with the Quantrills, raided in uniform supposedly for the cause of the Confed-eracy; however, any loot they confiscated seldom was turned over to the South. Actually, the two gangs were independent acting bandits who raided in their own interests.

Why the South did not resort to raiding on a larger scale during the Civil War puzzles armchair generals. They did not need to defeat the North, all that was necessary was to wear the Union down for the purpose of destroying their will to continue the costly business of war. With these circumstances in mind, raiding or guerila tactics seemed to offer promising possibilities. Why, then, were these tac-tics not implemented? Forrest and Stuart Confed-erate raiders par excellent have already been men-tioned; they were highly effective. The truth may lie in the aristocratic nature of southern values. Raiding was not as attractive as the cavalry, with its color and brilliant maneuvering. A man of honor did not pursue war like a bandit, he fought like a gentleman. Did this attitude deprive the South of victory? No one will ever know.

There were at least four different raiding at-tempts planned to grab Colorado gold, only one of these was successful. Raiding appealed to the ro-mantic bandit nature of the West, therefore, provid-ed an opportunity to gain fame and fortune. Attack-ing civilians was more attractive to some than the campaigns of the bitterly fought Civil War.

Some of General Henry H. Sibley's troops raid-ed Southern Colorado in 1862 by launching hit-and-run attacks. These raids were not thorough enough to be effective and preceded the confederate invasion of Colorado that was stoppd at La Glorieta Pass.

In 1863 another raiding party headed for the Colorado gold fields. The leader of the raiders was Charlie Harrison, Rebel sympathizer and erstwhile proprietor of Denver's Criterion Saloon. The Criterion was a popular watering spa and hangout for assorted types in fledgling Denver. It was advantageous for raiders to know the territory they planned to raid firsthand; consequently, many of the commissioned raiders were former residents of their victim's territory. With these credentials, Harrison successfully finagled a colonel's rank out of the Confederacy, with the promise of seizing the Colorado mines and instigating insurrection.

The most notorious name connected with raiding in the West was Quantrill. William Clarke Quantrill formed his band of guerillas in 1862 in Kansas and began to plunder Kansas towns; starting with thirty, eventually three hundred rode with this group. Many other famous names, including Jesse and Frank James, Cole and Jim Younger, along with lesser knowns, launched their careers by riding with Quantrill. The gang left a swath of death and destruction from Kansas to Kentucky, where Quantrill was killed in a surprise attack. Charlie Harrison boasted he would do the same in Colorado.

The Harrison Gang moved into Eastern Kansas on its way to the Centennial State. On May 14, 1863 they were attacked by a group of unfriendly Osage Indians and wiped out. The problem of trophies was solved on the bald-pated Harrison by substitution of his goatee. The Indians were not deprived of their battle trophies and Colorado was spared the trouble of dealing with this threat.

The raiding parties in the West were organized principally to raid the gold camps to gain the bullion so desperately needed by the South to back Confederate currency. Once acquired, gold was hard to relinquish, so little ever left Colorado to be used by the Confederacy. Jim Reynolds had been in South Park during the gold rush; consequently, he knew the territory. His gang of guerillas included his brother, John, and about twenty others; the group never had more than twenty-five members—not a very impressive force. However, smaller raiding parties had been responsible for considerable damage and Quantrill raided Lawrence with about thirty men. Reynolds threatened to raid Denver in the same manner Quantrill had raided and pillaged Lawrence, Kansas and arrived in Colorado during the summer of 1864.

The Texas Guerillas raided a wagon train on the Santa Fe Trail, then turned toward South Park, attempting to avoid Fort Lyon, Pueblo, and Canon City. They began to attack ranches, stagecoache and miners in South Park, presumably to raise mon ey for the Confederacy. The Reynolds' July cam paign soon attracted opposition, for a posse was or ganized with the purpose of putting a permanen end to the depredations. The posse originated a Fairplay and, after a determined hunt, the gan was located in Handcart Gulch and attacked. Esti mates put the loot in possession of the gang a about $75,000 when the showdown began. Treasur hunters enjoy speculating about the disposition o the Reynolds' loot, as the $75,000 has never bee accounted for.

In the gun battle that followed, three member of the gang were killed and Jim Reynolds wa wounded; the gang fled, leaving their supplies an plunder behind. Reynolds and five members of th gang were captured near Canon City a few day later. The remainder of the gang, including Joh Reynolds, escaped, however, John returned later t recover the $75,000, presumably cached in Handcar Gulch. When John returned to the scene, a fores fire had obscured all the signs left to locate the loot so it was never found.

The six captives, including Jim Reynolds, wer taken to Denver where they were tried before a mili tary tribunal for highway robbery and condemne to be shot. Feelings ran a little high on both sides moreover, there were several Confederate sympa thizers in the Denver area; consequently, the deci sion was made to take the five prisoners to For Lyon on the Arkansas River where repercussion would not be so likely to follow the execution of th six guerillas. Some accounts claim the plan was t eventually transport the group to the Federal Peni tentary at Fort Leavenworth, Kansas. The plan were insignificant, because the entourage neve traveled further than the distance from Denver nec essary to obscure rifle shots. The troops responsibl for transporting the gang members soon returne to Denver, claiming the gang had attempted to es cape, forcing the soldiers to shoot them. The ser geant in charge of the entourage suffered from som of the Reynolds' activities in South Park, accord ingly, Coloradans understood taxpayers were save the expense of transporting and executing the si men at a later date. The sergeant was a forme stagecoach driver who had been robbed by the gang whether he acted on his own behalf or on order from superiors is as much a mystery as the fate o the $75,000.

The New Governor

The circumstances that brought the term o William Gilpin to a rather abrupt and untimely en

JIM REYNOLDS

JOHN
REYNOLDS

S Grover

BRECKENRIDGE

GRANT
GENEVA
BASIN
HANDCART
GULCH
KENOSHA
PASS

KENOSHA MTS.

SO. PLATTE

BUCKSKIN JOE
ALMA

LEADVILLE

X ROBBERY OF
BUCKSKIN STAGE
6/24/1864

TARRYALL MTS.

CASTLE
ROCK

FAIRPLAY

COMO
ROBBERY OF
STAGE STATION
7/26/1864

SOUTH
PARK

NATHROP

CRIPPLE
CREEK

Reynolds Area of Operation

have been described. Maybe the first governor of the Colorado Territory was the unfortunate victim of peculiar circumstances. His successor, Dr. John Evans, was a Republican from the State of Illinois, an acquaintance of President Lincoln, and a staunch Union supporter. These factors put the doctor in a good position for the appointment, but did not prepare him for the challenges he would face in the Colorado Territory. Evans was not a military man, nor did he have any previous experience in the West or knowledge of the West, Indians, or their affairs. Dr. Evans was one of the founders of Northwestern University at Evanston, Illinois and the guiding light in the founding of Denver University, but his appointment was of the political variety, moreover, he was poorly equipped to cope with the multitude of problems facing him.

Governor Evans was more of a businessman-promoter than a politician or statesman, also, he shared the pathological fear many Coloradans had of Indians. An understanding of this intense fear is necessary to explain, not justify, the events soon to follow. Fear of Indians began during the French and Indian War when British and French bought each others' scalps from the Indians, who at first

had been encouraged to live peacefully. This practice of inciting the Indians continued through the American Revolution and the War of 1812, until the tomahawk became a well-known menace to be greatly feared. This fear was dormant or latent until stirred to recollection. It certainly did not discourage the affliction and fever that sent or pulled thousands of Americans westward. Volumes almost as high as the Rockies have been written trying to explain the phenomenon of "Western Fever;" none seem to do justice to this American passion.

The influx of miners into Colorado in the early 1860's upset the peace declared by the Treaty of Fort Laramie and caused the Indians' concern about the illegal activity on lands promised to them in perpetuity. To ease this concern the governor negotiated the Evans Treaty in Denver in 1863. According to the treaty, the Cheyenne and the Arapaho would go on a triangular reservation between the Arkansas River and Sand Creek, surrendering their hunting grounds. The purpose of the treaty was to acculturate the two tribes into the way of the white man, at the same time making these proud warriors of the plains into agriculturists. Each Indian adult would be given forty acres of land to farm as his

STAGECOACH

Gov. John Evans

own, therefore, their communal existence and method of holding land would be replaced by individual ownership. A grist mill and sawmill were to be constructed to pave the way for the building of houses to replace the tepee. Schools would be constructed for the Indian children to convert them to the superior culture; the Indians would cease to be wandering nomads and settle down to working for a living, as every righteous man should.

A resume' of Indian policy would transcend the scope of this volume, but some explanation seems pertinent. The United States Government, through the Bureau of Indian Affairs, preferred to treat the various Indian tribes as independent nations when it came to making treaties. A chief or tribal representative would be induced to sign a treaty, then the tribe would be expected to abide by this commitment; however, the political structure of the tribes was frequently so vague it was impossible for the tribe to be completely informed regarding the treaty, consequently, enforcing such an arrangement was completely beyond the realm of possibility. The democratic nature of the tribes, their communal concept of land ownership, the frequent congressional alterations of the treaties when they returned to Washington, and the consistent failure of the Congress to appropriate funds called for in the treaties for annuities, resulted in great misunderstanding. The Evans Treaty promised a subsidy to the Cheyenne and the Arapaho of $30,000 for fifteen years.

One of the most incredible facts in the relationship with the American Indian is that so many of the injustices that were forced on the red man were unintentional and were often suggested or carried out by sincere, well-meaning Americans who were righteously convinced that they were doing the In-

dian a favor, while at the same time doing what was best for him. Why they never consulted the Indian is another mystery.

The Evans Treaty was fashioned to pacify the Cheyenne and Arapaho—the most formidable of the Colorado tribes—and avoid the possibility of an untimely outbreak during the Civil War. It appeared to have been a success, because the years of 1861, 1862, and 1863 were quiet with no serious Indian problems. Governor Evans had ordered the victorious Second Colorado Volunteers to return from their impressive and decisive campaign in New Mexico and their presence in Colorado made the citizenry rest more easily. Maybe the Indians would make no attempt to use the war as an opportunity to avenge their losses to the whites.

The assumed peace was not long-lived and, when the Indian outbreaks occurred, they were extensive and costly. The change in the situation is not easy to assess. There were people in Colorado who would benefit from an Indian uprising which would bring in more troops and more money. An Indian war would stir up excitement and sell more newspapers, so many of the Colorado papers "beat the war drums" about raids in locations where Indians were seldom seen. Most of the irresponsible journalism consisted of printed accounts of alleged raids, with no effort made to check their authenticity. The officers of the Colorado Volunteers, including newly promoted Col. John M. Chivington, considered new avenues to glory. Many of the enlistments of the volunteers would soon be terminating, negating such possibilities, but paramount was the attitude shared by the majority of the populace that Colorado would be better off without its Indians and much better use could be made of the vast Indian holdings.

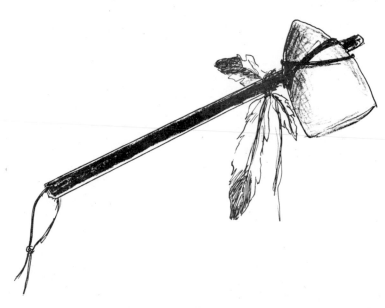

14—GOODBYE TO THE CHEYENNE AND ARAPAHO

Fear of the Indians had been paramount in the minds of Coloradans before the Civil War began, secondly the battles of La Glorieta Pass and Apache Canyon were about as close as the battles of the Civil War came to the Centennial State. The Reynolds Gang only touched a small part of the territory; consequently, concern about the Indians remained a troublesome worry for the more exposed settlers. As the Civil War dragged on and demanded an ever-increasing number of human resources, this anxiety increased. When the Colorado volunteers were mustered into the Union Army at Fort Garland preparatory to the New Mexico campaign, they were no longer militia, therefore, subject to be sent anywhere they were needed. Many of them left Colorado for places like Gettysburg, Lookout Mountain or Cold Harbor. News that the Sioux were on the warpath did nothing to ease worried Coloradans who realized the Sioux were relatives and allies of the Cheyenne. Many rumors circulated describing Indian confederations comprised of the tribes from Canada to Mexico, Confederate efforts to arm, aid and stir up the Plains Indians, plus the hazy knowledge of actual Indian atrocities and practice, had led many to believe the Indians were savage barbarians capable of the most gruesome actions imaginable.

Governor Evans had little experience or knowledge to guide him in his efforts to deal with the Plains tribes and was financially limited in bargaining. Having little to bargain with, he was forced into a "play-it-by-ear" diplomacy that had no chance of success and frequently did more harm than good. His dual assignment as governor of the territory and superintendent of Indian affairs was so conflicting it was almost impossible to carry out. He was expected to defend, protect and look after the welfare of the citizens of Colorado and the Indians, at the same time then try to keep peace with both.

Trouble started in the spring of 1864 when a report was received accusing a group of Cheyenne of attacking a wild horse contractor and making off with about 175 of his stock, quite a coup. Without checking, Col. Chivington led a contingent of troops out to investigate the incident. The troops caught up with a party of Cheyenne near the Smokey Hill Trail then ordered them to surrender their arms; when they refused, a skirmish resulted. After the skirmish the troops attacked a nearby village and killed about 175 Indians, mostly women and children. Chivington returned to Denver, claiming a victory in a major encounter. Governor Evans wired Washington that an Indian war had now begun in earnest, hopeful of gaining support to raise more militia or better, federal troops.

As the summer of 1864 approached, Indians were fleeing when they sighted troops, Indian camps were being raided and looted with mostly women and children the casualties. Gov. Evans announced that any citizen who wanted to engage in private war with the Indians could do so and keep whatever plunder he was able to confiscate. The Indians relocated their camps in more inaccessible places and avoided the main trails in an attempt to prevent trouble—the raids and depredations of both sides began to subside—maybe the threat of war was over.

Rumors still persisted on the front range, stories of Indian purchases of firearms, and depredations continued. Elbridge Gerry, the "squaw man" who lived with the Cheyennes, kept things warm with his stories of Indian confederation near Denver, along with planned attacks on Denver. Evans now wired Washington, "An Indian war rages that could wipe out the populace." His dire predictions in an effort to obtain aid from Washington were beginning to make him look bad when no trouble materialized.

On May 16th a hundred troops trotted down the Smoky Hill Trail; this trail drifted off southeast of Denver and was off the beaten path, used by the the Indians, but not by anyone else. Near the present town of Agate, they spotted an Arapaho village and began to approach. Sighting the approaching troopers, Chief Lean Bear rode out to meet the group and raised his arm in peace, asking for parley. As he approached the troopers, someone raised his rifle and shot the Arapaho chief from his horse, as the Indians hastily began to prepare an assault, the troops departed. After this incident Indian raids increased in earnest—wagons, ranches and even settled towns were attacked. On June 11th the Nathan Hungate ranch, twenty-five miles southeast of Denver was raided and Hungate, his wife and two daughters were tortured, mutilated and murdered, the women were raped. Roman Nose was accused of this atrocity. This resplendent Cheyenne, the ultimate warrior, now confirmed rumors about his actions. After the raid the mutilated bodies of the Hungates were brought to Denver to be placed in the main display window of one of the most prom-

CHEYENNE TEEPEE   DIORAMA STATE HISTORICAL SOCIETY

ROMAN
NOSE

SGrover

inent dry goods establishments. People of Denver went hysterical—the army warehouse was seized to arm the masses and barricades were erected all over the endangered frontier town. Evans wired Washington that a full-scale Indian war was now occurring along the front range of the Rockies.

The Indians were divided into "friendlies"— those who had gone into agriculture and put aside their weapons as agreed according to the Evans Treaty of 1863, and the Indians not yet settled, who were called "hostiles."

Indians that sought to be classified as "friendlies" were to gather at the forts to turn in their arms and become settled on their reservation. Indian raids did not subside and frequent accounts of raids appeared in the news, adding to the anxiety of the populace. People who lived in fear of attacks by barbarous savages for several months were becoming eager to be rid of their great fear, which had now also taken on the added emotion, intense hatred. This intense hatred and obsessive fear soon made any solution that would end the anxiety attractive and justified. The people demanded an end to the problem. The Third Colorado Regiment was raised, mustering in troops for an enlistment period of one hundred days.

If the Indians had a plan for a massive attack on Denver, as many believed, the assault never came. Maj. Edward W. Wynkoop, commanding officer at Fort Lyon who was acquainted with most of the Cheyenne and Arapaho chiefs, was approached by the Indians and asked to arrange a parley with Gov. Evans. Fall was approaching and the Indians wished to prepare for the winter, so seven Cheyenne and Arapaho chiefs were escorted to Denver. The Indians claimed misunderstandings were the cause of the trouble of the past few weeks. The Hungate Massacre, the chiefs claimed, was the work of a group of young Indians on a coup party led by Roman Nose, also it had occurred after the peaceful Lean Bear had been murdered. Raids had dropped off the past few weeks, therefore, the eloquent chiefs stated they were ready to live in peace with the white men. Governor Evans reluctantly agreed to the terms of peace, but told the Indians to report into the forts and turn in their arms, if they were sincere. When the Indians reported into the forts, they were fired on, so the tempo of the raids picked up and Elbridge Gerry reported a huge Indian army was gathering for an attack on Denver. Ranchers moved into town, women were barricaded in the brick buildings, some lost their minds. The terrified Evans wired Washington that, "The largest Indian war in history is now raging in Colorado."

Col. Chivington wired his superior, Gen. S. R. Curtis, in St. Louis, for permission to conduct a campaign against the Indians. In the same wire he reported Maj. Wynkoop, commandant at Ft. Lyon, was issuing supplies to hostile Indians, therefore, was unworthy as an officer. Shortly after the September 28th meeting with the seven chiefs in Denver, Chivington received a reply from Gen. Curtis, giving him an affirmative answer and telling him "to make the Indians suffer more." He did not show the telegram to Major Wynkoop, who was considered an Indian sympathizer. Many of the Indians had begun to report into the forts in peace, hence it seemed a solution may be approaching.

On November the 4th Maj. Scott Anthony reported at Fort Lyon and presented Maj. Wynkoop with orders to report to St. Louis to answer charges of trafficking with hostiles. About a week later Chief Black Kettle arrived with about 1,000 Cheyenne and Arapaho. Maj. Anthony, the new commandant, refused the Indians permission to enter the fort and would not take their arms, but told them to continue to hunt. The Indians signed a truce with Anthony then informed the Major they would go into camp on Sand Creek, which was located on their reservation. They asked that traders be sent to trade their buffalo robes for supplies they needed for the winter. On November 27th Col. John Chivington rode into Fort Lyon with 500 troops. As the Volunteers approached the fort, they fanned out and surrounded the walls to insure no one would leave, betraying their arrival. Their plan to attack the Indian encampment on Sand Creek was a conclusion easily guessed. Maj. Anthony protested because he had signed petitions of peace with Black Kettle and Lt. Silas Soule, one of Chivington's staff, was quite vocal in condemning the assault. Col. Chivington was the highest ranking officer, Anthony owed his promotion to the colonel, also the 100-day enlistments were about to expire without any taste of action. The Third Colorado Volunteers had been ridiculed by being called the "bloodless Third" and were anxious to demonstrate their mettle.

Governor John Evans was in Washington during the time of the Sand Creek attack, so his part in this complex and controversial event is vague. So many accounts and versions of what transpired exist that an accurate description is difficult. Eye witness accounts are of little help, because they are inconsistent. Joined with several of the regulars stationed at Fort Lyon, along with their cannon, the contingent pulled out on November 28th for an all-night march to the Sand Creek camp. The Indians were caught completely by surprise, and surrounded,

"Trouble"

BLACK
KETTLE

LITTLE
RAVEN

the first alert they had was when cannon balls began to fall among their tepees. The Indians ran from their tepees in wild disorder, some waving their arms in signs of peace, others trying to organize for protection and defense. The battle lasted for six or seven hours until all the Indians that did not escape were killed. Most of the Indians, including Black Kettle, escaped; the 400 or more that were killed were mostly women and children, as was the case with so many battles in so many places. Sand Creek became a name blotted into history, along with Washita Springs, Wounded Knee, Fallen Timbers, and many others. The bitterness and hatred unleashed in these thought provoking battles is hard to explain or fathom.

If the purpose of the Sand Creek affair was to bring the Indians to a lasting peace, it was the greatest and most colossal failure in history. The rampaging troopers and their commander now had a genuine full-scale Indian war on their hands. Raiding parties plundered all up and down the front range. The Platte River Trail was closed, telegraph wire and poles were torn down, Julesburg was sacked twice, many pitched battles, unusual for Indians, were fought and won by the Indians.

The triumphant Third Colorado Volunteers rode back into Denver, displaying scalps and booty that the Indians had in camp and were given a heroes welcome. On December 30th, a telegram arrived in Denver, ordering the arrest of Col. Chivington, who resigned his commission and left the territory. A congressional investigating committee was sent to the Mile High City to ferret out the truth. Silas Soule, the most important witness for the committee, was shot down in the streets of Denver and, when an officer of the law who had witnessed the murder tried to arrest the assassin, he, too, was shot. Feelings ran so high in Denver, the city was placed under martial law. Finally, the army sent in a team to investigate, after lengthy and contradictory hearings, the Sand Creek Massacre was condemned, but the case ended with this action.

A general campaign was ordered against the Indians, also the cavalry learned what an Indian war was. Washington dispatched peace commissions, more investigating committees and finally some treaties were negotiated in 1865. The Civil War ended in 1865, freeing thousands of troops for action in the Indian wars, therefore, Gen. Wm. T. Sherman became the commander in the West. Wagon loads of presents were sent west to bribe the Indians into submission, at the same time the pressure of more modern warfare was kept on the Plains Indians. Finally, the Cheyenne and Arapaho signed the Medicine Lodge Creek Treaty in 1867 and agreed to relocate in Oklahoma; their hunting privileges were retained for as long as the buffalo lasted. The last Plains Indian battle in Colorado was Summit Springs in 1869, which was a re-run of Sand Creek. By 1870 the Cheyenne, Arapaho, Kiowa and Comanche were resettled in Oklahoma, then the former hunting grounds of the Cheyenne and Arapaho were soon declared open for settlement. The Utes of western Colorado now, along with the formidable Apache near the southern border, were the remaining tribes. The story of their forced exodus will follow.

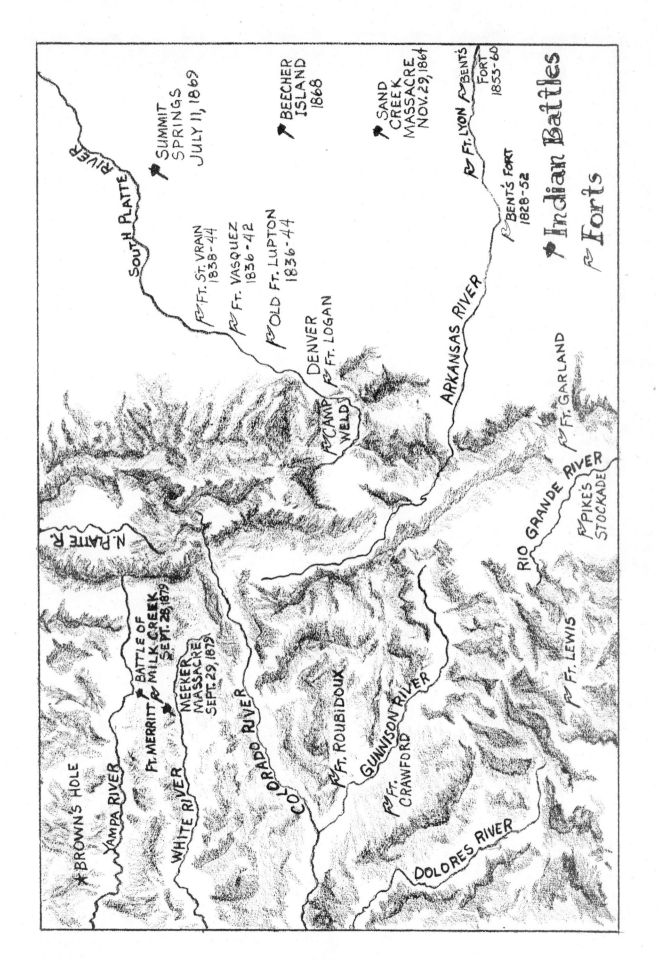

SOUTH PLATTE RIVER

SUMMIT SPRINGS JULY 11, 1869

BEECHER ISLAND 1868

SAND CREEK MASSACRE NOV. 29, 1864

FT. LYON

BENT'S FORT 1853-60

FT. ST. VRAIN 1838-44

FT. VASQUEZ 1836-42

OLD FT. LUPTON 1836-44

DENVER

FT. LOGAN

CAMP WELD

BENT'S FORT 1826-52

ARKANSAS RIVER

Indian Battles

Forts

FT. GARLAND

RIO GRANDE RIVER

PIKE'S STOCKADE

N. PLATTE R.

BATTLE OF MILK CREEK SEPT. 28, 1879

FT. MERRITT

MEEKER MASSACRE SEPT. 29, 1879

WHITE RIVER

COLORADO RIVER

FT. ROUBIDOUX

GUNNISON RIVER

FT. CRAWFORD

FT. LEWIS

BROWN'S HOLE

YAMPA RIVER

DOLORES RIVER

—113—

15—THE 1870's AND GREATER PROSPECTS

In the 1870's Colorado began to boom like never before. There are several reasons for this progress after a decade of doubt, frustration and Indian war. The "Iron Horse" was one of the most significant factors for growth, with the transcontinental being completed in 1869 and the Kansas Pacific and Denver Pacific connecting to it in 1870. Historians, at best, are a cantankerous lot so many argue the railroad was an overrated performer in the drama of the West. This allegation probably has elements of truth, therefore the statement that canals could have served as well bears some credibility, however, in the Rocky Mountains the canals would have had their problems. The removal of the Indians from east of the Continental Divide, followed by the opening of that vast expanse, also facilitated the spurt of growth in the 1870's. The silver boom with its by-products was another contributor; also, the open range cattle industry along with foreign capital invested in railroads, mining, and the cattle industry helped to get these industries going. Colorado began to beckon as a health spa, with its dry climate and sunshine, with tuberculosis sanitariums and hot springs hotels. The outbreak of spas leads one to suspect good doctors back East told a chronic hypochondriac to go to Colorado for a change of scenery instead of telling him where they would really like him to go. Liberal land legislation with the Homestead Act of 1862 aided the most important, if not most spectacular, industry of the West, soon dotting the plains with homesteaders' cabins and increasing agriculture, Colorado's number one industry until the 1940's.

By 1890, an intricate network of railroads crisscrossed the continent helping to make the United States the world's greatest railroad nation. The age of steam began in the 1830's in the East, with interruptions caused by the Mexican and Civil wars. After the Civil War the question of a southern or middle route for a transcontinental road was put aside and men with vision saw the potential of Colorado with the help of the railroad. Many such men had been in Colorado during the Indian wars—men like Gen. Palmer, Col. Dodge, and Gen. Custer, to name a few, mostly young men that were adventurous and aggressive who chose to seek their fame and fortune in the direction of the setting sun after the Civil War.

Transportation was a major problem pertinent to the economic development of the Centennial State, therefore, if this dilemma remained unsolved, it would sorely hinder the potential of an isolated state needing heavy equipment for its mines and farms. One hundred million pounds of freight was being brought across the plains and into Colorado by 1865, with the tonnage increasing each year.[1] Many negative reports were already circulating about the feasibility of bringing the "Iron Horse" to Colorado. The mountains seemed too much of a barrier, also the ill-fated fourth Fremont expedition, along with pessimistic comments in the Gunnison log, did nothing to allay the rather bad name Colorado had acquired for a location on the contemplated transcontinental.

The transcontinental was chartered in 1862, during the Civil War, but then delayed in construction until the end of the war. Denver citizens shared high hopes it would come through their fair city; Gov. Evans was on the board of directors of the Union Pacific, the most prominent company involved, also Denver was the largest city in the central Rockies.

However, the surveyors and engineers making the route designation thought otherwise and decided to go through South Pass, west of the hastily built town of Cheyenne. Maybe they had never heard of men like William Jackson Palmer or the diminutive Otto Mears, who did not share these doubts. At any rate, the sobering facts had to be accepted, Denver was going to be by-passed, as was the State of Colorado, moreover many began to predict the demise of the "Mile High City," meanwhile, speaking of Cheyenne as the new "queen city" of the Rockies.

If the transcontinental would not come to Denver, then Denver must go to the transcontinental; this was the next best alternative, consequently the Denver Board of Trade (equivalent to Chamber of Commerce) began to organize an effort to lay track to Cheyenne to make the important connection. Lucrative land grants and federal financing were now not as readily available for trunk lines, therefore financing was always a crucial hurdle for Colorado railroad promoters. Denverites also became aware of a competitive effort to build a rival railroad from Golden to Cheyenne, promoted by W. A. H. Loveland and E. L. Berthoud. Both these men were well known and capable, but efforts to consolidate their

venture with the Denver group were unsuccessful. The Golden group planned to follow a route close to the Front Range north and send feeder lines into the mining camps along the way, particularly Central City and Blackhawk. Inability to gain the support of Denver and other difficulties resulted in the failure of Colorado Central Railroad, as the Golden Railroad was to be named. The road did make it to most of the mining camps, but never connected with the transcontinental.

The Kansas Pacific announced its plans to follow the Smoky Hill Trail from Kansas City west into Denver, moreover, this news was heartening for the crestfallen Denver promoters, but then talk started of a change in plans to move south into the Arkansas Valley. The Kansas Pacific was having more than its share of difficulties from Indian attacks and shortage of funds. Finally, the energy and enthusiasm of the Denver Board of Trade began to bear fruit. Bond issues were floated, funds were obtained from the Kansas Pacific, meanwhile, the Union Pacific and Congress finally agreed to a grant for a right-of-way. People who were approached to contribute were told to bring a shovel and come to the construction site if they did not have any money and wished to help. Some were given stock for aiding in the making of roadbed. The Denver Pacific was completed to Cheyenne in 1870, giving Denver a transcontinental connection for the first time. In a few months the Kansas Pacific resolved its problems and connected to the "Mile High City." They were able to gain an increase in land grants and finish construction. The future of Denver was now assured, now the city began to grow rapidly with its two railroad connections, and soon Cheyenne was left far behind. Connections were made to Golden, Central City, Idaho Springs, and Blackhawk over the Colorado Central, therefore these mining towns began to depend more on Denver for supplies coming from the East.

"The Little Giant"

The story of the Rio Grande Railroad is well written in Robert G. Athearn's Rebel of the Rockies. The Denver and Rio Grande, as it was called, began in the 1870's and, before it was finished, laid track in some of the most spectacular mountain areas in the world. The D&RG, sometimes called "the dirty, rough and greasy" and a multitude of other less complimentary names, was mainly the brainchild of William Jackson Palmer. Palmer, who had risen to the rank of general while serving in the Civil War, was only 35 years old when he started his railroad venture, and definitely not a man without firm convictions. He had been in the West before

Gen. William Jackson Palmer

the war then returned to find his future as soon as the war ended. Palmer was an experienced railroad man, serving on the board of directors of the Kansas Pacific, but he did not think like most railroad men. The general was inclined to think big, was not afraid to defy convention, moreover, his visions included building a narrow gauge (three feet wide—conventional four feet eight and one-half inches), and in the wrong direction. It would run north to south from Canada to Mexico. He was even thinking in terms of Alaska to Tierra del Fuego. Everyone knew that commerce moved from east to west in the United States, but Palmer planned to connect his lines to gold camps running to the west and farming communities to the east. The narrow gauge would be cheaper to build and more maneuverable in the confines of the Rockies. (A later chapter will be devoted specifically to narrow gauge railroads.)

Palmer was a go-getter with important connections in the East; he married the daughter of a prominent Boston attorney after an abbreviated, whirlwind courtship. The railroad was planned and organized in 1870, with construction beginning in 1871 on the first leg south from Denver to Colorado City. Palmer was impressed by the beauty and surroundings of the Colorado City area and laid out the new town of Colorado Springs, following an English motif. The city was nicknamed "Newport of the Rockies" and began to flourish in its attractive setting. The next year the "Little Giant" headed south for Pueblo, informing the people of Pueblo that they would need to raise money to help the cause. Pueblo began to float a bond issue to pay for the privilege, as they knew Palmer would by-pass them and build a rival town if they did not come across.

At Pueblo, Palmer soon learned what most businessmen know so well—establishing a successful business venture is only part of the struggle. Competition can wipe you out after years of success. The Atchison, Topeka and Santa Fe, chartered in 1859, headed for Pueblo, therefore, the people of that city began to lose interest in Palmer's railroad and schemes. Palmer by-passed Pueblo and built the town of South Pueblo as a rival city, then started to lay track south to Raton Pass in an effort to get to Santa Fe ahead of his competition. Both railroads headed for Trinidad, with the Denver and Rio Grande, failing to gain financial support from Trinidad, building the rival town of El Moro about five miles away. The rival A.T.&S.F. went to Trinidad from La Junta. From Trinidad the two railroads began the race to Raton Pass with the A.T.&S.F. winning by about one-half hour.

When the silver rush in Leadville began, transportation was a major deterrent to the mining development, therefore, both the Rio Grande and the Santa Fe were anxious to take advantage of the heavy traffic that was expected. The two railroads began to send work gangs into the Royal Gorge Canyon of the Arkansas River where the race to the "cloud city" began. Old newspaper clippings with pictures show handcars filled with menacing looking men armed to the teeth as the Royal Gorge war ensued. Fortunately, no one was killed and most of the serious battles were fought in court, with the attorneys generally the victors. The issues between the two railroads were partially settled by the Treaty of Boston, which decreed the Santa Fe would be given the franchise south to Santa Fe, while the Rio Grande would have first rights into the mountains to the west. Both sides violated the treaty but the wasteful expense of building parallel track was at least abandoned. Also, Jay Gould gained control of the Rio Grande and had large interests in the Union Pacific and Kansas Pacific and did not wish to have his toys competing against each other.

After the Royal Gorge was finished, the town of Salida was built and became one of the operational centers for the Rio Grande; also, the company hospital was built there. From Salida the road went to Leadville then on to Glenwood Springs. Railroad construction in Western Colorado waited for the removal of the Utes in 1881 and the rapid settlement that soon followed. West of Salida the Rio Grande began to lay rails to Gunnison, arriving in 1881, then to Montrose and Grand Junction. All of these new towns were given the opportunity to "cough up" for the expense of construction, but they had little to offer. When the "Little Giant" approached Grand Junction, the town was but a few cottonwood cabins and had no funds for railroads. Finally, the city fathers surrendered a large portion of the lots of the Western Colorado town and the Rio Grande crossed the Grand in 1882.

The Colorado Midland operated through the heartland of Colorado, Colo. Springs—Leadville—Basalt—Aspen and Glenwood Springs, to the coal fields of Newcastle, where it eventually was connected with the Rio Grande. The Colorado Midland was a financially healthy railroad for a time so therefore gave Palmer considerable competition. It used standard gauge which forced the Rio Grande to convert. In many places the Colorado Midland and the Rio Grande had three-track railroads to accommodate the rolling stock of both narrow and standard gauge operations, with tracks three feet and four feet eight and one-half inches.

COLO. MIDLAND EXCURSION ENGINE

COLO. MIDLAND HIGH BRIDGE NEAR BUENA VISTA

DIORAMA STATE HISTORICAL SOCIETY

The "Little Giant" continued to put down track in Colorado. It also built feeder and spur lines into many mining camps and quarries, or wherever it seemed a railroad would prosper. Like all railroads at the end of the 19th century in the United States, the "Little Giant" overbuilt and suffered the unfortunate consequences. The history of the Rio Grande is another story of mountains, machines and men, and it is a fascinating account, too voluminous for detail in this book. Many question the means of William Jackson Palmer, but few question the results. His achievements are there for all to see, and his forceful pragmatism probably was the only route he could follow to success. The importance of the Rio Grande to the mining towns of the Centennial State is obvious, also, the state made rapid progress with railroads to move material.

Turntable

C&S   Five of Twenty   Feb 1976   Michael C Downing

16—THE GLITTER OF SILVER

Gold mining continued to occupy the attention of many Colorado "sourdoughs" in the late 1860's, but the first rush was over, accordingly the buying and consolidating of claims began to pave the way for the more sophisticated process required by the stubborn refractory ores. Gilpin County was the most active area, with the smelter at Blackhawk opening for operation in 1868, producing a continued scurry for ore. Oro City, deep in the Rockies, had been a good producer before most of the placers were worked over, but by 1865 many avered that the only thing that kept the town going was lack of enough people to give the place a decent funeral.

The presence of silver was long known in the Centennial State, but in the 1860's the argonauts were single-minded in the pursuit of gold and ignored or discarded the dark pyrites that collected in the bottom of their pans or rockers, often stymying their efforts. Silver, lead and zinc were looked at as more of a nuisance than anything else because, as yet, there was no market to encourage production. The increasing industrial activity in the United States and governmental purchase and support of silver helped to provide a healthier market for these minerals when the silver mining began.

A mining rush to California Gulch was instigated when William Stevens and Alvinus Wood made a strike that assayed about 65% lead, with silver and zinc of payable quantity included. After the report, the two prospectors hurried to make claims on the location at Fryer Hill while gradually word began to filter out in newspapers and mining journals. As early as 1873 some mention of silver finds were known, but after the Wood and Stevens strike, more interest and response began, consequently the rush began in 1876. The novelty and lower value of silver, coupled with the isolation and inaccessability of Oro City, caused this boom to be slower in development. The railroad did not arrive until the 1880's, meanwhile, freight struggled in from Dillon or Buena Vista at a charge of 5¢ to 10¢ a pound with a bonus if the goods were able to hold up and arrive after the arduous trip. Passengers found transportation more dear. The first wagon taken into Oro City was driven by H. A. W. Tabor and Augusta Tabor, his wife, was the first and only woman in the area for a long time.

The "Cloud City" grew rapidly from 200 in 1877 to 5,000 in 1878, until by 1880 the population exceeded 30,000 or maybe more. In a transient atmosphe. of the typical mining town, the excitement of looking for 'ches transcended such mundane considerations as a census. The "Little Giant" and the Denver and South Park raced to Leadville—renamed by Mayor "Haw" Tabor—therefore, the "Cloud City" gained a world-wide reputation with a steady flow of all human kinds and types during the decade of the 80's. Probably well over a hundred thousand wandered into California Gulch to prospect, work in some business, or simply to take in the sights.

Zinc on many occasions produced more income than lead or silver, moreover, the variety of ores added more diversification to the mining, which interacted with each other, making milling and smelter easier. Lead was the first big producer, then zinc, while, at present. molybdenum is the most valuable mineral coming from the mountains. By 1920 over $500,000,000 in minerals were produced by the mines. After the railroads arrived, coal and coke were imported, therefore, much of the milling was done in Leadville. However, it later proved more profitable to haul the ore to the mills in Pueblo and Denver. The Robert E. Lee was the most productive mine, with many others, including the Little Pittsburgh, Chrysolite, Matchless, with many more located on Pryor, Fryer, Breece, Derry, or Carbonate Hills.

The silver boom soon spread to other localities, with Aspen being next in importance and production to the "Cloud City." The ore in Aspen proved to be richer than any found, some as high as 93% silver. The largest nugget ever found came from the Smuggler Mine in Aspen; it weighed over a ton and had to be trimmed down to a paltry 1,840 pounds to get it out of the mine. The ore was so rich it paid a profit to haul it by mule pack train to mill. The Aspen Mine produced over $15,000,000 in silver and other minerals. The "Little Giant" and the Colorado Midland raced to Aspen, with the contest ending in a dead heat. The Colo. Midland had the best access to town. There were about 15,000 people of various sorts in the town at the time. After the panic of 1893, the population plummeted to a mere 700.

Gold and silver were found in combinations in the telluride ores of the San Juans when the mining boom began. The boom in the San Juans paralleled the Leadville and Aspen rush, therefore, the inaccessibility of this area was even a greater challenge. Gunnison became a new smeltering center for the mines in Western Colorado. Many new fortunes were made in the 1880's, while names like Pullman, Westinghouse, Guggenheim, Moffatt and Tabor entered the exclusive group of Colorado millionaires.

The Tabor Story

Frequently, the story of an important event in history can best be told by the experiences of someone who lived through it all. H. A. W. Tabor was a personification and an embodiment of the boom-to-bust nature of the mining period. The story of rags to riches then back to rags is better understood by this fabulous portrayal and tragic climax. Through the life of the Tabors, the story of silver mining in the Centennial State is vividly related while at the same time, unexpectedly, several other highlights on what life and people are all about came out into the open for all to see.

Horace Austin Warren Tabor was born in 1830 on a Vermont farm, with no indications of spectacular events in the future. The young Tabor learned the stone-cutting trade, then plied it during his more sober moments, without any impressive returns. His rather unpromising stock increased when he met his first wife, Augusta, who was the daughter of a wealthy quarry owner. Augusta was a fine woman who began to set the erring Tabor on the right track. It seemed everyone who knew this woman admired her for her honesty, sincerity and consideration for others. When Tabor began to wander into infidelity, he became unpopular with many, because they knew he was doing a loyal and good woman wrong. Augusta was not an overly attractive woman, moreover, sad, but nevertheless true men frequently seek women who do not bring out the good in them, but do otherwise.

Augusta encouraged the young Tabor to attend church, and he got caught up in the Abolition Movement which was gaining momentum in New England. When the Kansas-Nebraska Act passed in 1854, the territory was opened for settlement, where the new, questionable doctrine of popular sovereignty would be put to test in Kansas, allowing a plebecite to decide whether the Sunflower State would be slave or free. The shortsighted exponents of this doctrine never guessed that the South would challenge Kansas as a cotton-growing or slave state. Soon southerners with slaves began to move into Kansas, while the abolitionists responded by raising money to send anti-slavery people to keep Kansas free. The ultimate result is well known and not the topic of this story. The emigration fund provided by the abolitionists gave Tabor a chance to go west at someone else's expense, so he set out for Kansas, staked out a farm and returned to Maine to marry Augusta. The newlyweds returned to the farm in Kansas where "Haw" never did really get interested in the noble pursuit of agriculture. He spent more time dabbling in the politics of the new

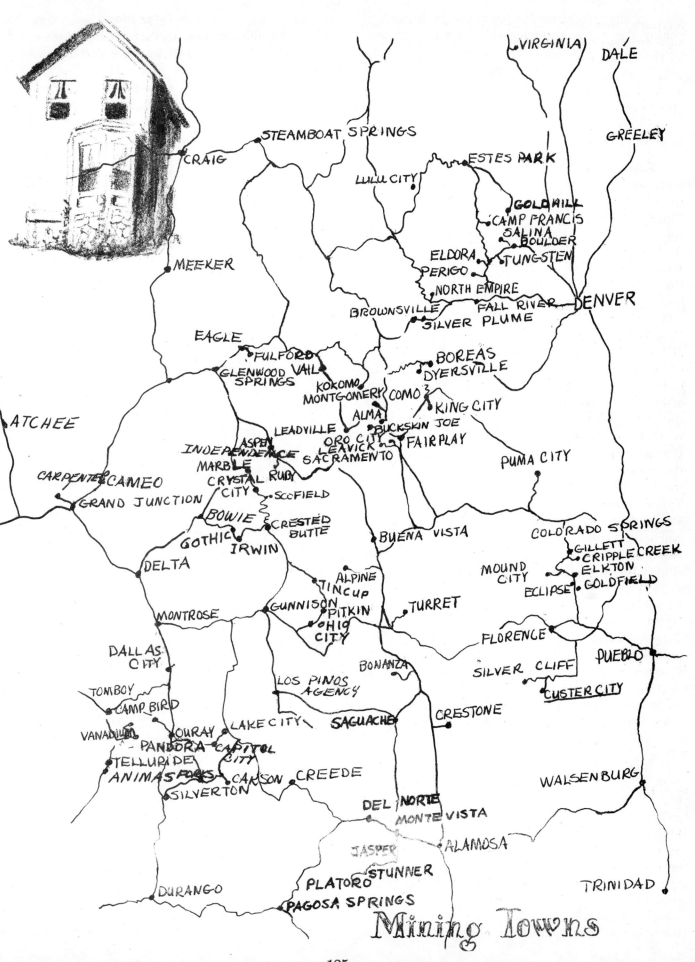

VIRGINIA   DALE

STEAMBOAT SPRINGS   GREELEY

CRAIG   ESTES PARK

                    LULU CITY   GOLDHILL
                                        CAMP FRANCIS
                                        SALINA
MEEKER   BOULDER
                                ELDORA   TUNGSTEN
                            PERIGO
                        NORTH EMPIRE   DENVER
EAGLE   BROWNSVILLE   FALL RIVER
                            SILVER PLUME

                FULFORD   BOREAS
        GLENWOOD VAIL   DYERSVILLE
            SPRINGS   KOKOMO
ATCHEE   MONTGOMERY COMO
                            ALMA   KING CITY
                LEADVILLE   BUCKSKIN JOE
            ASPEN   ORO CITY   FAIRPLAY
        INDEPENDENCE   LEAVICK
        MARBLE   SACRAMENTO   PUMA CITY
CARPENTER CAMEO CRYSTAL RUBY
                    CITY
GRAND JUNCTION   SCOFIELD   COLORADO SPRINGS
            BOWIE   CRESTED
                    BUTTE   GILLETT
        GOTHIC   BUENA VISTA   CRIPPLE CREEK
DELTA   IRWIN   MOUND   ELKTON
                                        CITY ECLIPSE GOLDFIELD
                    ALPINE
                    TINCUP
            GUNNISON PITKIN   TURRET
MONTROSE   OHIO
                    CITY   FLORENCE
DALLAS   PUEBLO
CITY   BONANZA   SILVER CLIFF
TOMBOY   LOS PINOS   CUSTER CITY
    CAMP BIRD   AGENCY
VANADIUM OURAY LAKE CITY SAGUACHE CRESTONE
    PANDORA CAPITOL
TELLURIDE   CITY
ANIMAS FORKS   CARSON CREEDE   WALSENBURG
    SILVERTON
                    DEL NORTE
                        MONTE VISTA
                JASPER   ALAMOSA
                    STUNNER
DURANGO   PLATORO   TRINIDAD
    PAGOSA SPRINGS

Mining Towns

—125—

territory, moreover, this avocation became almost an obsession with him. The Tabors were struggling on their Kansas farm when news of the Pikes Peak gold rush spread east. Tabor's gambling nature made it impossible to disregard the glowing possibilities of the Colorado gold fields, consequently, he was soon on his way, leaving the reliable Augusta to mind the farm.

Tabor hit all the gold camps in Colorado, therefore, was in Idaho Springs and Central City at the time both of these strikes began but had no luck. Finally, Augusta arrived, so they departed for California Gulch to try their luck. Tabor brought in the first wagon; after several weeks of prospecting, he found about $7,000 worth of gold. With the $7,000 the Tabors went into business in Oro City. They built a general store, Tabor became the postmaster and mayor, and he also kept the stagecoach station. Mrs. Tabor fed miners in her parlor, provided rooms and lent a helping hand in any way she could. Much of the time she was the only woman in California Gulch. During times of illness or difficulty, most often after an accident, she served as the area doctor. The Tabors became the most prominent and respected citizens in the rugged mountain town. As the early placers and gold began to dwindle, most of the miners became discouraged and forsook California Gulch for more promising locations. The Tabors stayed on and continued to operate their store. Augusta added a bakery to her other duties and gave birth to a son, their only child. Tabor's gambling nature would not let him give up the possibility of striking it rich, moreover, the general store provided only a mediocre livelihood which gave him an excuse to remain interested in mining. Oro City became almost a ghost town, but the Tabors stayed on and looked after the needs of the miners that moved in and out. They were still there when Wood and Stevens made their strike and the rush began in 1876. Tabor was in a good position to gain from the increased activity. As the town grew, Tabor changed his location to Leadville, then served as mayor and in many other capacities.

In the summer of 1877, the center of the silver rush shifted to the new town of Leadville, where the growth and discoveries surpassed the previous output of California Gulch. The rush to Leadville began in the spring of 1878, with a motley assortment of miners, adventurers, drummers, and camp followers descending on the formerly peaceful mountain valley. "Haw" Tabor still operated his establishment, therefore, was well known among the miners in the area, as many dropped into his store for supplies, frequently signing grubstake agreements when they were short of operating funds. The gullible nature of Tabor made him easy prey for many such propositions, therefore he grubstaked several of the hopeful miners. When he grubstaked August Rische and George Hook, his fortune soared because the two itinerant German shoemakers found a strike that turned out to be the fabulous Little Pittsburg, which produced almost $20,000,000. The intrepid Tabor bought out his original partners, then formed a partnership with Jerome Chaffee and David Moffatt. Tabor moved to Leadville to become mayor, then helped to plan the town along with its future; in 1878 "Haw" served a term as Lt. Governor. It seemed that everything the "magnate of the mountains" touched turned to silver, moreover, his booming successes lured him into the fantasy that he was a financial genius. With this misconception, he began to make poor investments, even buying a portion of the Gulf of Mexico. Chicken Bill of Pryor Hill salted a worthless pit with ore from the Little Pittsburg then informed "Haw" he was on to something but could not afford to develop his new find. "Haw" had his foreman check the pit where he reported that the mine had ore every bit as good as the Little Pittsburg. Tabor bought the claim for a thousand dollars then began to mine but his men concluded he had been taken when they found no new ore. The undaunted Tabor ordered them to keep on digging, moreover, they hit it rich resulting in the Chrysolite mine, one of the region's best producers. An unworked claim he purchased turned into the Matchless, which brought the Tabors $10,000,000.

His partnership resulted in a constant squabble with Senator Chaffee and banker Moffatt, so it was dissolved, with Tabor buying his way out, meanwhile, keeping the Matchless. Tabor's obsession to be a politician was pushing him to new adventures. He poured money into the Republican party of Colorado, donated money for public works, a new city hall plus a fire engine in Leadville; he replaced the telephone system in Leadville, then built opera houses in Denver and Leadville. To gain social prominence, Tabor bought a huge mansion in Denver which Augusta opposed, as both of them were more at ease with the people of the "Cloud City." Tabor's political ambitions embarrassed the Republican party because they were consistently willing to accept the Leadville millionaire's donations, but their lack of confidence in Tabor's political acumen made it hard to come up with a position that corresponded to both.

"Haw" Tabor spent very little time in his mansion in Denver, for he was not comfortable in the

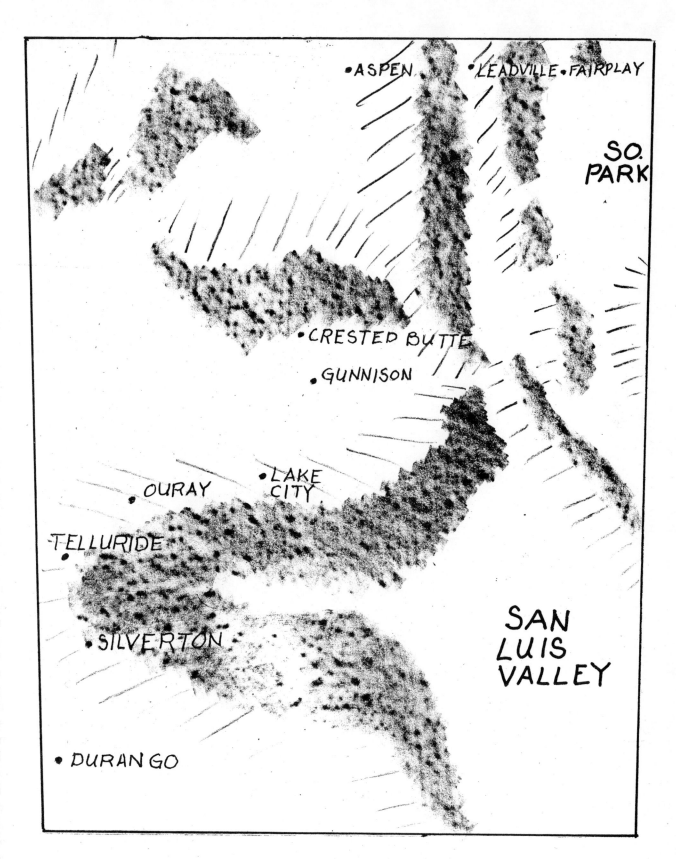

ASPEN •LEADVILLE•FAIRPLAY

SO. PARK

•CRESTED BUTTE

•GUNNISON

•LAKE CITY

OURAY

TELLURIDE

SILVERTON

SAN LUIS VALLEY

•DURANGO

SILVER PRODUCERS

"Haw" Tabor

Mile High City"; therefore, the silver king spent most of his time in Leadville, managing his mining operations, at the same time visiting with his cronies in the Leadville saloons and frequenting the brothels in the evening. One day he noticed an attractive young woman in one of the saloons and soon became acquainted with the young lady. Elizabeth McCourt, better known as Baby Doe, was the kind of woman who caught a man's eye. Although Baby Doe was thirty-two years younger than Tabor, the differential did not prevent the blossoming of a twenty-year romance. The two began to see more and more of each other. Tabor hoped to avoid any scandal, for he realized it would be detrimental to his political aspirations, so a secret divorce was arranged in Durango and a secret marriage followed in St. Louis. About the same time Tabor's political fortunes improved. The assasination of President Garfield caused a reshuffling of the cabinet, therefore, Colorado's Senator Henry Teller was made Secretary of the Interior. His unexpired term as senator had thirty days yet to run, moreover, this provided a safe way for the Republican party of Colorado to pay the debt to the Leadville benefactor. After arriving in Washington, Tabor staged a lavish state wedding that cost over $500,000 and invited most of the important people of the nation's capital. Shortly after the wedding, news was released that the Durango priest had refused to sign the divorce papers for Horace and Augusta, which opened legal technicalities that plunged the newlyweds into the scandal of living in sin, much like the experience so bitter to Andrew Jackson.

After the brief sojourn as U. S. Senator, Tabor returned to Denver, where he was now rejected by the self-righteous social leaders of the most wide-open town in the United States. Two daughters, Elizabeth and Silver Dollar, were born to the Tabors; notwithstanding their problems, the marriage turned out to be happy and secure. Baby Doe was able to enjoy the benefits of Tabor's income and appreciated the expensive things that Tabor showered on her. He continued to make wild investments, but his income could stand his extravagance, as it was over $400,000 a year.

Leadville Ice Palace 1896

COLORADO MOUNTAIN COLLEGE
Alpine Campus - L. R. C.
P.O. Box 775288
Steamboat Springs, CO 80477

When the Panic of 1893 resulted in the repeal of the Sherman Silver Purchase Act and the price of silver plummeted from $1.30 to 50c an ounce overnight, Tabor made the transition to poverty. He had spent over $35,000,000, but could recover practically nothing, therefore, was still a poor man, $1,000,000 in debt after he had sold everything. The Tabors moved to the edge of Denver and lived in poverty, "Haw" taking the abrupt change of fortunes with admirable grace. Winfield Scott Stratton, the Cripple Creek Midas, was one of the few who helped Tabor by sending him money. History is full of men who were responsible for helping many people and communities along the way. Curiously, when their affluence was with them and they were on top, their friends were everywhere, but, when they hit the skids, they had no friends to be found. Finally, in 1898, the Republican party condescended to make "Haw" a postmaster in suburban Denver at an income of $3,000 a year. Sixteen months later Tabor died from an appendicitis attack and was given a hero's funeral with over 14,000 in belated attendance. Before he died, Tabor told his wife how happy he was and urged her to hang on to the Matchless, no matter what happened. Baby Doe went to Leadville where she began the vigil that was to last for almost thirty-six years. Gradually the girls left—Liz was the first to repudiate her mother—Silver Dollar stayed on, tried journalism, then stated she planned to go into a convent. She was later found murdered in Chicago. Baby Doe kept her vigil in the cabin near the Matchless, where some of her Leadville friends helped her with her court battles to keep the Matchless. As she grew older, she kept more to herself and became demented. Occasionally, she would walk down to Leadville and charge a few groceries, with the people of Leadville or the mining company that owned the Matchless generally paying the bill. She became more suspicious and unfriendly to people she did not recognize who came near the Matchless. When she was not seen or heard of for several days, friends walked up to her cabin where they found her lying on her back in the middle of the cabin floor, with her arms spread like the sign of a cross, frozen solid. She was clad in rags and had gunny sacks tied around her feet. The cabin was a disarray of newspapers and gunny sacks stacked and piled on the floor. The glittering Tabor story ended in tragedy on this mountain cabin floor in 1935, during the time of another depression. The story stands out as a milestone in the struggle of man against the forces of wealth, poverty, and his weaknesses.

Baby Doe's Last Stand

17—UP AND DOWN COUNTRY

Old-timers claim, "there are only two directions in the San Juan Mountains, up and down; north, south, east and west don't matter". The geography of these picturesque mountains would not betray this appraisal. Located in southwestern Colorado and shaped like a triangle, the San Juans are the highest and most rugged mountains in the connected United States. There are fourteen peaks over 14,000 feet and hundreds reaching above 13,000 feet. The scenery is equally spectacular and matches the superlatives needed to describe the topographical ramparts of this range. Most impressive, however, is the awareness of the challenges offered and the breed of people that cast their luck and lot in this demanding environment. In the Centennial State the mining frontier is the most intact historical frontier available at present. The more isolated and difficult to reach, the more likely that there is something left from the ravages of man and nature for the historian or tourist. According to Hall, "The permanent occupation and development of the San Juan Country was accomplished under almost incredible hardships and by a mere handful of resolute people."

The mining periods experienced in other areas of Colorado also had their run in the San Juans. First, there was the disappointing gold rush of the early 1860's, then followed the silver rush of the 1870's and 1880's that was responsible for getting the San Juans opened. This was followed by a crash in 1893 that threatened to turn all the hamlets into ghost towns, when the gold rush returned to revive much of the San Juan Mining Frontier and save the day.

Western Colorado followed the same pattern of settlement that occurred on the Front Range. There were mineral discoveries in the San Juan Mountains that led to immigration; then came the removal of the Indians, this time the Utes; next, the arrival of the railroad occurred to put on the finishing touches.

The more venturesome types are inclined to believe the best hunting, fishing or, in this case, prospecting, have to be located in the most out-of-the-way and hard-to-get-to places possible. Such a man was Charles Baker, a restless fellow, always in search of something new. Baker prospected in California Gulch in 1860, but became discouraged and began to look for greener pastures. Somehow, Baker was able to gain financial backing for his party of seven and headed for the San Juans to prospect. How much "color" the party located is not completely known; no doubt they panned out some gold, but not enough to pay them for their time and trouble. Also, an effort was underway to build roads to the isolated region. The first jumping-off-place to the San Juans was Del Norte in the San Luis Valley. Besides the difficulty offered by distance and terrain, Indians were more of a problem in the San Juans than any of the other mining regions.

These problems, compounded by the coming of the Civil War, were enough to discourage further penetration of this remote region, so the mining there was postponed until after the Civil War. Also, the Utes let it be known that the miners were trespassing on their territory promised to them by treaty. The Apache backed the Utes by rolling huge stones down the mountain into miners' camps. Removal of the Indians seemed to be a foreseeable necessity or prerequisite before much prospecting could be effectively implemented, although it did continue on a small scale.

The history of the west has demonstrated poignantly the aggressive nature of the westward movement. Indian resistance sometimes slowed movement into Indian held land, but it seldom was able to prevent the eventual and inevitable resettlement of the Native American elsewhere. The Brunot Treaty of 1873 opened the San Juans to mining. Supposedly, this cession by the Utes permitted only mining and not farming, but it is of little importance because the second mining rush had already started in 1871. The Brunot Treaty was more a belated acquiescence to an existing actuality than a grant of permission. Prospectors in small numbers had continued to wander over the San Juans in the 1860s. Captain Baker returned from the Civil War in 1868,

but, after surviving the war fighting for the cause of his beloved state of Virginia, the resolute captain was killed by Indians. Baker Basin, the majestic location of the town of Silverton, was given this wandering soldier of fortune's name.

In 1871 and 1872, shortly before the Brunot Treaty, some impressive finds were made. Following the negotiation of the treaty there was a moderate movement of people to the region. With the increase of pressure, new and rich veins of silver were discovered. By 1874 Silverton became a county seat and the Crooke Smelter was located there. Lake City with its Ute and Ulay veins, plus the Little Giant vein in the Elk Mountains near Gunnison, all added up to increased activity. The San Juan Mining period now began in earnest. Fort Crawford was erected near present Ridgway in 1871 to attempt to prevent further difficulties with the Utes.

Until 1882 when the railroad began to probe the isolated San Juans, the region was forced to deal with this transport shortcoming in any way possible. Because of these hardships, the nature of the towns in the San Juans differed from those on the Front Range mining frontier, moreover, the mining was forced to proceed at a slower pace. The first step, getting there, was difficult enough, but only a beginning. Travel to the San Juan Mines was extreme-

Looking from Chattanooga South Over Mineral Creek to Sultan Mountain

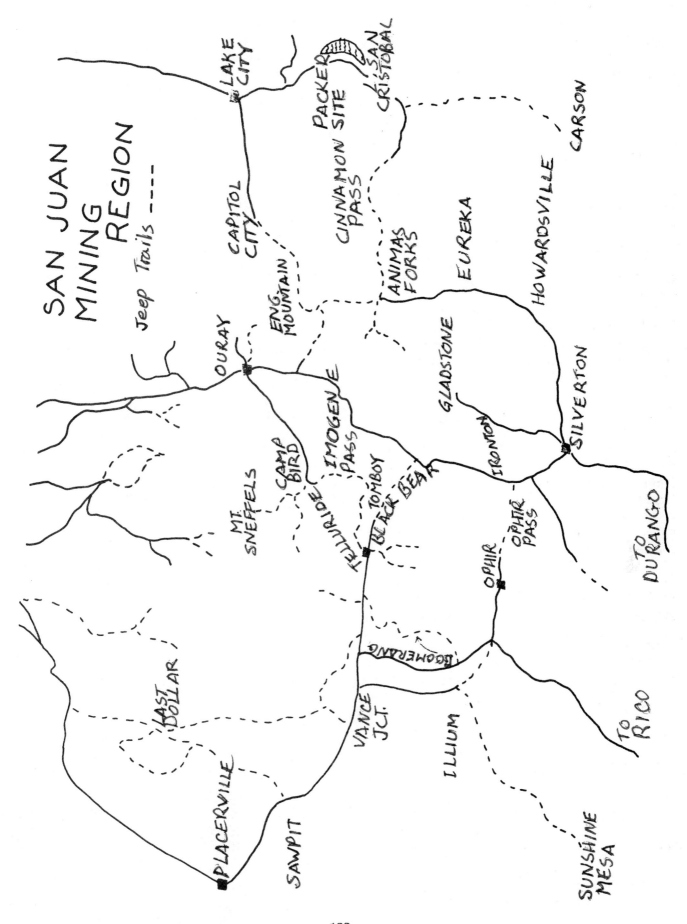

SAN JUAN MINING REGION

Jeep Trails ----

LAKE CITY

PACKER SITE

SAN CRISTOBAL

CARSON

CAPITOL CITY

CINNAMON PASS

ANIMAS FORKS

EUREKA

HOWARDSVILLE

OURAY

ENG MOUNTAIN

GLADSTONE

SILVERTON

IMOGENE PASS

MT. SNEFFELS

CAMP BIRD

TELLURIDE

TOMBOY

BLACK BEAR

IRONTON

OPHIR

OPHIR PASS

TO DURANGO

BOOMERANG

LAST DOLLAR

VANCE JCT.

ILLIUM

TO RICO

PLACERVILLE

SAWPIT

SUNSHINE MESA

ly difficult. Descriptions of the hardships and difficulty of reaching the area frequently appeared in the newspapers. Summittville was one of the first camps to prosper, furthermore, it was not too far from Del Norte; moreover, it soon played out, making it necessary to go over Stony Pass into the Animas Valley. The Animas River was one of the most productive mining centers in the San Juans, but before the coming of the railroad it was too isolated to completely take advantage of the valuable veins located there. Lake City, the other early center, was almost as isolated. The first year of settlement saw some of the worst weather in history. There were heavy rains in the summer followed by continual snow in the winter. This was the first winter any number of people tried to endure in this country. Normal winters produced 30 or 40 feet of snow, so the staying power of these first settlers was put to the ultimate test. Most of them were marooned anyway, but they developed a healthy respect for the San Juan winters. The San Juans are also the most precipitous mountains in the United States. This results in spectacular snowslides that rush down the mountain at 200 miles an hour. These slides wipe out roads, railroads, towns or anything else in their path.

The problems of isolation also contributed to poorer mining methods. The recovery yields were lower in percentage than any of the other mining camps. Gradually things began to improve a little. Spring arrived early in 1874, then a number of good strikes were made with the promise of more to come. Nevertheless, the transportation problem plagued the miners. Now, the prospectors used Silverton and Lake City as bases to probe further and higher into the mountains. Many of the best veins were discovered above timberline The problem of getting to these lofty mines and bringing out the ore was monumental. Also, some connection between the various mining communities was highly desirable.

Otto Mears, the Ultimate Success Story

The story of transportation in the San Juans is the story of Otto Mears.

Mears was born in Russia in 1840 of an English father and a Jewish mother. Since his father died when he was a year old the young Mears was raised among his mother's people. His early life was spent with various relatives until he was eleven years old. Finally, in 1851 Mears was sent to San Francisco to live with an uncle located there. When Otto arrived the uncle was nowhere to be found. Not a very auspicious beginning, to say the least, cast adrift in a foreign land at the age of eleven

without friend or relative, and unable to speak the English language. A more difficult beginning does not seem imaginable. But Mears had his health and wits about him, so soon he was making progress His first job was selling newspapers. From there he went on to other things, then learned as many trades as possible. During this ten-year period Mears also made and saved money.

In 1861 the young immigrant became a natural ized American Citizen and entered the Army with the California Volunteers. During the Civil War Mears served in Texas and New Mexico against the Indians. Finally, he was mustered out in 1864. For some reason, the recently discharged veteran de cided to remain in Santa Fe after being released from service with an honorable discharge in Mesilla rather than return to California. He worked as a clerk in Santa Fe for a year, then went to Conejos in Colorado and opened a store. Soon Otto was build ing a lumber mill, although he had no tools or nails At the same time Mears began to raise wheat which naturally, required a grist mill to produce flour. A mill was soon built. At this time Leadville began to open, so the pragmatic Mears, who wished to mar ket flour there and in the other mining camps that were moving westward, sized up the situation. The lack of a decent road barred his plans, so, with no previous roadbuilding experience, the undaunted Mears began to build a road from Saguache—a town he founded—to Nathrop. When the railroad came along later, Mears sold his right-of-way to the D&RG for $40,000. The success of this venture led to numerous other toll roads in the San Juans until nearly all the towns were connected by his arteries Many of these roads are still in use, now perhaps a highways—as in the case of the Million Dollar high way—or still in almost their original condition a jeep trails. Mears also built railroads and buildings but so far as the San Juans are concerned, these pur examples of free enterprize loom as his greatest ac complishment. The remarkable thing is the reali zation of the lasting nature of this contribution Most of Mears railroads and other projects are now long gone, but his roads and jeep trails make it pos sible for tourists to enjoy the most spectacula scenery and country in the world.

A list of the roads Mears built would includ Saguache via Poncha Pass to Nathrop, Saguache to Lake City, Silverton to Lake City, Cimarron t Ouray, Salida to Gunnison, Animas City to For Lewis, Dallas Divide to Telluride, Vance Junctio to Ames, Ouray to Sneffels and Ouray to Silverto the last probably his most impressive. His busines interests also included a mail contract from Lak

OTTO
MEARS

City over Engineer Mountain to Ouray. The contract demanded one delivery a week all year round. When Mears could not find someone to make the delivery for him, he did it himself.

Mears was probably best known for his railroads, which were also built with no training on his part, only determination to get the job done. The Silverton was completed from Silverton to Ironton in 1889. The Silverton Northern in 1894 from Silverton to Animas Forks was added to this, then the Rio Grande Southern, his greatest achievement, was built. Unable to go from Ironton to Ouray the short route, Mears undauntedly made a 160 mile circuit by way of Ridgway, Rico, Dolores and Durango to connect Ouray and Silverton. The reputation of the diminutive man of the mountains became so well known that he was called to Washington to build a railroad from Washington, D.C. to Chesapeake Beach. Besides his railroads, Mears owned an immense packing and freighting business, several newspapers, was one of the developers of the Mack Truck Company, was in the smeltering business in Durango, plus several other concerns too numerous to mention.

Mears tried politics only briefly, when he served one term as a Colorado State Representative. After one term his political career ended permanently. The roadbuilder was too impatient for politics and thereafter remained behind the scenes, but retained considerable influence. He was able to serve his state in other capacities as a member of the commission that built the state capitol. In this capacity, he served for 34 years and was a consultant on the construction of a good number of state buildings. His early trading with the Indians taught him the Ute language, so he was involved in treaty negotiations as an interpreter and negotiator. After the mining panic in the early nineties, Mears moved to New York, but returned to Silverton in 1907 to run his railroads because he was dissatisfied with their operation. After reviving his railroads and other interests in Colorado, Mears decided to retire in California where he went in 1917. After arriving there he built the Maryland Hotel in Pasadena at the age of 77.

Mears was a small man, quick of movement and speech. His speech contained an obvious accent, and was accentuated with demonstrative gestures and movements of his arms. The education he possessed was almost entirely of a practical nature. His greatest ability was to get things done regardless of the circumstances. For relaxation the roadbuilder indulged in poker, which he loved, but could find little time to play. Finally, in 1931 at the age of 91, the restless heart subsided and the undaunted spirit came to rest. The ashes of Otto Mears were scattered on Engineer Mountain, the joining rooftop of three counties, to be forever carried by the winds of eternity over the mountains he conquered and loved so dearly.

Life In the San Juan Mining Camps

The rugged terrain where the mines were located profoundly influenced the nature of life in the mining camps. Other than Baker and Eureka Basins, the San Juans had little else to offer in the way of perpendicular townsites. The horizontal country forced location of towns into the fringes of the mountains or available basins. Sometimes mining camps were laid out with little anticipation of settlement, but to mine ore and leave when the job was done. This attitude, along with the isolation and topography, gave the San Juan region an even wilder and more transient character than the mining towns on the Front Range. Men were even farther from home and family restrictions. Shortages of supplies and women were also greater, while miners were frequently isolated in their mines for longer periods before they would finally descend to "blow off a little steam." A goodly number of miners spent October to April at the mine then, they would head for town, money jingling in their pockets, looking for a bath, a bottle and a woman, hopefully in that order.

The towns that sprang up would try to get along with a minimum of accomodations because of the impermanence of their prospects. Saloons might serve as a schoolroom in the morning or a courtroom in the afternoon or anytime the judge wished to convene court, surreptitiously interrupting the proceedings with little concern for the revellers. On Sunday the same facilities would serve as a church. This was done by moving a piano and a few chairs into new places. Ingenuity, as well as ruggedness, was a prerequisite for success in that horizontal environment.

Towns of a permanent type did appear. Silverton, Lake City, Ouray and Telluride are the best examples of the more established locations. The successful venture of a town company was determined by various things. Location near productive mines was highly important, and this seems to be the case of the four above mentioned towns. Designation as a post office was also a valuable advantage to a town company, because the Post Office Department limited post offices, therefore, the first post office location had an advantage in such a cut-off area, naturally anxious to hear from family and friends. Ambition and dedication of residents was

Otto Mears' Beaver Creek Toll Station Above Ouray.
His Monument Rests on This Spot.

instrumental, however, location near rich mines that continued to produce has to be considered of greatest importance. These towns were fortunate enough to find gold when the silver crash came, which saved them from oblivion.

After the Brunot Treaty, the mining rush and the appearance of the railroad, some of the primitiveness began to disappear. Silverton and Ouray took on many of the accoutrements of civilization. Schools, churches, libraries, hotels, opera houses, parks, newspapers and other gentile institutions began to make their appearance. Later, isolated Telluride started to grow. When the Rio Grande Southern came to town in 1890, the town grew rapidly. The bulk of the ore in the San Juans is in the 250 odd square mile quadrangle which includes Silverton, Lake City, Ouray and Telluride. Geologists claim most of the ore is yet to be mined, so these towns will retain some of their early mining color. The tourist interest and winter sports will probably also help keep things going. The best thing for the tourist to do in the San Juans is to feast his eyes, but he must be wary to avoid the "crick in the neck."

Toll roads and railroads did not completely put aside the onerous transportation problems in the San Juans. The lofty location of the mines required ingenuity on the part of the miners. One question frequently asked by tourists and backpackers about old mines is, "How in the world did all this equipment get up here?" The answer is, a four legged critter named "mule or donkey." A subsequent chapter is dedicated to these valuable animals, and Colorado's mining period would have failed without them, but they will be given their just due later, so no elaboration will follow here. One of the most spectacular transport methods were the aerial trams that were used in inaccessible places. The remnants of some of the old trams are still to be seen in places like the Smuggler, Blackbear or Silver Lake mines. After a casual scrutiny of these operations, solemn respect is generally paid to the miners that rode them as a matter of course. Tram accidents could be hairy; if a miner stuck his head up at the wrong time, it could be fatal. The operator needed to keep track of occupancy to avoid leaving the shift with someone marooned high above the ground in zero temperatures. Some of the Scandanavian miners would jump into the trams with their skis then jump out near the top to ski back down, all without the tram stopping.

Some of the mines were so hard to get to that trams could not be built to them, or the mine was too small to justify such an expenditure. If possible, the ore was taken out with pack mules. Sometimes this was impossible, so other methods were tried. One method was to put the ore in leather bags and roll it down the mountain. Eventually, the harder to reach veins could be approached with a drift from another direction connecting to some more feasible operation. The first aerial tramway in Colorado was built at Silverton.

The story of mining in the San Juans tells the story of the people without relating it. They were a hardy lot. The miners, engineers, railroaders, muleskinners, mill hands, ranchers and other assorted residents were the highest skilled to be found. They had to be. Many of the miners were hard rock miners brought over from Cornwall, Wales. The snow slides were a constant menace and had names given to them. The miners would bet on when the Riverside Slide or others might run down the mountain. With two strikes against them, when influenza or other respiratory ailments struck, the people had slim chances. Most of the miners had some lung problems to begin with, if they had worked in the mines for any length of time. This was all compounded by the high altitude. Pneumonia was practically the "kiss of death" to young children. The cemeteries scattered on the side of the hills near towns give grim recordings of flu epidemics or slide victims. Between 1900 and 1906 over one hundred people were killed in slides near Telluride. In 1902 the Liberty Bell Slide killed eight people, then ran again during rescue attempts and killed eleven more. Group burials in the cemetery were necessary to intern all the victims. The ever present threat of dangers did not change their life nor prevent them from enjoying it as much as possible.

Where there is gold or silver men will go to mine it. It does not make any difference whether it is in the bowels of the earth or on the top of the highest mountain. "Pay dirt is where you find it."

18—POLITICS BEGIN

When the mining rush began in the 1860's, the Pikes Peak country was part of three territories—the Kansas, New Mexico, and Utah territories. The Western Slope belonged to the Utah Territory, the Eastern Slope was Kansas Territory. All of this had been promised to the various Indian tribes for as long as the rivers flow and the grasses grow. Efforts to legalize the mining scramble, and at the same time seize political advantage began in 1858 in Auraria. California did not go through the tedious six-step statehood process, nor did Texas plod along this path either. There were sufficient bodies in Colorado to meet the census requirements for territory and statehood, if the other prerequisites could be satisfied. Many attempts were made in 1858 and 1859 to make Colorado a territory; many groups were in Washington at different times, some simultaneously, to further the ambitions of their town and gain legal sanction from the nation's capital. A good number of meetings were held all over the Colorado Piedmont to facilitate territorial or statehood action. The lack of communication between these various political overtures caused considerable delay in the implementation of a territorial political structure.

One of the first meetings was held in the fall of 1858 in Auraria, which had a population of about 200. The Aurarians were from a multitude of states, therefore, not even legal residents of the area they were trying to represent. Their first step was to form a county and name it Arapaho, then they declared Auraria to be the county seat. After electing a delegate to congress and the Kansas legislature, the august body began to plan how they would dissect the western part of Kansas and make it into a separate territory, even though they were still under Kansas laws.[1] The influx of settlers in the spring of 1859 added to the census and made some sort of political structure more important than ever before. There were probably over 25,000 people in the region.

An election of officers was held in March of 1859 to establish a government, but the effort to impress the U.S. Congress with the need to add a new territory proved unfruitful. Perhaps congress did not understand the growth and potential of the Pikes Peak region, but with more gold seekers coming in every day, something had to be done to alert Congress to the political needs of Colorado. Consequently, a mass meeting was held again at Auraria in April for the purpose of pursuing a separate territory or statehood. The fact that Kansas was busy attempting to enter the Union did not deter the ambitions of the assemblage, because they expeditiously decided to by-pass the territorial hassle and began a petition for statehood. The chosen name for the new state was to be Jefferson. Then a call went out for the election of delegates, but as the gold rush diminished it began to discourage the miners. When they began to leave the territory, it looked like the statehood efforts were premature. The audacity of these early political leaders was remarkable; they were but a small group, many not established residents anywhere, who had delegated themselves to form a new state long before the mines had yielded any ore and agriculture had not been given any serious consideration. Their chances of acceptance without authority or sanction were, indeed, slim, but chances can rapidly change when circumstances are altered. This did not prevent the assembling of fifty appointed delegates and the beginning of the first constitution.

On September 4, 1859 people were given a chance to vote for or against the new constitution and for or against statehood. The total turnout was a poor representation of the citizenry, but they were scattered and looking for gold. Efforts now were organized to gain entry to the Union as the territory of Jefferson, a new constitution was written, and delegates were chosen, also a governor, and other officials were elected, all without any declaration or consent of congress. The political inuendos that followed are too lengthy to list—how many constitutions were written and how much effort was wasted before Colorado became a state is comparable to the experience of most states, but probably much less. Each area tried to read advantages or disadvantages into the proposals. The election of 1860 and the sobering possibility of national conflict left the question of the political status of the territory of Jefferson in the background, therefore, the ambitious political overtures were to be delayed until the election of the next president.

Without being accepted into the Union, the newly organized territory of Jefferson began to proceed with the mundane activities of electing officers and a two-house legislature, enacting laws and provisions, establishing a judiciary, creating counties and establishing governments. All of these preliminary actions were unopposed until the new government began to approach the harsh political reality of levying taxes. Residents were undecided and divided anyway; some wished to remain loyal to the Kansas Territory, and only nine counties were

organized under the territory of Jefferson. There was also widespread disagreement about the name for the territory with a host of potential names—some reasonable and others completely ludicrous, but, gradually the name "Colorado" gained acceptance. The territory of Jefferson never won acceptance and most of the efforts were in vain. When Congress appointed William Gilpin and made Colorado a territory, some of the work that had been done served as a guide and saved repetitive effort. The failure of the Jefferson project resulted mainly in Colorado being the permanent name of the territory and state. The steady Republican nature of the Centennial State would seem to make the name of Jefferson an unpopular appellation, so maybe the failure was providential.

The various and sundry enactments of the Territory of Jefferson were worked over, then the territorialship of state was launched, with one of the more thorny problems being the location of the capital. Colorado City was designated as the first capital, because the outback vote broke the impasse between rivals Golden and Denver, when the more isolated areas thought the urbanites were a little too high-handed. It remained in Colorado City for nine days, then moved back to the City of Denver. Golden threw its hat in the ring, therefore, the Third Assembly met there, but adjourned almost immediately and went to Denver. The Fourth stayed in Golden and the Fifth left Golden after one day. And so it went.

According to the old Northwest Ordinance, a territory was required to have 60,000 citizens to become a state and, moreover, there were six steps to be taken to be admitted to the charmed circle. Colorado made another attempt to start the proceedings in 1864, but it was voted down. To be accepted, a hopeful territory must make application, Congress had to pass an enabling act (which usually included an appropriation to pay for details), the territory would hold a constitutional convention to write its constitution. The constitution then had to have the approval of congress. The President then made an official proclamation and the state could hold elections to elect its officers, legislature and form its government.

The procedure, like many steps in the democratic process, was a long and drawn out affair, sometimes taking many years. Alaska had to wait for seventeen years; however, 1876 was not a typical year; it was an election year and the incumbent Republicans thought they may be in for a tough election year. The scandals of the Grant administration, the resurgence of the South, and the in-

crease in the number of voters worried the Republican hierarchy about the horrible possibility of the return of the Democrats to the White House. Three more electoral votes of the right kind might determine the choice for president. The party turned its eyes in the direction of the setting sun for new states of correct allegiance that were ready to be admitted to the Union. It was noted that two western states had applied—New Mexico and Colorado, neither had been recognized as yet. When checking, the majority of the citizens of New Mexico turned out to be Democrats and the majority of Coloradoans Republicans. It did not take much time to decide which of the two states should be admitted, moreover, congress immediately passed an enabling act, skipping step one. This was the centennial year for the United States, therefore, what would be more appropriate than bringing in a new state in 1876 and having the president make the proclamation on July 4, 1876. Even the democrats would have difficulty raising serious questions about the motives behind such a patriotic move.

The congressional revue of the constitution was also skipped, because of the haste, and congress was adjourned at the time. Coloradans were provided with a golden opporunity to come up with an unusual constitution, but they did not take advantage of the chance. Sentiment against statehood was still strong in the Colorado Territory, but by now the population was over 100,000, and the opponents of statehood were in the minority. The people did not vote anyway, it was all done by the legislature, therefore, President Grant issued the proclamation August 1, 1876, after the July 4th date had passed. It is a shame the deadline was missed. However, the Centennial State will have the honor of sharing its centennial celebration with the country, as the bi-centennial is to be observed this year in 1976.

Texas was the only other state to enter the Union in this way. In the November election Rutherford B. Hayes defeated his Democratic opponent in the Electoral College, 185 to 184. The disputed nature of the election of 1876 is well known. A special election commission was appointed to finally resolve the controversy; however, the fact remains that Colorado was brought into the Union to elect a president and it did not fail in its task.

The capital issue was finally resolved in 188 when Denver was selected by an overwhelming vote of the people. The issue was so torrid that the constitution had purposely omitted any decision. The capitol can be changed by a two-thirds vote. With statehood settled and progress and prosperity, the Centennial State could now move into the 1880's with confidence.

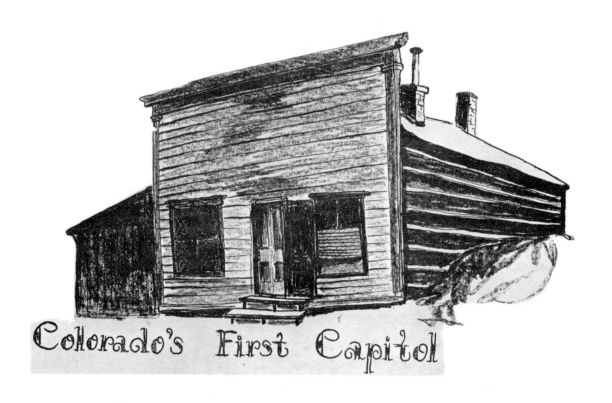

Colorado's First Capitol

19—NARROW GAUGES AND BROAD VISION

The history of the numerous narrow gauge railroads that operated in the Colorado Rockies is one of the most incredible facets of the colorful history of the Centennial State. It is a story that cannot be justly dealt with in one short chapter, but a humble attempt will have to be made because it would be a criminal act to do otherwise. In a sense, when the term "narrow gauge" is used, it is not completely correct to think only of the three-foot wide tracks that wandered over and through the mountains. Another narrow gauge operation was also operating underground in the numerous mine shafts. These railroads had tracks two feet apart where frequently the ore carts were pulled by mules or pushed with human hands or pulled with cable. Nevertheless, they were a type of railroad, moreover, the cable car ride down the mountain side would be refreshing for tired miners after a hard day's work. Some mines now have thousands of miles of underground railways operating.

The narrow gauge railroads represented a pragmatic approach to the problem of transportation in the Rocky Mountains. The diminutive narrow gauge was more economical to build because the right-of-way could be narrower and tunnels smaller. The smaller engines could maneuver around sharper corners and climb steeper grades, saving excavation. The engines and rolling stock were cheaper to purchase, easier to maintain, and not so difficult to operate in the mountains. Some of the routes followed by these intrepid lines were unbelievable, in addition the men that were responsible for the operation of the trains were some of the best railroaders in the world, proud of their challenging task and dedicated to its success.

Colorado's narrow gauge railroads were as various as the mountains they traversed. Some were several hundred miles long, some were only a few miles, or maybe not even one mile in length. Most of the railroads were a single-purpose operation, connecting some isolated mining town with civilization then hauling needed supplies into the town or the ore from the mine to a mill or smelter. This lack of diversity made them very vulnerable to the ravages of change in the town they served; in addition, when the town began to falter, the railroad became a victim. With the advent of the trucking industry, many of the small lines had difficulty competing for service; the trucks could operate cheaper and did not have the expense of maintaining their right-of-way. Many of the small lines were replaced by the ponderous trucks.

A description of some of these railroads seems like a good way to acquaint the reader with their operation. The Denver and South Park Railroad began in 1873 and added the "Pacific" suffix to its name later. (It seemed all railroads were heading for a plunge in the Pacific.) South Park had promising placer mines; there were timber and quarries with gypsum west of Morrison. The directors planned to follow South Platte Canyon out of Denver into South Park then send a branch line to Golden. To diversify, the plan included passenger service, hoping to tap the tourist trade out of Denver into the mountains and mining camps. Construction was delayed by the Panic of 1873, likewise, when the panic ended, the Leadville boom was beginning, so a change in plans was made to get to the silver mines of the Cloud City. John Evans and David Moffatt were among the directors of the railroad. While the track was being built, stages and wagons from Leadville connected to the uncompleted line, helping to pay expenses.

The ownership of the Denver and South Park changed so many times it was difficult to keep track of the various names and owners of the road. To Coloradans, it will always simply be the South Park. When Leadville began to boom, all railroads wanted a piece of the action and, fortunately, John Evans had included a branch to the headwaters of the Arkansas in Lake County in the original franchise, so the South Park, along with the Rio Grande, were in the best position to move into the Cloud City. The South Park was closest to the silver city, with its headquarters in Denver, 170 miles away, as the Rio Grande had to go by way of Pueblo, up the Arkansas Valley, a route 280 miles long.[1] Palmer had more experience, moreover, the knowledge that he was about to be denied the route won from the Atchison, Topeka and Santa Fe in court, made him eager for the fray. Jay Gould again stepped into the breach, as he owned a considerable part of each railroad, therefore, could see little advantage of competition under those circumstances; he suggested that the two roads use the same route.

The Alpine Tunnel project was one of the more unusual undertakings of the South Park and was built to tap the business in the Gunnison mining region. The tunnel was about half-way between Gunnison and Buena Vista through the Sawatch range at an altitude of 11,900 feet. The tunnel was completed, with great expense and loss of life, through about 1,800 feet of rock and conglomerate that was penetrated by underground streams. Shoring became a major problem and expense, requiring 12 x 12 redwoods imported from California—eventually more than 1,500,00 feet at $100 a thousand were purchased. Snow sheds were built on each portal—one being 150 feet on the east portal and a snow shed of 650 feet on the west portal. One mistaken dynamite explosion killed 48 workers; one contractor went broke, while a second completed the bore by keeping a thousand-man crew busy on a 24 hour schedule throughout most of 1880.[2]

The tunnel was completed and the South Park prospered from the Gunnison area mining until decline set in. Snow was a constant problem in the winter, moreover, the snow sheds at each portal had massive doors that were kept closed, making it necessary for the train to stop to open and close them at each end. The South Park was one of the largest and best known narrow gauges in Colorado, therefore, was an important part of the history of the late 1880s. There are many stories associated with the road—one claims a circus train, bound for Leadville, had the engine give out, an elephant was unloaded while it pushed the train into the Cloud City so the show could go on. The railroad and the people who ran the trains are now gone, with them a part of the history of the Centennial States comes to its conclusion.

Many of the mining centers became a network of small narrow gauge railroad tracks, with tracks descending on them in a number of directions, mostly from small railroads that connected some small mining town or mine to a mill or smelter. Georgetown was one of the railroad Meccas, with some unusual and interesting railroads in the vicinity. The Georgetown, Breckenridge and Leadville Railroad connected Georgetown to Silver Plume over the Georgetown Loop. The distance from Georgetown to Silver Plume as the crow flies is about two miles but the loop required four and a half miles of track to climb 143 feet a mile to its destination, climbing over itself on a high bridge and making several sharp turns as it wound its way to the Silver Plume depot. Other narrow gauges rolled into Georgetown and Silver Plume from the mines above, but the Georgetown Loop was the most notable, therefore a tourist attraction in the summer months, with tourists taking the trip to furnish them with something to brag about to their friends.

Colorado's Narrow Gauges

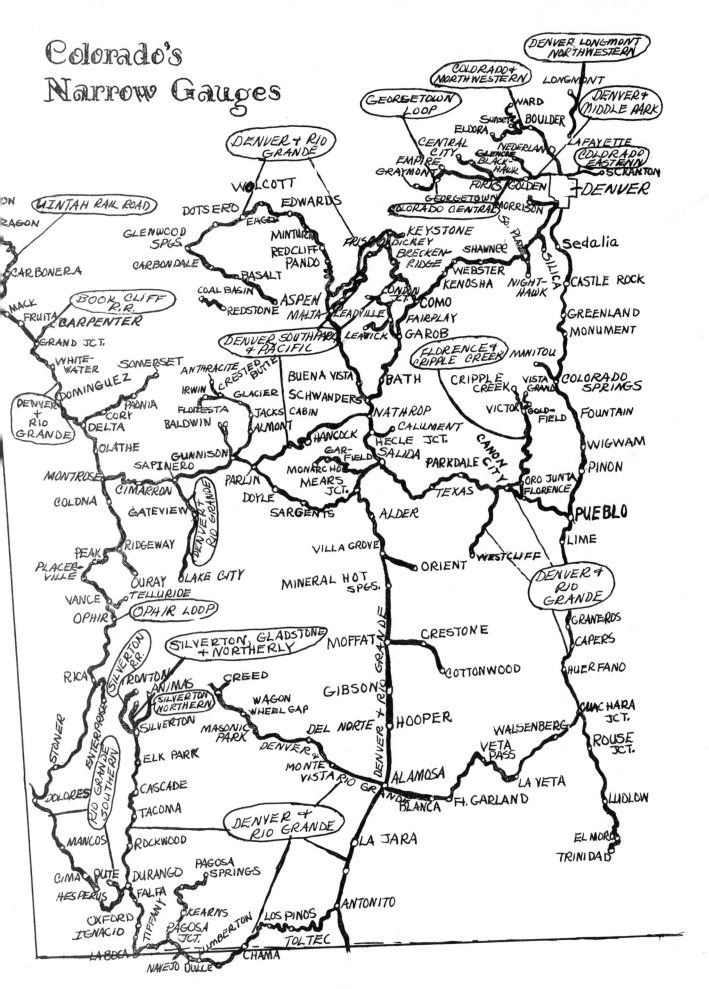

Otto Mears built several railroads in the San Juans to connect the mines with mills or smelters over some of his former toll roads. Three of his railroads had their origin in Silverton—they were the Silverton Railroad that went to Red Mountain and Ironton, the Silverton Northern which went up the Animas River to Animas Forks, and the Silverton, Gladstone and Northerly purchased by Mears went up Cement Creek to Gladstone. None of these railroads were very long, nor did they connect Silverton with any other line from the north, but, while the mines were operating, the roads ran a steady pace and provided a handsome profit for Mears and the stockholders. Mears' reputation gave him the ability to raise the immense capital necessary to build his roads. Many were constructed on the road bed of his toll roads, after he instructed the engineer to follow the ruts of his toll road with the words, "If wagons could travel over that road, a train could too."

Weather presented the same challenge to Mears that it did to other railroad men in the winter, therefore, he attacked it with all the ability he could muster. He built snow sheds on the Silverton Northern between Animas Forks and Eureka to try to meet a contract with the Gold Prince Mill at Animas Forks to transport ore on a year-round basis.[3] The 500-foot snow shed was well braced with timber, moreover, if it met the test, the diminutive Mears planned to build more; however, the first snowslide of the year wiped it out. Discouraged, he decided this was one battle with the elements he would have to concede.

Mears acumen for publicity is well known, moreover, his various promotional schemes are part of the reason he was successful. One of the most interesting ideas was his special passes to important people. They were made of leather, gold and silver, and were given to important people in a position to help his railroad dreams. His purchase of an elaborate Pullman car for use on his Silverton Railroad was another example of his sense for the unusual and unconventional. Many scoffed at his project and wondered how such a luxury could be used in the rustic atmosphere of the San Juans, but he used it for important people that were potential investors coming to survey the prospects of the mines. The people of Silverton, Ouray, Gladstone, Eureka, Ironton, Telluride, Placerville and many other towns depended on the railroads or toll roads built by Otto Mears to bring in food, clothing, supplies, liquor and, frequently, female entertainment. Seldom were they disappointed, meanwhile, the "little man of the mountains" grew in esteem. The Silverton Northern

operated the longest of the three roads out of Silverton, going into scrap in 1939.

The lofty cinnamon crags of Red Mountain prevented Otto Mears from following his toll road from Silverton to Ouray, but it is characteristic of the "roadbuilder of the San Juans" that he found another way. The Rio Grande Southern is the result of his determination and unwillingness to submit to overwhelming odds. It seemed that the cards were all stacked against Mears, but, when he realized he could not go over Red Mountain to Ouray from Silverton, he never hesitated a moment in his plans for the Rio Grande Southern. The fact that a 162-mile detour was needed to get to the rich mines of Ouray did not bother Mears—the railroad cost $8,000,000 to build and passed through territory few had ever traveled before and not too many frequent now.

The Rio Grande did everything possible to make life miserable for the Rio Grande Southern, charging exorbitant prices for rental rolling stock, terminals and leased locomotives. The Rio Grande gained control of 70% of the stock in the Rio Grande Southern then robbed its offspring blind. The route began at Ridgway, went over Dallas Divide to Placerville, past Sawpit to Telluride by a spur, from Vance Junction turned west to Ophir at the junction, and over the loop to Rico, then on to Dolores, Mancos and Durango. The 162-mile trip was not without scenic attractions and excitement and crossed about 60 tressels to complete the journey; some, like the high tressel above Ophir, were breathtaking. It required six months to build the four walls of bridge and tressels that made up the Ophir Loop. The Ophir Loop bridge was 92 feet high, 476 feet long with a 17-degree curvature and was the highest wooden tressel in the world.

Excitement and scenery could not keep the Colorado Southern in operation. Cancelled mail contracts, a drop in the price of silver, then the decline of mining in the region gradually took their toll on the road. During World War II the road began to use its famous "galloping Geese" to keep the road open. The single car geese, made out of auto bodies and engines, prolonged the life of the road about ten years and provided transportation and some freight shipment until 1950 when the road was abandoned. Freights were used when demand was sufficient.

One of the most unique of the narrow gauge was the Uintah, which was built in 1903 and abandoned in 1938. It served the purpose of hauling gilsonite from the Uintah Basin to the main line of the Denver and Rio Grande at Mack, Colorado. The road was engineered to save time, expense and space

Mallet Articulated Engine

It incorporated some of the steepest grades (7½%) and sharpest corners (66 degrees) of any railroad. The Uintah traversed Baxter Pass—named after the engineer who surveyed the route, and was planned so most of the sharp turns and steep grades would be on the side of the mountain where they would be exposed to the warming sun to melt the snow from the right-of-way as soon as possible.

Life on the Uintah was exciting, therefore, a trip over Baxter Pass was a ride to remember, like the Georgetown or Ophir Loops. The Uintah had the problems that beset the other roads in the mountains, plus washouts on the thirty miles of desert on the road. Snow was a constant challenge during the winter months when engines occasionally would go over a curve while pushing snow off the tracks going downhill when they gained too much momentum.

The Uintah used the principle of compensated corners to get around the sharp curves. The tracks were gradually widened as the train moved into the corner, and then gradually returned to the three-foot width. This widening decreased friction and allowed the trains to turn sharper corners. Special engines with the front trucks on a swivel, called articulated engines, were also constructed. The compensated corners were heavily reinforced to hold them together, moreover, the ties were fastened together with strap iron to prevent slippage; also, the road base was well packed, with the ties secured

with steel rods driven down for several feet. T tracks were banked to improve the curve and red friction. If the track was well engineered and bu it could be negotiated with surprising ease and spe and, when a train broke loose sometimes, it ma the curves to the bottom, to railroaders surprise, a after they had jumped to safety.

The Uintah was abandoned in 1938, after highway from Craig was extended into Utah wh it was possible to cut the cost of hauling gilsonite half by hauling it by truck. So the harsh realit of economics brought an end to the Gilsonite ro

For the first fifty years of the Centenn State's history of one hundred years of existen the narrow gauge railroads were the main arter of transportation and frequently the only connecti many small isolated mountain towns had with civi zation. The railroads were an important part of t period of history and provided Coloradans w transportation, food, supplies and luxuries, alo with the news of the outside world. The railro station was one of the town centers, where activ and excitement took place, moreover, one of sources of amusement was to take the kids do to the station to watch the trains arrive. Tin have changed and railroad depots are not what th once were. Old timers have parted with the age steam with great reluctance, others still cling to nostalgia of this bygone day, while many artifa survive to keep poignant memories alive.

20—OURAY, THE ARROW

The 1700's marked the extent of power and glory for the Utes, as this was a century of growth in numbers and expansion of territory at the expense of their enemies. The struggle for power wavered between the old chiefs and tribal elders and the young, aggressive, naturally ambitious war chiefs. Men with ability gained leadership of a band of Utes then pre-empted the title of chief for as long as they could meet the demands and needs of their following. These various chiefs were independent in spirit and action, resenting any encroachment on their autonomy and frequently rising in eloquent opposition to any tribal proposals or suggestions that might unify the tribe, but decrease their autonomy. The Utes were never united in mind and spirit; this inter-tribal factionalism was increased after Ouray was designated as the chief of the Utes, even though he was probably the greatest of Ute chiefs.

Ouray was born in 1833 at Abiquiu, near Taos, New Mexico, on the old Overland Trail. His father, Guera Murah, was a Jicarilla Apache that had been captured and reared by the Utes, later becoming a full member of the Uncompahgres and eventually reaching the rather unprecedented position of chief. Ouray's mother was an Uncompahgre Ute who died not too long after Ouray's birth, so Guera Murah sent the young Ouray to work on a hacienda near Taos. Growing up in this environment, Ouray learned to speak Spanish and English, but preferred Spanish as it was the spoken tongue of New Mexico; later, Ouray added Apache and Ute to his language repertoire. Guera Murah returned to the Uncompahgres, ruled by old Chief Nevava, and left Ouray behind with his brother, Quenche, to grow up in the Spanish culture of the Southwest. Ouray's sister, Susan, was born in 1845 after Guera Murah had remarried.

Guera Murah never cared for Taos, therefore, when asked to come back to the Uncompahgre country by old Chief Nevava, he did not hesitate. Antoine Roubidoux was burned out of his fort by the Utes because they felt the wily trader was overcharging them and taking advantage of the monopoly that was his as the only white trader within 200 miles. Guera Murah had urban and trading experience, so he was summoned to fill the void left by Roubidoux for the Uncompahgres.

Ouray and Quenche worked near Taos herding sheep, gathering pinon wood for the many fireplaces in the adobe hacienda, or packing the mules on the caravans traveling the Santa Fe Trail, with various wares for trade north, including the formidable "Taos Lightning." Ouray was brighter than many of the Indians working on the hacienda, so he attended Mass and received a rudimentary education, living and dressing like a white until he returned to the Uncompahgres. As he became more accepted among the more advanced class of Mexican sheepmen and more knowledgeable of their ways, he made several friends and learned to speak Spanish fluently. The priests and friars at the Taos mission added to his education and helped expand his unusual grasp of events and forces that were taking shape at that time in the Southwest.

When Ouray returned to his people and belatedly learned their culture, he became an embodiment and a personification of the three merging cultures of the Southwest. His perceptive background and experience with Spanish, Anglo and Indian culture, along with his insight, made him more aware and blessed with a much keener and broader understanding than almost anyone else other than Kit Carson. The Indians often said, "You do not know another's way until you have trod in his moccasins." Ouray had been in three pairs of moccasins. That he was misunderstood by so many, including his own people, is often the fate of a man of his wisdom.

In the 1830's and 1840's Taos was a dusty, dirty frontier town on the Santa Fe Trail where Ouray could come in contact with many different people, at the same time learning of many happenings from afar. Taos was over 200 years old at that time, older than the United States at present, moreover, indicative of the primacy of Spanish culture in the Southwest. Taos was a fur center and also the last Mexican frontier outpost in the north, making it a crossroads of trade and culture. The 500 odd population was a mixture of Spanish aristocrats who were in power and possessed most of the wealth, Mexican herdsmen, American trappers who would seem poor examples of Anglo culture, plus a dozen kinds of Indians—free and slave, in and around the village. Ouray was partly a product of his environment of gambling, fandangos, religious parades and processions, brawling drunks and the casual Spanish culture of the frontier.

Ouray was in Taos in 1846 when Col. Stephen W. Kearney came through with his dragoons on their way to California. The young Ute saw or heard about their number, witnessed cannons and equipment, then perceptively realized their total strength

outnumbered all the Utes in Colorado. In 1847 the Pueblo Indians went into revolt against their new masters, not able to distinguish any improvement over what they had experienced from their previous tormentors. Charles Bent, the first appointed American governor of New Mexico, was scalped and murdered in the presence of his family, also a good deal of blood was shed before the enraged Pueblos could be pacified. Most of the blood spilled was Indian blood however, therefore, Ouray had a good opportunity to observe the futility of trying to oppose the whites with the use of force. His perception and wisdom did not let him forget these lessons learned in his youth, sometimes when the most vividly imbedded lessons are learned.

In 1850 Ouray returned to his people and made his home with them for the next ten years until he became chief, putting on the buckskins and ways of the Uncompahgre Utes. Despite his mixed blood he became a full-fledged member of the tribe; now his education turned abruptly in a new direction. These ten years between 1850 and 1860 were enjoyable for the young Ouray, also he quickly made the adjustment from Spanish to Indian culture learning to love the mountains and meadows of the Uncompahgre country. Shortly after his return Guera Murah died, leaving behind the expected inheritance of a dozen ponies for each grown son, a possession treasured more than anything by the Utes.

Belated puberty rites were held for Ouray; he was smeared with the blood of a mountain lion to make him wise and quick, followed by a night in the tepee of a young Indian girl. In the spring of 1852 at the traditional bear dance, Ouray was paired with a young Tabeguache maiden named Black Mare, whom he married shortly after. A son, Queashegut, was born in 1857, but in 1863 was kidnapped near the present Fort Lupton while Ouray was on a buffalo hunt north of Denver. He was kidnapped presumably by an Arapaho raiding party that attacked the camp. The boy, who was six years old at the time, was never recovered and, as expected, this was a source of great sorrow to Ouray.

In 1873, ten years after the boy was lost, Felix Brunot, a federal negotiator, promised to help Ouray find the lost son at treaty talks. Ouray promised to help facilitate the negotiation of the Brunot Treaty and convince the Utes to give up their lands in the San Juan Mountains. The boy was found and taken to Washington, D.C., but refused to acknowledge any relationship with Ouray. Black Mare died in 1859, so Ouray married Chipeta, who was sixteen years old—Ouray was 26. Chipeta was noted for

OURAY

her intelligence and beauty, moreover, these two remarkable Indians were devoted to each other. Chipeta cared for Queashegut like her own son and shared Ouray's sorrow in his loss. Chipeta never had any children of her own, so they adopted three orphans and reared them to adulthood.[1]

Chipeta was a good wife and the typical condescending mate the Ute male expected—devoted, hard working, shy and quiet of mouth, keeping her temper and performing the multitude of tasks that kept the Indian household together, leaving time for her husband to partake of the male prerogatives such as gambling all night, resting late to prepare for a leisurely day of hunting and fishing or simply sitting around the campfires, fed with wood by the women, telling tall tales.

Ouray's bent for leadership appeared early when he would sit around the council fires listening to the elders, absorbing as much as he could. Conejo was the Ute tribal headquarters where Ouray made many trips to councils to take part or listen in on the discussions that occurred, taking it all in for later use. Indian politics were exciting to the young Indian, moreover, the councils whetted his appetite for more of an active role in the tribal affairs. His knowledge and ambition pushed him up the political ladder of the Uncompahgres, consequently, he probably realized Chief Nevava was getting along in years.

Ouray fell into his new life in Colorado with great zest and soon became one of the most adept warriors of the tribe. This still was a warrior culture, where the only way a man could rise to the

Chipeta

top was to prove his ability in this capacity. Chief Nevava and War Chief Benito quickly turned Ouray into a warrior of the highest type. He was a fine horseman, became a crack shot with a rifle and pistol and a calm, quick man with a knife in a duel, surprisingly quick for his stocky build. Ouray loved to fight, both for ambition and sport, moreover, he killed several Utes for Chief Nevava and, later for himself, to enforce tribal discipline.[2]

Once a year, with a group of his warrior friends, Ouray would head east for a buffalo hunt. This meant several good days of hard riding and perhaps skirmishes with the Cheyenne and Arapaho, sometimes resulting in tragedy, as the loss of Queashegut. The Utes enjoyed this lark into the land of their enemies, besides, Ouray relished the opportunity for the diversion. During his younger years, Ouray was a fine physical specimen, with a large head and stocky frame, about 5 feet 7 inches tall. Ouray's gift of statesmanship helped him to gain the knowledge and respect of his people, while gradually his influence increased. His power, ambition and scheming were naturally resented by other ambitious Utes, but he was still respected for his perception, wisdom, honesty, foresight and courage.

More and more Ouray became a man of several worlds; he could live and relate with the Utes or Apaches, could speak English, Spanish, Ute, Apache, and could get by in some of the Pueblo tongues.

During his second life with the Utes, Ouray learned their ways and came to love his people. When he became chief, it became his responsibility to guard them from their enemies and protect them from danger. The most serious threat came after 1860, with the gold rush, when the white encroachment on Indian land increased and there was more interest in the lands of the Western Slope of the Centennial State. Gold was discovered in the San Juans in 1859, bringing the whites closer to the Uncompahgres and their land.

In 1854, Kit Carson became Indian agent for the Muaches at the Indian agency at Conejos. Ouray and the well-known mountain man became close friends, frequently discussing problems between their two peoples. Carson was also a man at home in several worlds who understood the Indian and his culture better than any other white man in the region. Carson advised Ouray that the Utes should obtain a treaty that would confirm their holdings in Western Colorado. Ouray relayed this advice to Old Chief Nevava in 1860, but Nevava said the Rockies would belong to the Utes forever, therefore, it was not necessary to obtain a treaty to confirm this ownership. "Did not Ouray realize the Utes had

been safe and secure in their mountain sanctua for 700 years?" Finally, Ouray entreated the c chief for permission to take a group of warriors investigate the gold rush on the Front Range and the San Juans. When the Utes witnessed the 100,0 gold seekers scrambling over both areas, they we alarmed and realized the overwhelming numeric superiority these whites had over them.

Ouray returned to Nevava with the soberi news of the increase in white encroachment, b Nevava was still stubborn; he said, "The Utes cou stop the soldiers with sticks and stones as the came through Ute or Mosca Passes." It was at th time, in 1860, that Ouray seized command of t tribe and became chief of the Uncompahgres. was not long until Ouray headed for Conejos inform Kit Carson he was ready for treaty tal Maybe old Nevava was wiser than Ouray realize because when bargaining began Ouray soon foun he had to give up some of his land to gain a gua antee regarding Ute ownership of the remainde However, the young chief soon became a wise ar forceful negotiator for his people's interests. Ouray first experience with treaty making came at Conejo in 1863, during the Civil War. The treaty was eve tually signed in Denver, when the Utes gave up th San Luis Valley in return for a guarantee of the 16,000,000-acre holdings, mostly in Western Colo rado. This was the first treaty-signing by the ne chief, moreover, he soon learned that when he wer looking for something, he had to forfeit somethin else to obtain his goal. He signed this treaty "Uray or "Arrow"; the treaty was amended in 1868, whe his name was changed to Ouray on the documen Ouray's hold over the Utes was precarious, but h arose as their top leader and came into prominenc anyway. The Muaches of the south and the Whit River Utes were leaders in the opposition agains his selection and rule thereafter. During these ne gotiations, Ouray used the force of his personality patience and diplomacy to accomplish his goals. Hi power as an Indian chief was of little help to hir among the whites anyway.[3]

The Hunt Treaty was negotiated in 1868 i Denver without any problems. It simply opened u the mining areas of the Front Range and legalize the activity of the past ten years. The Brunot Treat was signed in Washington in 1873, after the gol and silver rush began in the San Juans, therefor the towns of Ouray, Silverton, Creede, Telluride an Lake City soon resulted. Ouray and Chipeta an several of the other Utes made the trip to Washing ton to be impressed by the power and wealth of th "Great White Father." By the treaty, Ouray wa given two homes—one at Los Pinos, on the junctio of Los Pinos and Cochetopa Creeks, the other at Montrose. He was also granted a pension of $1,000 a year. These grants were particularly resented by the White River Ute chiefs who considered themselves more worthy. Annuities of $25,000 annually forever were to be given to the tribe, mostly in goods and services and not cash. The annuity problem was one of the most annoying sources of grief, because the House of Representatives frequently forgot to appropriate the money, moreover, it was almost impossible to distribute them over the terrain of Western Colorado to the widely scattered Utes. All Utes had to be included in the allocation, besides it was never easy to distinguish between different Indian bands. The administration of annuities was so troublesome that the awards frequently did more harm than good and was one of the main causes of the rebellion of the White River Utes.

The Brunot Treaty, like the Evans Treaty with the Cheyenne and Arapaho, was an attempt to induce the Indians to a new way of life. Part of the annuities was to be used to establish cattle ranches in the Gunnison and White River country to convert the Utes to a more productive existence. These cattle ranches were stocked with cattle and the Indians given the opportunity to undertake a new way of life. Neither ranch was a glowing success, moreover, the White River operation turned out to be a colossal failure. However, the experiment only lasted six years. The Ute tribe successfully sued the U. S. government for back pay in the annuities not paid according to the Brunot Treaty and won over five million dollars.

Ouray's position as the chief of the confederation of Utes, recognized by the U. S., if not by all the Utes, was a great responsibility that weighed heavily on his shoulders, because his previous life made him aware that the future would inevitably bring changes for his people, whether they wanted them or not. He tried to follow a middle course and reconcile the differences between the two cultures, trying to preserve as much of their land and way of life as possible. The Ute chief would not hear of talk of violence, likewise, on many occasions spoke out bluntly against suggestions from other chiefs to take up the war ax.

Ouray's persistence in opposition to violence and his friendly treatment of whites won him many friends among the whites, but frequently led to the "sell out" allegation among his own people. The following speech, given by Ouray in Denver in 1874, after the signing of the Brunot Treaty, eloquently portrays his wisdom and foresight in dealing with the white man:

I realize the destiny of my people. They will be extirpated by the race that overruns, occupies and holds our hunting grounds, whose numbers and force, with the government and the millions behind it will in a few years remove the last trace of our blood that now remains. We shall fall as the leaves from the trees when frost or winter comes, and the lands which we have roamed over for countless generations will be given over to the miner and the plowshare. In place of our humble tepees, the white man's towns and cities will appear and we shall be buried out of sight beneath the avalanche of the new civilization. This is the destiny of my people. My part is to protect them and yours, as far as I can, from the violence and bloodshed while I live and to bring both into friendly relations, so that they may be at peace with one another.

JOSEPH
McCOY

21—THE NEW LORDS OF THE PRAIRIES

The American Cowboy has assumed a position in the folk culture of America—the whole world, for that matter—that is amazing. Originally, the men or boys that herded cattle across the country were referred to as drovers and the cattle they dealt with were comparatively tame ranch cattle. The Texas cattle driven to railheads in Kansas was a different breed altogether. The longhorns were wilder than buffalo and more dangerous. In the early days of the open-range cattle business it was almost impossible to pay a man top wages to herd cattle. For this reason, young men or boys were hired on to do the job. Some herds were driven the 1,000 miles north from Texas to Kansas with the oldest member of the group, generally the foreman, only seventeen years old, while the rest of the drovers were even younger. Hence, the term "cowboys" was derived from the young nature of these early participants and it remains to this day.

Sometime after 1500, European cattle came to North America from Mexico. These Spanish, or Andalusian livestock were first brought to Mexico by Cortez in 1521. Then, after this date, several more followed, to be driven north by Coronado or other conquistadores. Some were turned loose or broke loose, others were shipwrecked on the islands of the gulf or on the mainland. Gradually, the Texas Longhorn, the hybrid of the Texas brush country, emerged, a new entity entirely. For a more complete and colorful treatment of the longhorn the reader's attention is directed to **The Longhorns** by J. Frank Dobie.

The Santa Fe Trail taught another lesson to westerners. To their surprise, their oxen and horses grew sleek and fat on the trip over the trail while hauling freight. This could only be because of the nutritious nature of the grass that covered the prairies. It was good cattle feed and, better yet, it was free, and seemingly, limitless. As this knowledge became widespread, the day of the buffalo and Plains Indian was as good as over. There were yet three more ingredients necessary to launch the open-range cattle industry—they were, cheap cattle in Texas, railheads in Kansas and a demand for meat in the East. After the Civil War these factors began to fall into place.

The first commercial use of the Texas Cattle was for their hides, horns, hooves and tallow, because they were poor meat producers anyway. The hides were twice as thick and tough as regular rawhide, therefore, it had a multitude of uses in a country and age that resembled its sterling qualities. The hooves and horns were used for glue and utensils; the tallow was used to make candles and cooking fat. The cattle were shipped to Missouri and California before the Civil War, but so far the possibilities of large cattle drives had not attracted attention. Two men, one at each end of the trail, helped to change the past and usher in the open range cattle industry and the trail drive. Joseph McCoy realized the best way to get cattle to a beef-hungry East was by rail. McCoy's next step was to build stockyards along the Kansas-Pacific Railroad in places like Abilene, Kansas then send word a thousand miles south to Texas to bring cattle.

At the other end of the trail was a sturdy Texan by the name of Charles Goodnight. Goodnight was one of the first to ship cattle north; he carefully laid out the Loving-Goodnight Trail, scientifically designed the first chuckwagon and worked out a code of conduct for the trail that was harsh, but fair, for his cowboys. McCoy and Goodnight were followed by a host of others at both ends of the trails who added more trails, cattle towns and competition. The cattle trails were opened and the herds began to move north. The young drovers, pressed into this demanding enterprize because of competition and low prices for cattle, matured with the industry to become "the shining knights on horseback" of American folklore.

Texas cattle multiplied during the Civil War when many of the long-horned critters were turned loose on the Texas plains to forage for themselves, where they flourished. The Battle of Vicksburg gained the Mississippi River from the Confederacy and cut Texas off from the rest of the southern states. The Texas cattlemen could not reach southern markets, moreover, it would have been disloyal to sell to the North so, with few buyers in Texas, there was a considerable surplus roaming the Texas plains after the war.

With the surplus of Texas cattle, many head, unbranded or unowned and free for the taking, along with the demand for beef in the North at war-inflated prices, the trail drive to Kansas railheads was a natural consequence. When the war ended, the railroads pushed westward, giving Texas cattle access to northern markets with free "government hay" in between. The cattle went to slaughter in eastern slaughter houses or were fattened on the plains for later use, while some were used to make up the beginning of the cattle industry in states north of Texas. The first cattle brought into the Centennial State were brought into the San Luis Valley in the late 1840's, but the industry did not flourish until Texas cattle began to make an appearance in the 1860's. Territorial Colorado had laws prohibiting importation of Texas cattle. With new interest aroused in the cattle industry after the Civil War, the law was repealed in 1870. When the Kansas Pacific Railroad came into Colorado, the cattle drives entered the state, and the open range cattle industry began in Colorado.

The herds were driven to the northern railheads for a cost of about $1.00 a head, depending on the trail and the distance traveled. There were several routes taken for the Texas cattle; only the Dawson and Goodnight Trails came into Colorado.

The routes moved further west as the homesteader moved into Kansas and plowed and fenced the open range. The open-range cattle industry operated on the plains of Colorado, in South Park and the San Luis Valley, until it came to an end. During the good years, profits were high and money could be made quickly, so soon many began to make an effort to enter such a lucrative business.

The climate dictated that the cattle industry would develop on the plains of Eastern Colorado. A pastoral existence could tolerate the arid expanse while agriculture could not make it with the limited moisture available. As the gold rush brought more people, cognizant businessmen bought old worn stock and pastured them east of the supply towns of Denver, Boulder and Colorado City on the free and open range, then sold them to the beef-hungry miners for a good profit when they were fattened. The removal of the Plains Indians in 1870, along with the arrival of the cattle drivers from Texas, added impetus to this infant Colorado industry.

The buffalo and grama grass were nutritious summer and winter, without losing their food value after freezing; moreover, best of all, it was free. As more pressure was placed on the cattlemen for grazing land, like the Utes before them, they pushed up into the higher mountain valleys, finding the same nutritious grass the Utes had fed their ponies two hundred years earlier; also, their cattle flourished from the feed and surroundings in the same way. In the beginning, the open range cattle industry was an open operation without regulation or restrictions, with no officials to check on the industry. As could be expected, the cattlemen solved their own problems in their own way, sometimes at the expense of the sodbuster or sheepman. The cattlemen followed the Indians into the West and naturally, felt they had a primacy that gave them first rights; they had little patience with anyone who disagreed with their appropriated sovereignty.

Land offices and marshalls eventually came West to handle the transfer of property and to begin the regulation and restriction of the activities of the open-range cattle industry. In most cases these new restrictions did not hamper these primates of the plains, as they continued to use their high-handed methods without much restraint. The time when everything was free except cattle and labor began to pass, then the cattle barons began to move for control of land near water by gaining deeded control. John Wesley Iliff, John Wesley Prowers and James C. Jones were three of Colorado's early cattle kings, well known in their time in the cattle industry in the Rocky Mountain region.

CHARLES
GOODNIGHT

Iliff fed Union Pacific construction gangs as the roadbed was constructed westward, then stayed in Colorado and began to amass his cattle kingdom which, by 1889, consisted of over 15,000 acres along the Platte from Greeley to Julesburg. Prowers was one of the first to pioneer the white face or Hereford strain in Colorado and try to improve on the stringy longhorn and produce more pounds of beef per ton of feed. Prowers gained control of about forty miles of frontage along the Arkansas River; Jones was another of the Arkansas River cattle barons.

The federal government remained liberal with the cattle industry, moreover, the land laws of the time, fashioned for the East but to be used in the West, left much to be desired and, therefore, were constantly abused. The Homestead Act of 1862 allowed a claim of 160 acres for improvements, therefore, during the winter when chores were light, cattlemen would send their cowboys out to file on 160 acres and then would work with a land marshall for the certification of improvements, which were sometimes small "dollhouses" moved to each 160 acres for substantiation of improvement which was, at best, a rather ambiguous requirement. The Timber Culture Act of 1873 required the planting of trees on forty of the 160 acres, because it was believed that the planting of trees would bring rain to the treeless plains and change the arid climate to that of the East where trees were located.

The Desert Land Act of 1877 finally admitted that some places in the West a farmer could not make a living on 160 acres and permitted the purchase of 640 acres at the going price of $1.25 an acre. Supposedly, the new owner was to irrigate this land and improve it in other ways. The Timber and Stone Act of 1878 applied to quarry, mining and timber land and land not suitable for agriculture, but the price was raised to $2.50 an acre, then 160 acres were allotted to each individual. Some of the finest timber lands in the world went for the incredible price of $2.50 an acre, as the laws were abused with fraudulent claims by employees to amass huge cattle, ranch and timber holdings, even though the laws were intended to provide these allotments to individuals for their own use, not for the use of huge cattle companies or timber enterprises. However, it was not the laws that were wrong, it was the people that misused them, moreover, the purpose of the laws, to settle the West, was eventually realized.

As the cattlemen strove to protect their interests and perpetuate their bonanza, they ran into competition from various sources. Gradually, they began to organize, therefore, the Colorado Cattlemen Association made its appearance in 1871. They also realized the open range could not last, so they began to lobby for a permanent cattle trail, unfenced, stretching from Texas to Canada—a strip of free government hay, fifty miles wide, from the Gulf to Montana. At first they demanded permanent range areas be set aside for their use, but finally compromised on the cattle trail which they first asked to be one hundred miles wide. The invention of the barbed wire fence in 1874 brought an end to the open range, as fences were erected by both the farmer and the cattleman, frequently on government range. The cattleman's argument of primacy was a valid one, so far as he was concerned, because he did not regard the Indian as a human, but his argument was similar to the Indian's. The cattleman was, in a sense, a nomad much like the Indian who did not make intense use of the land; therefore, replacing nomads with nomads was not enough to prevent the farmers from moving on to the open range, although the cattleman relinquished his hold grudgingly.

Restrictions gradually arrived and roundup districts were arranged. In 1879 the State of Colorado was divided into sixteen roundup districts, with an inspector in each. After the 1880's, the open-range cattle industry began to decline. More and more of the land was taken up by the homesteader, quarantine laws restricted the movement of cattle from Texas, when many died from hoof-and-mouth disease. The attractive possibilities offered by the industry resulted in too many cattlemen; then the over-supply resulted in a surplus which, in turn, led to a drop in prices, so soon the range was over grazed until there was not enough feed, causing the cattleman to buy or produce feed for his cattle greatly increasing costs.

The coming of the railroad opened the cattle industry to Eastern markets, but the railroads began to fence their right-of-ways, because of the cost of cattle destroyed by the trains. In 1886 2,242 cattle were killed by trains in Colorado and according to the law of the open range, the railroad was liable for the destroyed cattle. It seemed the cattle that were killed by the trains were almost always prime beef that cost the railroad the limit. The railroad went so far as to accuse cattlemen of driving decrepid stock on the tracks to spare them the trouble of disposing of the unmarketable critters, therefore, giving them an opportunity to turn a loss into a considerable profit.

Like many farmers, the cattlemen were guilty of poor methods of farming; consequently, their mistakes cut into their profits until they became

JOHN
W.
ILIFF

more adept in meeting the challenges of that rigorous business. Frequently, they had poor stock—too many bulls or horses that consumed a lot of the feed. After the mining ended in the San Juans and other areas, burros were turned loose to fend for themselves, moreover, the hardy little animals multiplied until their numbers were so great they had to be killed off by cattlemen to preserve food for cattle in the mountain areas where they were located. Wild horses were other consumers of the range, resented by cattlemen and coveted by dog-food producers, and they can easily become a thing of the past if efforts to protect them are not implemented.

The mustangs arrived in the Southwest in the same way cattle were introduced. These wild horses multiplied in South Texas and other grassed areas until their numbers were in the thousands. They were sought by the Indians, cattlemen and the army to replenish stock when they were needed. Gradually, the pressure of civilization brought an abrupt end to their existence. Present wild horses are not mustangs, but escaped or turned loose ranch horses. As the open range was over-grazed, cattlemen did everything they could to eliminate animals that might compete with their cattle for feed. Buffalo, wild horses, wild burros or any other animal that grazed was held in contempt. This contempt was amplified with the arrival of sheep. The history of the west is filled with the antipathy between these two industries. Conflict and destruction were brothers and sisters to the friction between the two industries. It was the lonely sheepherder that most often felt the brunt of this contempt. Sheep were driven over cliffs, camps were raided. A favorite cowboy practice was to hitch a rope between the saddles of two riders by tying each end to the saddle-horn, then riding side-by-side with the rope taunt through a sheepherder's camp, much like the huge caterpillars with their log chains used to destructively reduce sage brush and trees in order to expedite grazing. The cowboys would reduce the sheep-herder's camp to shreds until the battle-weary sheepherder devised a way to teach the cowboys a lesson. After a few of these unwelcome visits, the sheepherder would pitch his tent over the sturdy stump of a tree that had been trimmed off at the top. The boisterous cowboys were in for the surprise of their lives when the rope hit the tent.

A credit to the West is the dissipation of this animosity between the two industries. Ranchers frequently raise both cattle and sheep on the same ranch at the present time, which gives them more diversity and provides the opportunity to utilize the advantages of both. The bitterness is not completely gone, but things have improved. The sheep industry, although not as heralded, is as much a part of the history of the West as the cattle industry. A good example would be in the case of the state of Texas; Texas is known for the cattle industry, but it so happens it is also the largest sheep producing state in the United States.

The late 1880's saw Mother Nature plague the cattleman with some of the worst winters in history, when many cattle perished on the plains as they were marooned and feed could not be taken to them. When cattlemen lost hundreds of their cattle, they were not able to absorb the losses and survive; the hardest hit or most marginal outfits were forced out of business. Like the proud and stately Plains Indians before them who lived from the buffalo that grazed on the plains, the cattlemen replaced the buffalo with Texas cattle, and they became the new lords of the plains, claiming land for as far as their eyes could reach. Their sacrifices and efforts hardened them, much like the mountain men were changed by their environment. They had paid a high price for the land they loved and could not be expected to part with a way of life that was dear to them without trying to preserve it. Yes, their story is more like the Indian than they would ever have admitted.

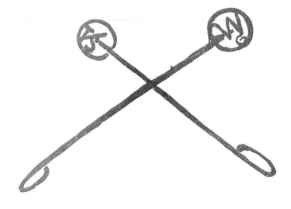

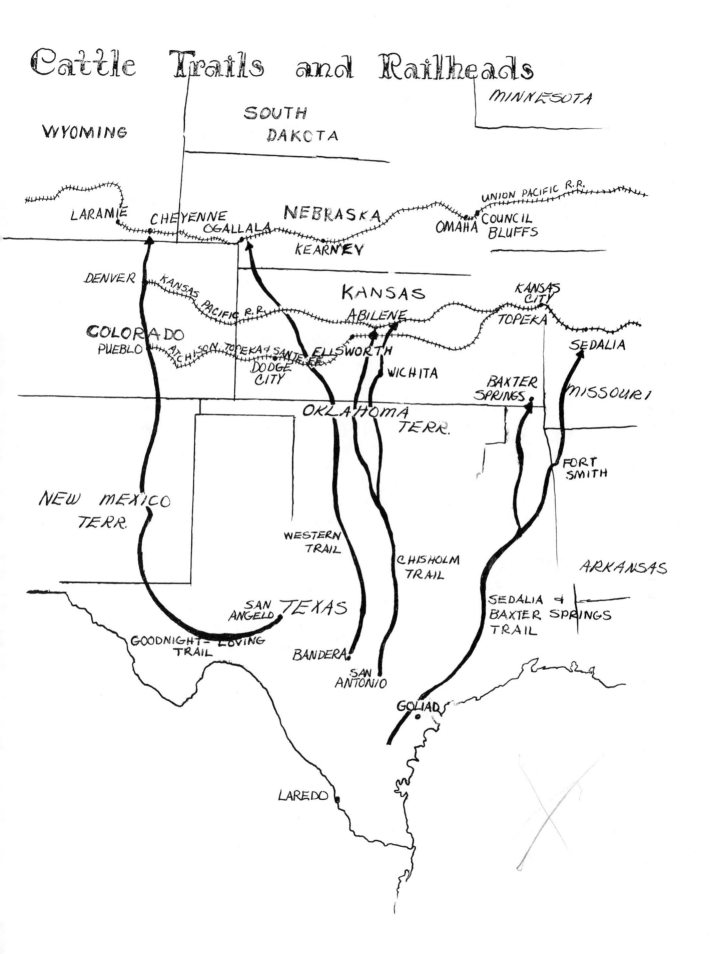

Cattle Trails and Railheads

MINNESOTA

WYOMING

SOUTH DAKOTA

UNION PACIFIC R.R.

LARAMIE CHEYENNE OGALLALA NEBRASKA OMAHA COUNCIL BLUFFS

KEARNEY

DENVER KANSAS PACIFIC R.R. KANSAS KANSAS CITY

COLORADO ABILENE TOPEKA

PUEBLO ATCHISON, TOPEKA & SANTA FE ELLSWORTH SEDALIA

DODGE CITY WICHITA

BAXTER SPRINGS MISSOURI

OKLAHOMA TERR.

NEW MEXICO TERR. FORT SMITH

WESTERN TRAIL CHISHOLM TRAIL ARKANSAS

SAN ANGELO TEXAS SEDALIA & BAXTER SPRINGS TRAIL

GOODNIGHT-LOVING TRAIL BANDERA SAN ANTONIO

GOLIAD

LAREDO

—163—

- 1892 -

Companies in parade in downtown Grand Junction

(original photo given to Department by Charlie Peeore)

22—TOWNS, FARMS, FUN AND GAMES

To create the territory of Colorado, it was necessary to arrange for the cession of parts of the Utah, Nebraska, Kansas and the New Mexico territories. After this was accomplished, the business of setting up a government and making political divisions within the new territory was expedited. Early efforts connected with the territory of Jefferson have already been mentioned. Before Congress created the Colorado Territory on February 26, 1861, local problems in unorganized areas were dealt with by setting up People's or Miners' Courts.

People's Courts were improvised assemblies convened to settle criminal cases. They were presided over by a probate judge or justice of the peace. Miners' courts were better organized and generally were established in a mining district that had been set up for political purposes in an isolated region. These courts had fixed limits within the district, had worked out and adopted a miners' code and had defined the duties of their officials. Besides the trying of criminal offenses, the Miners' Court settled all claim disputes. Both of these courts served well in the Pikes Peak Region from 1858 until the territory was created in 1861. It would appear that these judicial efforts were crude and chaotic; however, evidence indicates they were orderly affairs that were handled with dignity and decorum.

Another political task that the new territory faced was the division of the new territory into counties. In the beginning, seventeen counties were designated. The Arapaho and Cheyenne Reservation in Eastern Colorado and the Ute Reservation in Western Colorado were excluded from these original counties. Most of them were quite large in size, many more than equaled the size of the smaller eastern states. Weld County occupied the entire northeastern part of the territory and remains one of the three largest counties in the State. New counties were gradually added later by dividing these seventeen original counties or moving into the Indian reservations.

Efforts of political organizations on the territorial level were paralleled by the forming of town companies. The early companies that were organized in 1859 were largely affiliated with the gold rush as mining camps or supply towns. A good portion of these hopeful sites withered away and disappeared from the scene, however, others remained to survive and become the embryos of present cities. Dreams and applications for charters were only the beginning—much more was needed to complete a successful town. Production of the mines in the region and accessibility to transportation were two important determinants of success. Ambition and ingenuity could help, but were not enough to insure a permanent town.

The year 1870 was a turning point in the history of the Centennial State. The arrival of the railroad, coupled with the removal of the Cheyenne and Arapaho from Eastern Colorado, convinced would-be settlers that the rudimentary ingredients of civilization were attainable in the territory. The period of colonization began.

Colonies were organized in the east and came west in groups. Frequently, they were sponsored by a church or a national group. The Chicago Colony was the first to come. In 1870 eighty-six families settled in the Wet Mountain Valley and laid out the town of Colfax. The colony soon failed because of dissension between its members and lack of strong leadership. The second colony was inspired by the words and efforts of Horace Greeley, the editor of the New York Tribune. Greeley had visited Colorado in 1859 and was awed with the potential of the region. His famous words, "go west, young man", helped to encourage settlement. Nathan C. Meeker had colonial experience and was a Tribune writer; in 1869 Meeker made a trip to the Colorado Territory and was impressed by the South Park area. Later, he was fortunate to change his plans and decided on Weld County, a better choice and a much wiser decision than the fateful one that later sent him to the White River Country as agent of the White River Utes in 1878.

Upon the return of Meeker, an active advertising program was initiated that praised the merits and potential of the chosen colony site. Such advertisements appeared frequently in eastern newspapers between 1850 and 1900. Their contents were similar: "Wanted, sober, godfearing citizens to form a colony to settle in the Colorado Territory." Each head of the family must contribute $150 to $250 (depending on the colony) to the company. Upon arrival in the territory, members will receive 160 acres of land. Once the assigned number was gathered—perhaps a hundred families—the business of electing leaders was taken care of, then a compact was worked out that listed regulations, travel orders and maximum gear allowed. With this done, the group headed in the direction of the setting sun with high anticipations and expectations, mingled with some trepidation. The Union Colony was only the beginning. Others followed with all races, religions and philosophies represented. Eventually,

colonies pushed to all parts of the State. Some we successful, as in the case of the Union Colony, othe were quick to fail. Choice of location, resources the area and the people involved were the determi ants in the experiment.

The West provided the opportunity for all zea ous and righteous prophets of all types to test the convictions by attempting to recreate heaven earth in an isolated, uncontaminated, virgin lan Communal settlements were formed with Utopia principles of the wildest nature employed. Althoug heaven did not reappear in the Colorado Territor in the isolated and unfettered Utopias, a good nun ber of the colonists did find what they were lookir for. Some could not have been more pleased, whi others were bitterly disappointed. The organizatic and leadership of the colony was undoubtedly instr mental in its success. The Union Colony, along wi several of the religiously motivated colonies, we inclined to try to protect their Utopia by enacti rigid blue laws regarding consumption of alcohol beverages and moral conduct. One of the stipul tions in the real estate deeds given to its membe was that no intoxicating liquor could be manufa tured or sold upon the town plat. Most of the ear colony or farm-oriented towns included simil clauses—the mining towns had no such stipulation Colorado Springs began with blue laws, but the were eventually repealed. Another factor that add to this dilemma was that several of the towns wi these blue laws became college towns, which add to the difficulty of enforcement. The first solutic was the incorporation of a small town on the ou skirts that provided the college students and othe with the drinking, gambling and assorted privileg they were seeking. Garden City and Rosedale, "O South" of Greeley, are pertinent examples.

The fact remains that many families came the Centennial State as a part of a colonial ventur and some of the most stable communities were e tablished in this way. Once the colony or communi was established, the next item of business was attract others. Leaders of these communities aga advertised in eastern newspapers, extolling t merits of their haven beyond the limits of credib ity, making wild claims about fertility of soil, purit of air and water, and even claiming the air ar water possessed medicinal qualities that would cu anything from tuberculosis to dropsy. The ra roads aided in this promotion by publicity and tou with prospective settlers. The claims that we made were somewhat exaggerated, but not a who lot more than the chambers of commerce with the propaganda of the present. Anyway, how can t natural attributes of the Centennial State be exaggerated?

The colonists came to the West with agriculture in mind. The problem was that their previous experience did not prepare them for the new problems connected with farming in an arid region. When they trekked past the 100th meridian and twenty inches of annual rainfall, the rules made an abrupt change. The average rainfall in Colorado is seventeen inches; in some areas it is much less than that. In Europe or the eastern United States, water was ample. The first white settlers that came into Colorado went into the San Luis Valley, but they came from even more arid regions to the south and, consequently, were prepared to cope with this lack of moisture. These first settlers realized irrigation would be necessary. They had previous experience in irrigation and methods to allot water. Most of Colorado's first farmers had to work these problems out with the same method used in the mines—trial and error. Canals were dug to convert the waters of the Platte and Arkansas. At first they were small because of the immensity of the undertaking; eventually, insurance companies formed water companies and dug canals. Water prices were so high farmers rebelled until most of the canals became cooperatives owned by the farmers. After the Newlands Act the federal government began to build canals through the Bureau of Reclamation.

Perhaps it was on the Great Plains of Eastern Colorado, where water for irrigation was not available, that the farmer faced his greatest challenge, a challenge comparable to the one the miners grappled with in their rugged terrain. The demands were as rigorous and the people that met them were every bit as rugged. Mother Nature seemed to be at her worst with the "bag of tricks" she unfurled on the plains. The contest began in the 1870's after the removal of the Cheyenne and Arapaho. The plains were opened and the settlement began. The first to arrive were the cattlemen and they pre-empted most of the best land. On their tails came the unwelcome but dogged "nester". The Homestead Act of 1862 made it possible for these early ranchers to gain 160 acres and launch their agricultural enterprises. When they arrived the plains were covered with a verdent carpet of buffalo grass. Although there was practically no wood, they used buffalo chips for fuel and built sod houses. While they were about the business of getting settled, they began to plow up the rich carpet. The grass had stored moisture, humus and richness of the ages in the soil. Their first crops were promising, even if abundant moisture was not available from rain. It was at this time that Mother Nature began to open her "bag of tricks".

The new settler has been promptly set-up. Encouraged by his early success, he expanded his operation and mortgaged to the limit. His expansion took him into marginal areas where soil was not as rich. The 70's were blessed with adequate moisture; it was the 80's that turned dry. The prolonged droughts wiped out the dreams of most of these hardy ranchers; the 90's was the decade of foreclosures. The less determined gave up and left; the hardier, for some unknown reason, remained. Poorer but wiser, they began to learn to deal with the challenges of the plains. Walter Prescott Webb brilliantly portrays this Great Plains Frontier in his classic work, **The Great Plains.** They built windmills and sunk wells to obtain water. They wondered where else in the world were similar conditions and found that Russian farmers had coped with similar conditions for centuries. From these farmers of the Caucusus they obtained hard-grained wheat that would withstand the prolonged droughts. Gradually, they won the hard-fought battles, at least temporarily. Mother Nature again opened her "bag of tricks" in the 1930's and wiped out another generation. They scratched their heads and worked with the Department of Agriculture until they persevered. Today, wheat is the most valuable farm crop produced in Colorado. The farmers of the Great Plains continue in their struggle. A century of experience aids in their success and keeps them wary for the next quirk of Mother Nature.

Success in agriculture was responsible for prosperity in the Centennial State more than any other industry. This unsung, but valuable and reliable, enterprise was Colorado's most important industry much of the first century. Perhaps thinking in terms of their forefathers and the first Thanksgiving, a phenomenon was launched that exceeds anything of similarity; the food festival mania started in the 1870's. It consisted of free meals of a type best suited to the resources of the area where they occurred; also included were food-eating contests, beauty contests, fairs or anything else the imagination could conjure. Colorado is the only state where they became widspread and once they started, they seemed to become contagious.

The purpose of these food festivals was to reveal the agricultural bounty of the Centennial State, show off climate and soil fertility and, at the same time, share their good fortune with others. The movement spread rapidly until every summer weekend was involved. A state coordinating board was organized to prevent duplication and aid in providing publicity. It was the unusual Coloradan that was unaware of his blessings. He wanted to share them and, at the same time, have some fun. With careful planning it was possible to attend festivals continually, eating free food and participating in various events and contests. Every other year an election was held and there were campaigns during the summer, these festivals providing aspiring politicians with a splendid opportunity to meet their constituents and wear out their lungs and right arms. If people with money to spend in the community were attracted, this was another plus.

George Swink was the apostle of the festival movement. In 1878 Swink was blessed with a bumper crop of watermelons, far more than he could hope to market. It seemed a shame to let them go to waste, so he conceived the brilliant idea of sharing his bumper crop. He first went to the railroad station and then began to share with neighbors— the food festival was born. In 1891, 8,000 people came and ate 20,000 melons. Special trains to the Arkansas Valley were scheduled for the event; melons of the Arkansas Valley became famous; the movement began to gather momentum.

In 1890 Monument, Colorado staged a potato bake. Each new festival followed the original pattern of exalting the most important crop in the area. The next year, Grand Junction inaugurated Peach Day. Palisade peaches were taken to Denver and given away downtown and at the railroad station to advertise the luscious fruit. Not to be outdone, two years later, in 1893, Lamar joined the movement with the Lamar Jackrabbit Festival. "Fighting Parson" Uzell sold the citizens on the idea with the promise that the pesky jackrabbits could be brought under control and a festival of their meat could be a part of it. The first jackrabbit roundup produced so many rabbits it was decided to dress them and take them to Denver and give to the poor. Contests, parades and festive events were added, plus the free meal.

The same year, 1893, Colorado Springs, in a more sedate effort, started its Flower Festival with parades, floats and a barbecue. Greeley countered with its Spud Festival, with 10,000 people appearing the first year and 15,000 the next. The event included the free barbecue and the usual fun and games. In 1895 Loveland launched its Corn Festival. The free feast included all the roasting ears you could eat; Kuner's turned over its steam cookers to cook all the corn. In 1898 Strawberry Festivals began in Boulder and Glenwood Springs, replete with queen contests, parades and gala activities.

The festival idea began by honoring the chief agricultural product of the community. Eventually, it became difficult to avoid duplication, or some communities, high in the mountains, did not have an agricultural product to exalt. Steamboat Springs,

one of these mountain communities, entered th[e] movement with a game and fish barbecue. Thre[e] thousand people attended the free barbecue and fe[s]tival the first year it was held. Gunnison starte[d] its free fish fry. Local citizens went out to th[e] nearby streams and lakes and caught the trout f[or] the meal. It added the additional events to mak[e] the day a memorable one and soon gained a larg[e] following. In 1899 Longmont opened Pumpkin P[ie] Day. By 1909 this event had grown to be one [of] the most popular, with 10,000 pumpkin pies disa[p]pearing in the twinkling of an eye. In 1908 Fo[rt] Lupton started its Tomato Festival with a parad[e] and free barbecue. Each town tried to be origina[l] and come up with some event that was one of the[ir] own and, at the same time, an expected part of th[e] festival. Fort Lupton's massive tomato fight wa[s] such an event. The more red-blooded participate[d] and the rest of the crowd watched at a safe distanc[e.]

In 1909 Apple Pie Day began in Rifle. The firs[t] year 7,000 people appeared and disposed of 6,00[0] apple pies in the barbecue and pie-eating contes[t.] The special event was a huge tug-of-war with 1,00[0] on each end of the rope, on each side of Rifle Cree[k.] Fort Collins started Lamb Chop Day the same yea[r.] Every town of any size in Colorado staged some kin[d] of a food festival on an annual basis. People planne[d] their vacations to allow them the opportunity to par[ti]cipate in as many of these colorful events as pos[]sible. For some reason the food festivals began t[o] decline in the 1920's. The local chambers of com[]merce took them over and the free food—probabl[y] the main attraction—disappeared. Vestiges of th[e] old event still remain, however.

The Fourth of July was the most importan[t] holiday of the year. It was celebrated by fireworks[,] patriotic speeches and events, picnics, games, con[]tests, home-made ice cream and whatever the im[]agination of the local citizenry could conjure. I[t] was particularly important in the mining communi[]ties, because they did not have a reason to have [a] food festival; also, Christmas was at the time whe[n] heavy snow and cold weather made festivity diffi[]cult. The holiday was generally about three day[s] in duration. The contests included mining-oriente[d] contests such as hard rock drilling. Horse and mul[e] races and pulling contests were another type of con[]test. The "hook and ladder companies" were fre[]quent participants in the food festivals and Fourt[h] of July holidays. Hose companies were equally in[]volved. It was the passion of the time to win thes[e] contests. The hose companies and hook and ladde[r] outfits were decked out in uniforms that would pu[t] a Prussian officer to shame. Men were vigorousl[y] recruited for their running speed and not necessaril[y] or their fire fighting ability. Contests were held all over the state. A frequent item that appeared on the books in the towns of the state were expenditures to pay the local companies' expenses to some such contest. Cort Thompson, one of the husbands of Mattie Silks, was fast of foot and well known as a successful participant in these contests, as well as his other activities. No wonder so many Colorado communities burned to the ground; their firemen were at some contest or convention.

These food festivals were spontaneous displays of community pride; an attempt to show the world

what the Centennial State had to offer while, at the same time, have a good time. The Mineral Palace at Pueblo, the Ice Palace in Leadville and Aspen's Silver Queen were very similar in their purpose, but on a more grandiose scale. The Mineral Palace was a resplendent exhibit of Colorado ores and minerals held each year. The Aspen Silver Queen was built in 1892 and 1893 by Hiram L. Johnson, a Pueblo sculptor. It required six men working for nine months to complete the statue. It consisted of an 18 foot statue made of silver and white glass. The Silver Queen depicted the ideal maiden of seventeen years of age—the age of the State of Colorado at the time. The statue was valued at $20,000 and was displayed at the Chicago World's Fair. It last appeared as a part of Colorado ores and minerals display in Pueblo in 1942. After that, the Silver Queen was crated for shipment to Denver but has never been seen since. The Aspen City Council has appropriated $5,000 reward in an attempt to locate the statue for the Centennial observance.

The idea of constructing an ice palace in Leadville was the result of community pride and an interest in some kind of a winter carnival that had been discussed for several years. The appearance of the Mineral Palace in Pueblo in 1890 added to the interest in this project. The panic of 1893 cooled such ambitions, but by 1895 the plan emerged with new fervor. Such a palace would bring thousands of people to Leadville and, because of the isolated nature of the Cloud City, they would all require food and lodging. Letters were sent to other locales with previous ice palace experience and Capitol Hill was chosen as the site; construction was begun in November of 1895. The place was braced with timber and, when cold weather began, the ice was added. How could they forecast that the winter of 1895-96 would be unseasonably warm with temperatures from 45 to 65 degrees? Some of the ice had to be hauled in from other locales. Finally, on December 28th, the Palace was opened for public scrutiny. Twenty-five hundred appeared to look at the mar-

velous palace the first day. The interior of the palace was divided into three large rooms—the center section housed a 16,000 square feet skating rink. The ceiling, though made of wood and steel, was completely frosted and had icicles hanging down. On each side of the skating rink were two large ball rooms, 80 x 50 feet. The three-month winter carnival and Ice Palace were a huge success. The only sour note was lack of cooperation from Mother Nature. Spring came early in 1896 and the palace had to be dismantled ahead of schedule. The town had subscribed and invested over $20,000 in its unusual project and few would complain of the money not being well spent.

The Festival of Mountain and Plain was Denver's contribution to the Colorado festival movement. The celebration lasted a week and was held in Denver each October from 1895 to 1912. Festivities included a parade with lavishly decorated floats along with a masquerade during which people danced in the downtown streets. Silver was the underlying theme of the festival because of silver's part in Colorado's wealth and heritage. A Mystic Silver Serpent was paraded in a float to the Silver Serpent Ball. A queen was selected to reign over the ball and was cloaked in long, flowering silver robes. While her reign lasted, she was attended by the Slaves of the Silver Serpent.

In the parade, a silver serpent a block long slithered its way along. It was made up of hundreds of people covered by shiny silver cloth with a head like a Chinese serpent. The parade included hundreds of floats from all over the state with numerous themes and designs. During the week of festivities bicycle races, hook and ladder competition, rock-drilling contests, horse races, along with other contests, occupied the young in heart. This event was a highlight eagerly anticipated for many years. After it was abandoned, it was sorely missed. Efforts to revive it were never successful, however, Denver has inaugurated other events to take its place.

Douglas   **Johnson**

23—THE PURITAN MEETS THE RENEGADES

The various Indians that made up the White River or Northern Utes roamed over the largest segment of the Ute lands. Their isolation and large holdings tended to make them the most casual and loosely organized of all the Utes. They were inclined to be the least receptive to Ouray's leadership, moreover, had their own thoughts about what was best for them. During the summer they roamed the high mountain valleys of northwestern Colorado, hunting deer and elk, while at the same time, visiting their Indian relatives. They did a lot of fishing along the White River, where a fish smokehouse still stands that was built to smoke their trout. They traveled in small groups, therefore, seldom gathered together for any purpose. During the winter months some would come to Powell Park, where their ponies could forage for grass. (Powell Park, west of Meeker, was named after the one-armed John Wesley Powell who camped on that location before he went down the Grand Canyon to explore.) Winter was the time for enjoyment and social activities, while the Utes were gathered in one place, moreover, there were frequent visits among the tribes while they were more settled, when the weather permitted.

The White River Utes were especially transfixed with the horse, which was an item of prestige and wealth. They adored their horses maybe even more than the other Utes, consequently, most of

them had from ten to forty ponies. These ponies, naturally, ate a lot of grass, therefore, were a source of friction to the cattle-conscious whites, who were trying to convert the White River Utes to cattlemen and their country to cattle country. The Indians did not give much cooperation to this endeavor. The view held by a good number of westerners was that Indian horses were more important to the Indian than the buffalo. An unpublicized, but nevertheless, concentrated extermination program was launched against the Indian ponies simultaneously with the effort to eliminate the buffalo. Hiram Bennett of Colorado, asked Congress for a law protecting the buffalo, but his plan was rejected with the claim it could not be enforced.

During the winter the Indian passion turned to horse racing, where Powell Park was the horse pasture and racetrack, consequently, the scene of most activity. These Indian horse races were a sight to behold, therefore, anyone with sporting blood, Indian or white, made a considerable effort to witness or participate. The race track was about a quarter mile long but generally not a circuit, because the Indians did not use bridles or saddles on their ponies during the races—the only thing on the pony, besides the rider, was paint. The young teenage Indian jockeys were attired in the same manner as their ponies, stark naked except for the paint daubed over their faces and bodies. Many accounts claim Indians guided their ponies with the pressure of their knees on the pony's neck, but when the race began there was a lot of yelling, shouting and flapping of arms, trying to get the most from the eager ponies. When the horse came to the end of the race, it was impossible to stop or turn the excited animal, so the jockey generally slid from his back, thereby allowing him to return to the pasture to rest and feed until he was called upon for his next contest.

The White River Utes would gamble almost anything on their horse races, including their wives and children. The promoter of these races, while at the same time the winner of most of these contests, was Johnson, sort of a medicine man and chief of the Utes, who was married to Susan, Ouray's sister. Johnson owned a good number of horses, most of the fastest, moreover, he had a keen knowledge about horses and their abilities which he put to advantage in his races. Johnson also had a pet bear that was trained to dance, therefore, when the bear became inebriated, it was quite a spectacle. Usually, after a day of racing, the Utes would settle down to Spanish Monte, a gambling game, where they again would gamble about anything they possessed. Sometimes they would gather around a huge bonfire to watch the antics of Johnson's bear. There was an itinerant old settler by the name of Charlie Lowry who played the harmonica and was in frequent attendance at these occasions, so he would play while the bear danced, then sometimes the Indians would play moraches or tomtoms. To the White River Utes, this was a great life that left little to be desired. These happy people had no wish to change their ways, moreover, they could not see how they could improve upon their Utopia.

In 1878, Nathan Meeker was appointed agent to the White River Utes. The puritan idealist planned on spending two years in the White River Country, as he estimated it would take about that long to convert the barbarians to the Christian faith, and to a more respectable and practical way of life. These religious and economic transformations were diligently approached by the undaunted Meeker. Many aver that a more articulate and knowledgeable student of Indian affairs could have succeeded where Meeker failed. This is hard to believe, as the forces in Colorado, Utah and Washington were already in motion. A more understanding agent probably could have delayed violence, but the trouble would have surfaced sooner or later, regardless.

"The Utes must go" was a slogan appearing frequently in the Colorado press in the 1870's. Eastern Colorado was now free of Indians and many

were anxious for the opening of the Western Slope. Inquiries about the Western Slope resulted in the answer, "That is the Ute reservation." "How many Utes are in Western Colorado?" would be the next question. "Oh, about 3,500." "What do those damned redskins do with all that land?" "They just roam around on it, hunting and fishing and doing as they please because they all have a pension from the government." "Hell, they don't need all that land for just that, they can roam around somewhere else." So it went—the Utes were communist wards of the U. S. Government, living in sin and iniquity in Western Colorado. "The Utes must go!" "The Utes must go!"

Meeker arrived at the White River agency in 1878, along with his wife, Arvilla, and his youngest daughter, Josephine, who was 18 years of age. The first agency was up the White River about fourteen miles from Powell Park, a good arrangement so far as the Indians were concerned, but impractical for the ambitious Meeker. His decision to move the agency to Powell Park was not a popular one with the Indians, but old Chief Douglas was easy to persuade, so the move was implemented. This brought the Meeker family into closer contact with the Utes, meanwhile, the two older Meekers were somewhat offended by the activities they witnessed in Powell Park. However, the young Josie watched the horse races in wild-eyed amazement, moreover, her emotions were anything but those of distaste.

Captain Jack, sort of a war chief of the Utes, who was raised by the Mormons, then served as a scout for the army, along with Johnson, rose in opposition when Meeker moved the agency. The duo went to see Meeker and vigorously protested the change, but Meeker was a self-righteous and stubborn man, who was sincere in his conviction that what he was doing was right and best for the Utes. How many times the American Indians have been the victims of self-appointed experts to manage their affairs, at the same time firmly convinced about the righteousness of their actions and nobly sincere in their efforts, is unbelievable. Probably most annoying to the Indian was the fact that he was never consulted about what he wanted or thought was best. The Utes were equally stubborn and uncooperative with the plans of their new agent.

Meeker realized that the one obstacle to any progress he attempted was the multitude of ponies owned by the Utes. Nothing he could do would change the ways of the Utes or induce them to embrace cattle raising as a way of life so long as they had their beloved ponies. It was at this time that he conceived a plan that would do away with the

White River Ute Indian Horse Race

ponies and show the Utes the power of the Great White Father. He could plow up Powell Park with the excuse of adding to the farmland and destroy a den of iniquity at the same time. Shadrack Price, an agency employee, began the plowing of Powell Park with a steam tractor near Johnson's house. Immediately, Johnson rushed to the agency to protest, but Johnson had always been peaceful, so Meeker was not too worried. A series of meetings were held where several of the Indians protested the action, but the plowing continued. Finally, Johnson, who was an excellent shot, began to take pot-shots at the tractor, so Price decided to recess the plowing. Johnson again went to see Meeker and accused the agent of plowing his land and sending lies to Washington about the Utes in his reports. "This is not your land," replied Meeker. "It belongs to the government of the United States." That a white man believed land given to Indians by treaty was still the property of the government, therefore, public land, was a principle that was shared by most whites, but certainly incredible to Indians. Meeker had made this statement before, moreover, it had done nothing to put the Indians at ease, but land was not their most precious possession, they prized their ponies most of all. Alarmingly, this was the next Indian institution attacked by the determined puritan.

Meeker had lost his temper and told Johnson, "You have too many ponies, you should kill some of them." To Johnson, this was comparable to suggesting he commit suicide, therefore, he promptly grabbed Meeker and tossed him over the porch rail, but this only shook him up, but did not injure the agent. It was at this time that Meeker decided his life was in danger, therefore, he decided to send for troops. The White River agent had considered the possibility before, but realized the anxiety such action would create among the Indians. To them, troops or the presence of troops meant the danger of removal from their land, because this frequently followed their appearance, therefore, they lived more in fear of troops for this reason than any concern about war or battle. Meeker decided, however, the situation was desperate enough to send the request to Governor Pitkin.

Trouble had been building up in the White River country for sometime, but Nathan Meeker had little to do with most of it; he may have been the unwilling and unsuspecting catalyst that started things moving, but he was not the instigator of many of the problems. The annuity issue was the great provocator of bitterness, because by 1879 a considerable backlog of undelivered annuities made the In-

dians impatient. The annuities were to be shipped to Rawlins, Wyoming on the railroad, but were frequently not there when the Utes made the long trip to claim them. On one occasion, they had arrived but the freight bill was unpaid, therefore, the Indians were forced to return home empty handed. They returned the next spring to find the material blankets, food, and grain destroyed by weather and rats, consequently, it was not worth the trouble of transporting. The annuity problem was a constant source of strife. In most cases, conscientious agents made a great effort to deliver the goods, but sometimes the agents, who were generally political appointees, were dishonest and tried to bilk the Indians or had sold their annuities.

The Indians disregarded, or did not understand boundaries, therefore, they thought such concepts applied only to the whites. It was necessary to restrict them to a reservation and halt their wandering before they could be transformed religiously or economically. They simply did not respond to these restrictions, but continued to hunt and ramble. Sometimes they were destructive when they burned grass or forests to expedite their hunting. The White River Utes never took to the cattle-raising experiment, moreover, they would occasionally ridicule Meeker by conducting a mock hunt by stalking one of the herd, then shooting it, then celebrating their "glorious" hunt with a barbecue. Many of their cattle disappeared, however, there were some cattle outfits not too far away with similar brands. With these circumstances, the herd dwindled instead of increasing.

There had been some Indian depredation in parts of Colorado—a report claimed a group of Utes had attacked whites in South Park, therefore, troops were sent out from Fort Garland to investigate. Josie had been brought to the White River country to start a school for the Indian children in hope of making progress with the young where it was difficult with the adults, who were more set in their ways. She received very little cooperation from the Utes, who refused to allow their children to attend her school. Most of the time the only Indians that attended were the older Indian boys that were more interested in Josie than they were in her school. One of the young suitors named Persine proposed to Josie—the fact that he already had two wives did not trouble him, because plural marriage was not uncommon among the Utes, but it was a serious matter to Josie's father.

The subject of Josie weighed heavily on her father's mind, moreover, his young, attractive, and impressionable daughter seemed to be changing

Nathan Meeker

Arvilla Delight Meeker

Major Thomas Tipton

Thornburgh

Joe Rankin

more herself than she was able to alter the Indians. She admired the Utes and their customs, meanwhile, participated in many of their activities. The horse races were exciting to her; she played Spanish Monte and was reputed to have smoked with the Indians. She became a good friend of Susan, Johnson's wife and Ouray's sister, and went fishing with her up the White River. As she altered her appearance and related with the Indians, who were the only people in the area that were her age and unmarried, Nathan Meeker worried about the possibilities presented by this circumstance. The agent was becoming more uneasy, while the Indians were doing the same. Captain Jack had gone to Denver to see the governor and had visited Chief Ouray to report that Meeker was unfit for the job as their agent, because he did not understand them; moreover, when the governor received Meeker's plea for troops, he sought and gained approval from Washington, then ordered the troops to be dispatched from Wyoming to the White River country.

Three companies of troops gathered at Rawlins for the march to White River. They were to be commanded by Major Thomas Tipton "Tip" Thornburgh, as fine a looking young cavalry officer as could be imagined. Thornburgh had kissed his new bride goodbye, then headed for Rawlins with great anticipation; that was an opportunity for action and promotion, in addition, the young officer had great potential. The White River country was so isolated that a jurisdictional problem arose as to whether the territory was under the command of Gen. Crook or Gen. Pope. This ponderous problem was eventually settled, accordingly, the contingent began to gather for its journey south. The next dilemma was that none of the soldiers had ever been in the White River area, so a guide would be necessary. Joe Rankin was eventually appointed, the troops were assembled, along with supplies, including a huge threshing machine the intrepid Meeker had optimistically ordered. The contingent left Rawlins in late September of 1879, leisurely approaching the White River Reservation. Joe Rankin, the guide, and Lt. Sam Cherry went ahead to visit with Meeker to check on just how serious things were on the reservation.

About the same time the troopers moved south, a group of Utes headed north to Wyoming for their fall buffalo hunt. Captain Jack was their leader. When they came upon the troops camped and fishing, they were very alarmed, consequently, Jack abandoned his hunt to watch the troops. Rankin and Cherry stopped at Peck's store, just north of the reservation, to inquire what the Utes were do-

ing. They were informed that the Indians were buying up all the ammunition in the region. Then they met Captain Jack and Sowerick at the store and they realized that Captain Jack was furious about the approach of troops. Jack said he planned to go north to meet with Major Thornburgh and try to stop him from bringing the troops on the reservation, because it would be disastrous. Rankin went on ahead with a message from the Major to Meeker.

When Jack met with Thornburgh, he again complained about the restrictions Meeker had placed his people under and urged it would be a mistake to bring the soldiers on the reservation. After meeting Thornburgh on the Little Snake, Jack returned to the reservation, where, on September 27th, he began to round up the warriors of the tribe. He established a guard camp on Coal Creek, then told old chief Douglas that the Utes must unite to meet the threat they all faced.

When Joe Rankin talked with Meeker, the agent agreed with Captain Jack about the danger of bringing troops on the reservation and concurred with the suggestion that only Thornburgh, with his officers should visit Meeker, while the bulk of the soldiers would remain outside the reservation. Thornburgh also was in favor of this plan. Why the soldiers were moved onto the reservation and into the battle of Milk Creek is a question that is difficult to resolve. The Utes were uneasy, moreover, it would not take much to stir them into action. Meeker suggested sending five soldiers to allay fear, but Thornburgh moved the complete force. The Battle of Milk Creek began the morning of the 28th, with Major Thornburgh one of the first casualties. He was shot in the ear while riding on the flank, then the battle commenced at that time. The valley was flat and open, providing little cover, forcing the soldiers to dig in and use their horses for cover. A deadly barrage of bullets poured down from the Indian positions on the hills on each side of the valley—most of the horses were killed on the first day. Joe Rankin slipped out the first night to summon help to the beleaguered troops and, miraculously, was able to slip through the Indian lines and hurry to Wyoming. The next day Col. Dodge arrived with a black cavalry to join in the action. That night more troops were requested by sending out another messenger.

At the same time a group of Indians attacked the agency then killed, scalped, and mutilated Meeker. Finally, a split barrel stave was driven into his mouth to impale him on the ground. Before this atrocity, a log chain was fastened around his neck to drag his body around the compound. Meeker had

IGNACIO

made a noble effort to succeed in his appointed task; he did not understand the Utes, but he was sincere in his belief that he was doing right, therefore, he did not deserve such an ignoble fate.

All the men on the agency were killed—Shadrack Price, along with the other agency employees, died quickly. The Indians began firing while the men were at work on one of the buildings in the compound. There was no warning or planned attack, the shots were spontaneous. The women first hid in a storehouse, then moved to the icehouse where they were unnoticed until later in the day. The attack began about two o'clock in the afternoon. The women—Mrs. Meeker, Josephine, Flora Ellen Price, and her two children—were taken from their hiding place about 6:00 P.M. Mrs. Meeker was told to bring all the money she had because they were going to make a long trip. When she returned with the money, the women, with their captors, left the White River country.

News of the outbreak at the agency and the battle of Milk Creek soon hit the front pages all over the United States. Most Americans were more concerned about the fate of the women than the course of the battle. When things broke loose, Ouray was hunting and Chipeta was in the White River area. She quickly returned home as soon as possible to notify Ouray of the bad news, in hopes that a major uprising could be averted.

Col. Wesley Merritt arrived to aid the surrounded forces at Milk Creek, while the Utes, with the odds heavily against them, scattered in several directions. The troops moved into the White River valley, where officers' quarters were built at the present site of Meeker; construction of the town soon followed. The three buildings are still standing north of the courthouse—one is a fine museum. To prevent a full-scale war, troops were brought to the Uncompahgre Valley where Fort Crawford, built in 1871, accommodated them. Troops were also sent to Fort Lewis, as it was rumored the Southern Utes were about to join with the other Utes. Although there were a few altercations, no serious Indian uprising ensued. There was a demand that Captain Jack, Johnson, Douglas and others be delivered for prosecution, however, Ouray could not have produced these men if he had been so inclined. When he was asked to produce them, he asked, "What crime have they committed?" When he was told of the murder of Meeker and the agency employees, he asked about witnesses and was told the Meeker women witnessed most of the murders. Ouray responded in typical Indian fashion, "Indians do not take the word of women." The only White River Ute

to be arrested was Captain Jack, who spent abou eighteen months in Leavenworth and was then pa rolled.

As soon as possible, Ouray tried to arrange th rescue of the women, because he realized the reper cussions that could occur if they were harmed. Ger Charles Adams, Indian agent at Los Pinos, was giv en the responsibility of leading the rescue mission Along with Ouray's spokesman, he left as soon a possible. Douglas and Persine had taken the women to a camp near the present town of Mesa. After sixteen days of captivity, the mission approache the camp where the rescue was carried out with very little difficulty. The women seemed to be un harmed, but somewhat worn from their experiences They said they had not been molested in any way although they later changed their story. They wer returned to the Meeker home in Greeley. Flora Elle Price and her two children went to Greeley with Mrs. Meeker and Josie.

The Ute chiefs made a trip to Washington t make a new treaty, because the slogan, "The Ute must go" was now changed to "Either they go o we have to go, and we are not going." The treaty that was eventually formulated resettled the Whit River and Uncompahgre Utes on the Uintah reser vation in Utah, the Weeminuche stayed in Colorad on the Sleeping Ute Reservation, the Capotes an Muaches went to Ignacio. The treaty also gave th Utes $1,800,000. Ouray's quick action averted major showdown in Colorado. When he visite Washington in 1880, President Harrison called hin "the most intellectual man I have ever converse with." Ouray died August 24, 1880 while on a visi to the Southern Utes near the Pine River Agency He was secretly buried in the rocks about two mile south of the town of Ignacio. Forty-five years late most of his bones were recovered and properly bur ied in a marked grave in the cemetery south o Ignacio.

To avoid the claim by Indians that they wer not represented or had no knowledge of treaties t which their tribes were committed, the Ute Treaty of 1880 included an effort to acquire the signature of all the male members of the tribe. Otto Mears who could speak the difficult Ute tongue, was des ignated to gather the signatures or attested marks He wandered around Western Colorado visiting th Utes and gathered a total of 1,400 signatures, fo which he paid $2.00 each.

The Uncompahgre Utes continued to procrasti nate when they were told to leave Colorado as th treaty required, countering, "We want more talk."

McCook

Successor to Ouray

Finally, in September of 1881, they were told to gather their belongings, next, they were escorted out of Colorado by the troopers, down the Gunnison River to the Grand, across the Grand and west toward Utah. As they left the Grand Valley, they paused and looked back at the San Juans, Gran[d] Mesa, and the land that had been theirs for almos[t] a thousand years. Turning their eyes in the direc[-] tion of the setting sun, they slowly trekked towar[d] the Uintah Basin and their new home.

"Josie"   Captain Jack

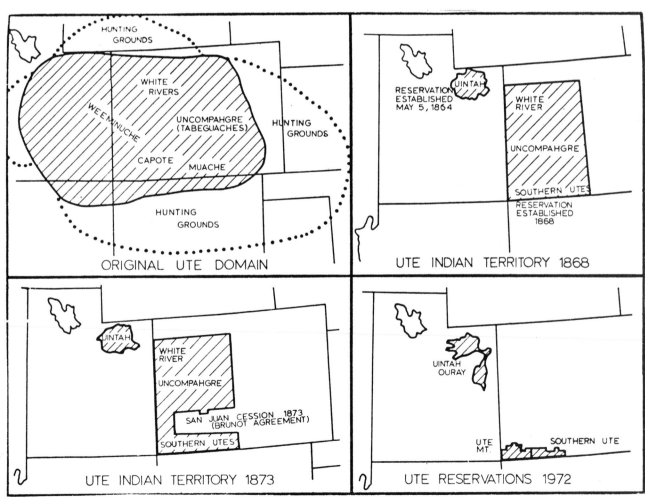

COURTESY SOUTHERN UTE[S]

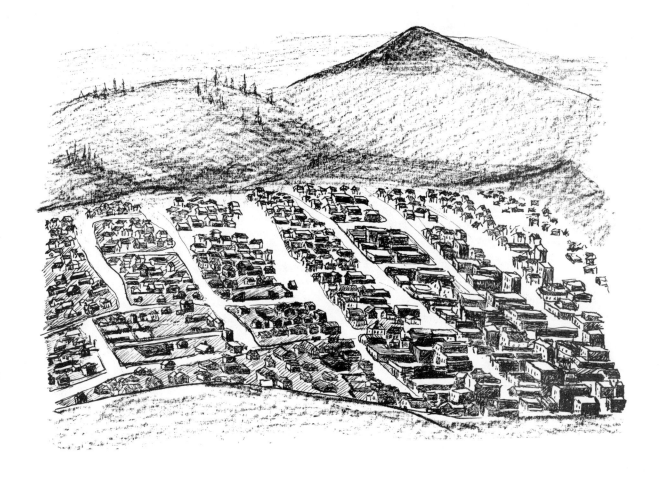

24—THE BOWL OF GOLD

The six-square-mile bowl that became the richest gold camp in the world hid its wealth until the 1890's from the anxious gold seekers of Colorado, then blossomed at the most opportune time, during the silver crash, giving the Centennial State a needed tonic. Many weary prospectors had dug in the Cripple Creek area without striking the bonanza, moreover, this frustration continued for almost twenty-five years. All of these unsuccessful efforts were not the work of amateurs, so why was the gold overlooked? The area had gained a bad reputation because promising finds had turned sour overnight, in addition, many seasoned prospectors had experienced bad luck. Miners are a superstitious lot anyway, therefore, they began to refer to the Cripple Creek area as "hoax country." Likewise, names like "Poverty Gulch" were tacked on to the region.

Bad luck and discouragement were not the only reasons for failure. Nothing in this location resembled typical gold-bearing geological formations. Further, to visit Cripple Creek or Victor today, one readily notices the green mountain landscape resembles cattle country much more than a typical mining region. The wierd geology present was created by volcanic action, because the bowl of gold rested in an extinct volcano crater; therefore, the gold was often found in the floor of the valley rather than in the outcroppings above. The valley was full of shafts and holes to attest to the efforts of many eager prospectors, but the bounty remained unclaimed.

Bob Womack, a cowboy with a big mouth, along with an equally large craving for whiskey, never gave up on the potential in the region, but stayed and continued to prospect after his father sold his ranch near the present site of the town of Cripple Creek. His biggest problem was to get someone to believe him after he discovered gold in Poverty Gulch. Womack was not considered to be capable as a prospector, therefore, the poor reputation of Womack, as well as the unpromising character of the valley, caused experienced miners and men with money to invest to shy away from Cripple Creek, especially after the Mount Pisgah Hoax. Finally, in 1890, Womack took some ore out of Poverty Gulch for assay and a few began to take the windy cowboy seriously after a favorable assay, and a mild rush began. Prospectors could not follow the usual guides in their search, consequently, luck played a large role in the success of the more fortunate. The ore was difficult to process, found combined with tellurium or other minerals in varying combinations, requiring complex smeltering processes for separation.

Womack shared the fate many prospectors like him have endured in not realizing a portion of the huge profits produced by his efforts. The gold which he found assayed about $100 a ton when he sold his claim for $500; then the prospector promptly went on an extended drunk. The first year his former claim, the Gold King property, paid $200,000 with almost $5,000,000 in total production. Womack died penniless in 1909, spending the remainder of his life around Cripple Creek. He was well known and had a gift for conversation, which was generally good enough to induce someone to set him up for a drink or two. Between 1890 and 1920, $800,000,000 worth of gold came out of the Cripple Creek gold fields, to make Womack's discovery one of the most remarkable ever found. His failure to cash in, although somewhat ironic, is not unusual in the history of the mining industry and the role of the prospector.

Once the word was out, people began to flock to Cripple Creek, hence the population rapidly increased to 10,000 in 1893. It continued until 1900 when there were close to 60,000 people in the region, along with thirteen towns and 150 saloons. Cripple Creek had a population of 25,000, hence was the third largest city in the state. Victor was the second largest city in the region, with about 7,000, while some of the other area towns were Altman, Independence, Elkton, Anaconda, Arequar, Goldfield, Lawrence and Gillett. These towns had the typical characteristics of mining communities, but were not quite so rustic. When this rush started, Colorado was no longer a frontier outpost, moreover, Colorado Springs, close to Cripple Creek, made it possible for the town to provide its citizens with more of the

comforts and conveniences of the 1890's. The tow were not built in such a haphazard manner; th included parks, baseball fields, opera houses a other refinements not found in some of the earl or more isolated gold rushes. Cripple Creek a Victor both suffered the ravages of fire and had be rebuilt, therefore, providing the opportunity improve over the first construction and make m adequate provisions for the needs of the people.

The bizarre geology and difficulty encounter in processing the ores made mining a rich ma game. Much of the gold was deposited by volca eruption as underlay of the lava on the floor of t valley. In some instances, pure gold was foun moreover, most of the towns were surrounded mines and mills. Excavation for a hotel in Vict struck gold ore while digging foundation trench thus changing the prospective hotel quickly into producing gold mine, the Gold Coin property, whi paid off far beyond the anticipated return expect in the original investment and project. The Portla Mine, the richest in the state, has produced $65,00 000 and is still operating.

The Cresson Mine had formerly been consi ered a jinx when it was purchased by a Chica Insurance company, who hired an experienced mi ing engineer. The shaft was sunk deeper until t mine produced $1,000,000 the first year. In 1915 new shaft in the mine hit an underground chamb 1,200 feet long, 30 feet wide and 18 feet high th was lined with pure gold. The chamber was mine with the most stringent security precautions po sible, as could be expected. The ore was shipped i closed, guarded box cars in place of the tradition open-ore cars, moreover, much of the ore produce over $1000,000 a ton in gold. In 1900, $20,000,000 i gold was taken from the Cripple Creek area mine while the region accounted for three-fourths of th gold produced in the United States. An unbelievabl sum of $800,000,000 was yielded before the mine began to decline, justly supporting the claims o Bob Womack and finally giving the Centennial Stat a gold rush that was no hoax.

The richness of the ore was tempting to th men working in the mines, so highgrading was no uncommon. The highgraded ore could be easil marketed in all the towns without embarassin questions. It is hard to estimate how many of th miners supplemented their income in this rathe questionable practice. It was impossible to preven some highgrading, regardless of the attempt, more over, when a miner stumbled onto a good sized nug get or rich piece of ore, the temptation was too grea for most of the men to overcome. Many of the min

WINFIELD SCOTT STRATTON

ers had their own crushing and smeltering operation in their homes where they worked in their spare time on this often lucrative enterprise. As the companies developed ingenious devices to prevent highgrading, the miners responded with imaginative methods to circumvent their employers' precautions. The amount of gold that was carried out of mines in lunch boxes from Colorado mines would probably match the gold leaf on the capitol dome and possibly provide an ample veneer of the metal for the domes of the capitols of the other forty-nine states.

Things were not the same in Cripple Creek after 1900, when a gradual decline set in. Labor troubles, along with water problems, helped to diminish the luster of the greatest gold camp. When the silver crash came in 1893, a horde of unemployed silver miners descended on the productive Cripple Creek area and presented employers with a temptation they could not ignore. Many of the mines paid $3.00 a day, which was the highest in the Centennial State in the 1890's. The surplus of miners encouraged the owners to press for advantages and ushered in a decade of labor strife. The Western Federation of Miners—a hard-rock mining union—had its headquarters in Cripple Creek where most of the gold mining existed in the 1890's. The mine union was anxious to organize the mines, therefore, by 1904, the conflict gravitated to one of the most serious labor wars in history. Property damage and loss of life marred the demands of the union and cost them the chance of gaining any public support, even though they were no more to blame than their antagonists. Their efforts to gain recognition were unsuccessful.

The water problems were compounded by the location of the mines in the valley. Many of the mines experienced such difficult flooding problems that the cost of pumping the water prevented a profit from the operation. Various measures proved inadequate, moreover, the tunnels that were dug to release the water from the valley through the mountain and into lower valley streams proved as costly as other methods and resulted in the abandonment of the poorer yielding mines.

The gold rush in the 1890's extended to the western part of the Centennial State, with mining operations in the Gunnison area around Irwin, Tincup (where gold was reputably measured in tin cups), Gothic and Crested Butte. Tom Walsh opened his Camp Bird Mine near Ouray, the second richest mine in the state. It is still producing and operating. The Tomboy, Black Bear and Smuggler Union, in the Telluride region, began to produce paydirt about the same time in some of the more inaccessible locations of the San Juans. The San Juan mines were often connected to supply and smelter by Otto Mears' toll roads, which provided the more intrepid tourist with some of the most spectacular scenery in the world. The shelf road from Telluride up past the Smuggler Union Mine to Tomboy, or the road from Telluride to Black Bear are two of the more breathtaking of these routes.

Winfield Scott Stratton

There were many fortunes made in the Cripple Creek gold strike. Men like Spencer Penrose, A. E. Carleton, William Fernay and a host of others found wealth in the "Bowl of Gold." The name of Winfield Scott Stratton is permanently engraved on the tablet of history surrounding the gold rush in Cripple Creek, where this unusual man, more than any other, seems to serve a role similar in the 1890's to "Haw" Tabor in the silver mining era in the 1880's. Tabor, however, went from rags to riches to rags while Stratton never completed the third step of that circuit. His story is the story of Cripple Creek, Victor and the mining days. His eccentricity frequently resulted in labels like "that crazy Stratton" or others, but his kindness and generosity, along with his love for all the facets and characters of the mining activity, made him an object of admiration to the people of the Pisgah region.

Stratton was born in Indiana in 1848, at the close of the Mexican War, which accounts for his first two names—being named after "Old Fuss and Feathers," the most decorated General of the war at a time when he was unable to protest. From the beginning, Stratton was a moody, melancholy type with a wandering spirit and technicolor dreams. He learned the trade of carpentry and cabinet making but his restless nature and lofty yearnings led him to ask his father for his inheritance to later head for the Colorado gold fields at the tender age of twenty. He spent about two years in Lincoln, Nebraska working as a carpenter, arriving in the Pikes Peak area in 1872. In his spare time, while he was working as a carpenter in Manitou Springs, Stratton would prospect in the nearby mountains, sometimes traveling to more distant areas. The determined Stratton spent most of his time alone and saved his money, hoping to possibly enter into some mining partnership, as he realized a one-man operation with much of the difficult mining in Colorado would be impractical. In 1874 he was offered the chance to invest in a mining venture in the San Juans, so decided this was the opportunity he was seeking, unfortunately, investing all his savings. The mine turned out to be a hoax, leaving Stratton penniless but not defeated. Instead of trying to build up his savings again, he gave up carpentry and began to prospect full time. During these years, Stratton ate poorly, frequently drank too much, but doggedly continued his search for gold.

In 1876 Stratton ventured into matrimony, but was soured on women for life, because of an unfortunate circumstance. His new wife turned out to be pregnant; moreover, he realized he could not be responsible for her condition, so the marriage ended, leaving him with a bitter attitude toward women. His prospecting proved to be equally frustrating, but he continued to comb the mountains for paydirt. In 1878 he headed for Leadville and prospected in California Gulch; during the 1880's, his footsteps took him to most of the gold camps, but still without any results. Finally, in the late 1880's, he concluded he could know a lot more about prospecting and decided to go to college to study geology and mining before he continued to prospect. After his college

studies, he returned to the hills with renewed hope and determination, but without any better results.

When Stratton heard of the strike in Cripple Creek in 1891, he went to the region and earnestly began to prospect. Talking Leslie Popejoy into grubstaking their efforts, Stratton and Billy Fernay, his partner, increased their efforts. His geology confused his thinking because there were no quartz formations or other indications generally used to locate gold. His reputed "vision of gold" on July 3, 1891 may be a true account of his strike, because something seemed to lure him to the mine on Battle Mountain at sunup the morning of the fourth of July, where he quickly staked the Independence and Washington claims in honor of the holiday. Popejoy had become impatient, so Stratton bought him out for $175 and then made an effort to gain as much of the surrounding property as possible. The rest

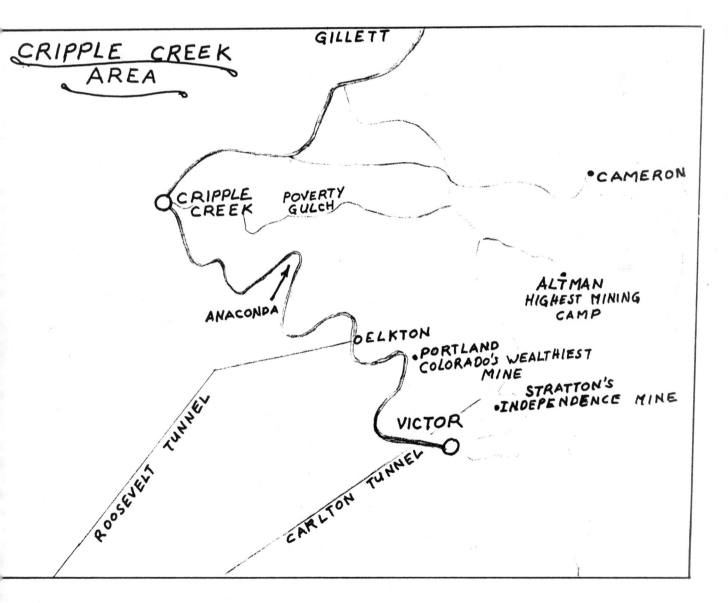

of the story is legend. Both mines paid handsomely and Stratton's wealth multiplied by leaps and bounds. He continued to buy everything he could and several of his investments added to his immense wealth, but Stratton continued to live, wisely managing his own operation without a bookkeeper, as a simple proprietorship with no one aware of the extent of his mining empire other than himself.

As his fortune multiplied, Stratton began to give away large sums to chosen recipients. His bitterness caused him to avoid church charities, moreover, by this time he had developed a passionate loathing for lawyers, because of the many suits he had to fight by various claimants who wanted to share in his fortune. Some of his donations included a new courthouse, a site for a post office to encourage the federal government to build a new post office, a new trolley system, a municipal amusement park and many gifts of cash to a large number of people whenever he felt like it.

By 1899 the 53-year-old Stratton looked more like 70 and his health was gone, forcing him to spend about half of his time in bed. His periods of melancholy and loneliness did not leave him when he became wealthy, therefore, drink seemed to be an alternative that he sought on too many occasions. Although he was well known and had many acquaintances, he had few close friends that he felt he could trust. His black housekeeper who tried to look after his health and well-being by seeing that he ate enough good food, often without any cooperation, his doctor, and a bootmaker, who was his closest friend and confident, were among his few close friends. Stratton had a passion for new shiny boots and had numerous pairs; his bootmaker became his financial advisor and the executor of his will when he died.

After 1900 the ailing Stratton began to talk of selling his mines and finally sold the Independence and other claims for $11,000,000 to some British investors. There was one more dream the white-haired and mustached millionaire wanted to put into action. He theorized that the mother lode of the "bowl of gold" never had been located and was about 5,000 feet in the center of the valley floor. He spent $8,000,000 trying to prove he was right; when he was ridiculed, he simply said he had plenty of money and through his efforts he was helping his friends by buying their claims and providing work for many that needed jobs. He never found the mother lode.

Death claimed Stratton in 1902; his will was naturally a matter of great interest. What would this eccentric man do with the vast fortune that remained? He had already proven himself to be unpredictable and uninterested in social or political advancement like Tabor, but many hoped to be favored. His estate amounted to around $6,000,000 of which about a million was distributed among friends and relatives. The bulk of the estate, about $5,000,000, was to be used as a trust fund to build a home for the aged, poor, and dependent or orphaned children. This home was to be called the Myron Stratton Home in honor of his father. The will was challenged by a multitude of claimants and suits. Thirteen women claimed to be the deserted or neglected widow of Stratton, moreover, several had documents to prove their allegation. The crafty bootmaker knew Stratton was not married and was able to beat these claims. Many miners, including Popejoy, made sizable claims. Finally, in 1913 the home was finished, almost eleven years after the death of the intrepid magnate. Many resented what they considered to be the last act of "that crazy Stratton." Some considered the will an insult to Colorado Springs, by creating a home for waifs and foundlings in the Newport of the Rockies. Cripple Creek expected some civic improvements and Colorado Springs had similar hopes. The Myron Stratton home still stands as a testimonial to the wisdom of this unusual Coloradan.

25—KING OF THE CANNIBALS

Cannibalism is a word that is often associated with humor, while many jokes have used this unusual subject to advantage, however, this rather morbid topic is probably more of a reality than guessed. Moreover, occurrences of this phenomenon have dotted the pages of history since the beginning of the written word. What is the circumstance of extreme deprivation that causes man to eat of his own kind? How many would respond to starvation with this deplorable solution in a time of great need? These are questions worthy of resolving before choosing associates for a safari or prolonged expedition of any kind. Who is capable of such degradation, and what causes the dissipation of principles that results in this gruesome crime?

Many mountain men were accused of cannibalism in hard times, also, it would be difficult to find a group that would be more likely to stoop to this level when food was absent. Phil Gardner has been accused of disposing of his Indian guide on a trip from Brown's Park to Fort Laramie and his squaw at an earlier date. When he arrived alone at Fort Laramie after being caught in a blizzard, he was in good physical condition and looked no worse for the ordeal. "Parson" Bill Williams came out of the LaGarita mountains after guiding the ill-fated fourth Fremont Expedition and was in unexpectedly good condition, with his partner missing. He was suffering only from snow blindness. An old trapper in Brown's Park is reputed to have had two squaws —one skinny and bony, named "Monkey," and the other, more on the plump side, was called "Beans," whom he considered as reserve rations. Several trappers referred to their squaws as "Beans," however, how many were forced to resort to such measures is hard to estimate.

Although cannibalism is a highly questionable act, unless it is preceded by murder, it would be hard to punish in a court of law. The only case to reach the docket in recent history was the well-known Packer case in Western Colorado. The Donner episode of California involved several incidents of cannibalism, but no murder, moreover, forty of the original eighty-seven members of the party survived to describe the ordeal. Only the Packer case was tried in court; the Donner survivors were not charged with homicide. This rather delicate subject does not die with these examples in the 19th century, however, as there are plenty of stories that suggest this tendency survives. The crime is occasionally suggested after people become lost for a long period of time with some members never being completely accounted for, as in the case of an airplane crash in an isolated region. The nature of the crime makes it difficult to produce the evidence required for conviction of homicide.

The story of Alferd Packer has been told and retold so many times by so many people that it is difficult to arrive at the actual truth; however, the story always seems to attract interested ears. The incident begins in Provo, Utah in 1873 and ends in Littleton, Colorado, with the death of Packer in 1911. Actually, the story continues to the present; although many wish for a permanent funeral, the tale will probably never die. A description of Packer is another interesting challenge. Pictures are available, but written accounts are inclined to mould the depiction to fit the crime, as is often the case in unusual crimes. Packer was born in 1842 in Pennsylvania and came west. In 1873 he was lodged in the Provo jail for the crime of counterfeiting. He is portrayed as being about six feet in height, weighing nearly 200 pounds, (several accounts record him as being smaller), lean built with wide shoulders, probably a good man physically, with dark hair and beady blue eyes. His unusually high-pitched voice was out of character with his physique and noticable enough to recollect. From this point, the account deteriorates, for Packer is described as having an unusual slanting forehead (like a primate), a pallid countenance, and an introverted personality. No writer is kind when he speaks of Packer's acumen, so there is little reason to believe otherwise. The colossal question or dilemma is, was Packer mentally unequipped, explaining his unusual actions, or, more startling, was he an ordinary person much like anyone else, who was submitted to unfortunate circumstances and responded to difficulty in what he felt was a practical manner? A perusal of **The History of the Donner Party,** by Chas. McGlashan, moves one to a posture sympathetic with Packer.

After hearing the story, no one accused Packer of being without a vivid imagination, moreover, he was talkative enough to attract the attention of a prospecting party headed for Colorado. His boasts of a knowledge of Colorado led to his freedom when the prospecting party bailed him out of jail, with the promise that he would guide them to the newly opened gold fields near Breckenridge. The route from Utah to Western Colorado was well known by 1973, so Packer's chances of getting into trouble by exaggerating his knowledge of Western Colorado was unlikely. When Packer left the Utah jail, he

was completely broke and had no possessions. H benefactors informed him they would pay him whe he had successfully guided them to their destina tion. The offer could not help but induce the despe ate Packer to embellish his ability to serve the ex pedition as a guide.

It was late in the autumn of 1873 when th twenty-one-man expedition left Utah and heade east toward Summitt County, hoping to be amon the first prospectors to arrive in the spring of 187 and get in on the expected bonanza. The part seemed to be jinxed from the onset, because the lost most of their provisions when their raft cap sized while they were attempting to ford the Gree River near the present site of Green River, Utah Undaunted, the group continued eastward and a rived at the Grand River near the present locatio of Grand Junction, where they forded the river the Indian ford and headed toward the Uncompahgr and Ouray's winter camp. Their journey had take them through trackless wastes, deep snow, an broad rivers, moreover, as they looked to their lef they saw snow on Grand Mesa, then snow on th San Juans to the right, therefore, some of the les intrepid members of the expedition began to thin in terms of finding a place to stay the winter an forget about making it to Breckenridge. While the were camped near the Grand (now the Colorado, th Utes called it the Bunkara), three Utes approache their camp and informed them that Ouray's winte camp was only "three sleeps" away. After askin more definite directions, the party headed for th Uncompahgre chief's camp.

O. D. Loutsenhizer was the spiritual leader o the expedition, moreover, by this time Packer ha gained the contempt of most of the members be cause of his sullenness and because of the bad luc that befell them which they blamed on the unfor tunate guide. Loutsenhizer decided that a sanctuar for the winter would be worth risking the enmity o the Utes, actually, he really had no other recours After his prospecting venture, "Pappy" Loutser hizer remained in Western Colorado and was on of the founders of Montrose. The citizens of Mont rose passed up a golden opportunity by not namin their town after "Pappy."

The group reached Ouray's camp on the Un compahgre in the middle of November, 1873. Oura was cordial, as usual, but resented the encroachmen on the Ute reservation. The Brunot Treaty had bee negotiated earlier that year, and Ouray had give up the San Juans for mining development. It wa difficult to explain to his more restless warriors th presence of the white men on their land, so recentl

Packer and Skeltons

reserved for Indian use; however, the noble chief treated them with hospitality and advised them to spend the winter in his camp. Every sign pointed to a severe winter with unusual snowfall.

The twenty-one members of the hard-luck expedition accepted Ouray's hospitality and stayed through December and January; finally, in February, some of them became restless because they had been away from communication with their families for over three months, or they were just anxious to continue on to Breckenridge. Some just wanted to return to civilization and were informed by Ouray that the closest town was Saguache, about one hundred miles. The white men were aware of the imposition they were placing on the Indians and fully realized the burden of twenty-one extra mouths to feed. Loutsenhizer wanted to end the free-loading as soon as possible, moreover, Packer offered to guide the men who wished to leave, claiming he knew a short cut to Saguache. The men had little confidence in Packer, so early in February, Loutsenhizer and four others left without Packer. Later, Packer persuaded five of the men remaining to leave for Saguache, accordingly they departed on February 9, 1874.

Ouray gave permission for the trip and sagely advised both groups to stay in sight of the Gunnison River and attempt no short cuts. A cattle ranch had been established near the present location of Gunnison by the Brunot Treaty to attempt to introduce the blessings of cattle ranching to the nomad Utes. Attempts to make farmers out of the Plains Indians had met with failure, so the Bureau of Indian Affairs decided to try a new approach with the annuity money provided by the treaty. The cattle ranch in the valley of the Gunnison was called Kelley's Cow Camp and was about 70 miles from the Ute camp. The Ute chief had furnished them with a small stock of provisions for the trip after he gave up trying to convince them to wait until spring. The five men that accompanied Packer were Shannon Bell, the leader; Israel Swan, an older man; George Noon, a teen-ager; Frank Miller, a German; and James Humphrey from Pennsylvania, Packer's home state. What transpired during the ensuing weeks until Packer returned to civilization can only be speculated upon—two facts are clear, five men died and parts of them were consumed.

The Loutsenhizer group arrived at Kelley's Cow Camp in mid-February, about two weeks after they had left the Ute headquarters. They had been staked to provisions for seven days by Ouray and were in deplorable condition when they finally stumbled into the cow camp. James Kelley had to nurse

them back to health for almost six weeks before they could continue to Saguache, but they were more fortunate than Packer's companions.

Three days after the Packer group left on their journey they were in serious trouble; night-time temperatures were dropping to 50 degrees below zero and the snow was two to three feet deep. All the food Ouray had provided for them was gone along with their supply of matches, adding to their dilemma. They kept fire by carrying embers from the last fire smoldering in their coffee pot, as most mountain men did on such occasions. Food was scarce, as the game had migrated to lower elevations, so they survived by eating roots, buds, bark, berries and an occasional squirrel or rabbit. When they began to boil their moccasins and eat them they realized their predicament and sought some way out of the mountains. At the lake fork of the Gunnison River, just twelve miles from Kelley's Cow Camp and safety, they made the decision to turn south. This was a fateful detour, and maybe they made it because Packer claimed this was the short cut he knew about, or maybe it was a miscalculation. At any rate, they soon became aware of the error of such a choice.

After fighting heavy snow and cold weather for several days, the desperate group camped below Lake San Cristobal to assess their situation. Since leaving the Gunnison River, the party had pushed southward, hopeful of finding a shorter way to Saguache. One can only speculate as to what did occur, but it is a good bet that the other five members of the party, already unenthusiastic about Packer as a guide or person, began to severely criticize the slow-witted guide and place full responsibility for their plight on his shoulders. The men were weak from exhaustion and lack of food, therefore, panic-stricken by the harsh realities of their predicament. Packer must have had to face the brutal facts that they were lost, if only to himself which forced him to take the action of which he was accused later. He may have done some exploring before he was fully convinced, but a look around Lake San Cristobal would be enough to demonstrate that to continue south would mean to go higher into the San Juans. Whether Packer was really guilty of killing all five of his companions while they were sleeping will never be known conclusively, but evidence points strongly in this direction.

The more incredible part of the story is the time Packer spent at his lean-to camp, casually devouring his former companions, while making no effort to dispose of their remains; not even moving them except enough to cut off some portions for meals, meanwhile, camping in the presence of these former companions. Two and a half months after leaving Ouray's camp, Packer trudged into the Los Pinos Indian Agency at the junction of Los Pinos and Cochetope Creeks, looking not too bad, considering his ordeal. He arrived at the agency April 16, 1874. General Charles Adams, the regular agent, was absent at the time, and Stephen A. Dole was in charge. The name General Adams is well known in the history of Western Colorado; he was a close friend of Otto Mears and responsible for the rescue of the Meeker women and the delicate task of interviewing them afterward. The industrious agent also brought Packer to justice.

Showing few signs of hunger or exposure, with the exception of two missing front teeth, Packer first asked for whiskey, then told this story: He explained how they left Ouray's camp and headed for Saguache, running into difficulty in a short time when Packer hurt his leg and was unable to continue. The rest of the party was forced to leave the injured guide to fend for himself, as they could not carry him with them and were out of food; it was expedient they made as good time as possible. The rest of the party decided to try to make it to Baker Basin, which was closer than Saguache, and should have already arrived, according to their former guide. If the party did not make it to Baker Basin (now Silverton), they were probably in the Animas Valley (now Durango), and would be heard from sooner or later.

The sympathetic Dole listened to Packer's story and offered him a job to help him make enough money to get to Saguache, as some help was needed at the agency, but Packer refused and said he wanted to get back to his home state of Pennsylvania, he was sick and tired of Colorado. He sold a rifle he was carrying with him to Dole for ten dollars and headed for Saguache. Not too many days later an Indian brought some strange strips of flesh into the agency and said he found them on Los Pinos Creek, the trail Packer had followed from Lake San Cristobal. The agency doctor examined the flesh and identified it as human flesh; naturally, Dole and the doctor began to concoct a story of murder and cannibalism with Packer as the culprit.

After arriving in Saguache, Packer spent most of his time drinking, gambling, and shooting-off his mouth when his tongue was loosened by liquor. He displayed considerable sums of money for someone that was broke when he left Ouray's camp. Packer bought a horse from Otto Mears for seventy dollars, but the founder of Saguache was aware of Packer's former arrest for counterfeiting and closely scruti-

nized the certificates, forcing him to refuse to accept one of the ten dollar bills. The diminutive Mears was not one to be careless with money. After the rejection, Packer pulled out another pocketbook and produced a second ten dollar bill, which Mears accepted, although wondering about a man that carried two pocketbooks with money in each. Packer became acquainted with Larry Dolan, who was a barkeeper in Saguache and had a good knowledge of what was going on in the area—one of the tools of his trade. Packer helped Dolan tend bar occasionally and also roomed with the colorful barkeeper, who was responsible for relating some of the more glamorous accounts of the Packer case.

Gradually, the other members of the original Loutsenhizer expedition began to arrive in Saguache from Kelley's Cow Camp. Packer had used the same story in Saguache as he had given to the agent at Los Pinos, so he related the same incidents to these men when they came into town. However, facts were beginning to add up that looked incriminating for the loud-mouthed Packer. One of the most perplexing puzzles was why Packer made no more effort than he did to cover his trail or to leave the territory of Colorado as soon as possible. There are many defenders of Packer that insist he was guilty of no crime and believe some of his incredible stories, citing his lack of effort to hide his actions as evidence that he considered himself guilty of no crime. Murder is a serious crime; eating flesh of the deceased, admittedly highly irregular, is seldom considered worthy of indictment.

During times of intoxication, Packer was inconsistent in his stories and revealed articles like a pipe, pocketknife and watch that were known to belong to his former traveling companions which had been in their possession when the men left Ouray's camp. About a week after Packer arrived in Saguache, Gen Adams came through on his way from Denver back to Los Pinos. Suspicious members of the Loutsenhizer expedition convinced Adams that there may be a case of multiple homicide and cannibalism worthy of his attention in the offing. No word from the Animas Valley or Baker Basin had reached Saguache about Packer's companions, also the finding of the strips of human flesh was now known, so circumstantial evidence began to fall in an avalanche on the shoulders of Alferd Packer.

Gen. Adams was authorized to enforce the law in the area where Packer had been, so he desired to return him to Los Pinos, which was under his jurisdiction, then make an effort to pin the goods on the burly Packer and force a confession, if possible. If not, then he would be held until a full investigation could be made. To induce Packer to return to Los Pinos, Adams suggested a search party for the missing men with Packer again serving as guide, since he was the last person to see the men and maybe some kind of a trail could be picked up from where they were last seen. Packer was not at all enthusiastic about the proposition, but Adams offered to pay his expenses and he finally, reluctantly agreed to accompany the group, which included Otto Mears. On the return trip, Packer threw some articles in Cochetope Creek and claimed it to be trash. When they arrived Adams asked Packer where all his money came from and he replied, "I borrowed it." "Who from," asked Adams." "I can't remember," answered Packer; a search of the accused was unproductive. Adams was able to tear apart the previous story used by Packer bit by bit, as the slow-witted defendant was caught in one lie after another, so he was forced to change his story. He claimed his five companions had died from hunger and cold resulting from the bad weather and heavy snow, since it was impossible to bury them in anything except snow, he left them where they fell.

Packer was again pushed into a corner when Adams confronted him with the strips of flesh for the first time, again Packer changed his story to what was perhaps his masterpiece. According to the incredible story, Israel Swan, the old man, had died and, since they were starving, it was decided to eat his flesh. He was lean and tough, but, nevertheless, better than boiled moccasin; however, he was small and did not last long. After disposing of Swan, the remaining five voted to draw lots to see who would be next on the menu. James Humphrey was killed by Shannon Bell and eaten, then Frank Miller died; later, Bell shot sixteen-year-old George Noon, leaving only Packer and Bell. After the last of Noon was gone—a starving man does not have much meat on his bones, Packer claimed he noticed Bell eyeing him in a strange manner and confronted him, resulting in a fierce fight which Packer won in self-defense, but lost his two front teeth in the affray. So, according to the account, he was not guilty of killing anyone. Packer must have given a great deal of thought to the preparation of this tale and, regardless of what thought one may have about the desperate Packer, it is difficult not to respect his imagination. Packer concluded his tale by relating that he ate as much of Bell as he could, then packed some to carry with him on his way to civilization, casting the remainder aside shortly before he reached Los Pinos.

Adams told Packer he did not believe this story and suggested they begin the search for the five missing men. The members of the party were no convinced that Packer was guilty of a horrible crim and began to openly accuse him during the searc On one occasion, Packer tried to stab one of tl searchers who had accused him, and, after tw weeks, the search was abandoned when the guic claimed to be lost. When the party returned to L Pinos, Adams arrested the accused but, lacking jail in Los Pinos, the prisoner was taken to Saguach to be placed under custody in the log jail that Mea had built to make his town respectable. The bizar story of Packer had already spread far beyond tl rugged San Juans, bringing people from far an wide to view the cannibal of Saguache. Mears ha experienced second thoughts about the notorie Packer and his trial would bring this fair town a rival Del Norte was enjoying this publicity immens ly. Many of the residents of Del Norte rode over Saguache to relish the prospects of seeing the def mation of their rival town. Some went so far as claim the man-eater was an honored resident Saguache.

Mears worst fears materialized when the r mains of the five missing men were found in o spot near Lake San Cristobal, around a single cam fire. J. A. Randolph, a photographer for **Harper Weekly,** was the first to stumble on the grisly scen which later he committed to posterity by sketchin Four of the bodies were in a row within arms-lengt of each other; the fifth body, later identified as th of Shannon Bell, was several feet away. The skul of all the men had been split with a hatchet, an Bell was also shot in the back, suggesting he ha awakened and tried to escape and was shot. Prestc Nutter, of the original Utah party, made the sombe trip to the macabre site and identified the fi bodies as Packer's five companions. The bodies we buried on the spot with a monument on which tl five names were inscribed. This grave site remai to this day.

The evidence was conclusive, so preparatior for the trial and the building of a gallows were soc underway. Mears considered the forthcoming tri and the accompanying adverse publicity that wa impending for Saguache on a nationwide scale. Son say Packer escaped, using a key fashioned from pen knife which was passed through the bars his cell; others claim the door of the jail was co veniently left ajar to permit him to wander out in the night and spare Mears' town from more notor ety. At any rate, Packer disappeared and was n seen or heard of for about ten years.

Packer made good his escape in September 1874, moreover, his whereabouts were unknow until March of 1883, when one of the members of the Utah party heard a familiar high-pitched voice through a thin partition in the wall of one of the barracks in Ft. Fetterman, Wyoming. The authorities were promptly notified and the unfortunate Packer was taken into custody for the second time, to be held until General Adams could come to Wyoming to return him to Colorado. The new town of Lake City now graced the San Juans, with smelters and frenzied mining activity, and Hinsdale County began to prepare for a trial and hanging. The trial did not take long, for, on May 19, 1883, less than two months after Jean Cabazon had recognized his voice, Judge Melville B. Gerry sentenced Packer to be hanged on May 19, 1883. Larry Dolan, the barkeep and former acquaintance of Packer, gives the classic account of the sentence described in Wilson Rockwell's **Sunset Slope.** Judge Gerry was a southerner who had arrived in Colorado shortly before the trial, therefore, being from the State of Georgia, was an ardent democrat. According to Dolan, Gerry stated:

"Stand up, you voracious, man-eating son of a bitch, stand up! They was seven democrats in Hinsdale County and you ate five of them. God damn you, I sentence you to be hanged by the neck until you are dead, dead, dead, as a warning against reducing the democratic population of the state."

Again the gallows was deprived of its victim as technicalities began to encircle the case. Hinsdale County did not exist when the crime was committed, so its right to try Packer was questionable. Colorado was a territory, not a state, when the crime occurred, furthermore, the people of Hinsdale County were prejudiced and incapable of giving the accused cannibal a fair trial; anyway, Packer was far too interesting journalistic material to be disposed of so quickly. Finally, the Supreme Court of Colorado ruled that a person could not be hanged for committing a crime in Colorado before Colorado became a state. It was decided to try Packer again in Gunnison, where people were not so prejudiced. The charge was changed to voluntary manslaughter.

On August 5, 1886, after being tried twice in Gunnison and once in Lake City, Packer was sentenced to serve forty years in the state penitentiary at Canon City. After serving fourteen years of his sentence, Packer was paroled in 1901, due to the efforts of Polly Pry, one of the personal interest reporters for the Denver Post. Miss Pry had visited

Packer at Canon City and realized his copy potential, so began to take up the cause for the wronged man. She published letters Packer wrote to his family in Pennsylvania and some received from his relatives. Other writers and newspapers took an interest and joined the cause. Soon the name of Packer was on the lips of residents all over the state. Sympathetic Coloradans began to concur that Packer was a victim of unusual circumstances, therefore, they felt his actions were warranted; it was known that Packer was not overly articulate, making him more unaccountable for his acts, anyway.

History of the Donner Episode vividly portrays accounts of the moaning and crying of starving people, enough to drive a person mad—surviving members of a family maintaining life by eating their departed relatives, a dying father urging his children to save their own lives by eating his flesh, and a wife saving her meager rations and setting them aside to hand to her husband before she dies as her last gesture of devotion in order to save him, or at least prolong his life.

Governor Charles Thomas paroled Packer, and according to Marshall Sprague in **Massacre, the Tragedy at White River,** resigned the next day. The parole required that Packer remain in Colorado, be-

cause he had threatened some of the members of his family in Pennsylvania, so he spent his remaining years in Littleton, Colorado, dying in 1911. During his last years, Packer was a model citizen, doing chores for needy neighbors, even occasionally baby sitting when the need arose. He prospected a little did odd jobs, provided a sanctuary for stray cats and had the respect of his community and the thousands of curious that came to look at him or shake his hand, because known cannibals were a rarity in the United States. He became a confirmed vegetarian and seemed to relish the attention and interest he received. When he died in 1911, although he was not a veteran, he was given the distinction of being buried in the Civil War Veterans Cemetery in Littleton, where his body still rests, but tombstones are hard to keep on the grave and frequently disappear.

The Packer incident still attracts attention and interest. The plateau above Lake San Cristobal has been christened "Cannibal Plateau" and the students of Colorado University named their cafeteria in the University Memorial Center "Packer Grill," to commemorate one of Colorado's best known citizens and, perhaps, to express something about the food served in the cafeteria.

Old Homestead, Myers Avenue

26—VICTORIAN DAYS

Life styles in the Centennial State during the 19th century varied with the locale. It has been frequently stated that saloons, gambling and brothels were brothers and sisters of mining, railroading and cattle towns, and it would be difficult to argue otherwise. However, these institutions were a part of almost all of Victorian America during "The Gilded Age." The West, with its disparity of women, presented a different picture. The shortage of white females made prostitution a more attractive institution and men, without the civilizing influence of womanhood, fell into horribly sloven housekeeping ways. Most of the mining towns had more saloons than all other business establishments combined. Miners preferred to hang around the saloons rather than depart for their miserable mine shacks or boarding houses which they considered a place to "flop" and nothing else.

The "get-rich-quick" atmosphere of the mining towns added to the moral flexibility that existed—towns were built in great haste and often died as quickly, so there was a sort of transitory impermanence that hovered over the heads of the citizens. People drifted in and out and became a part of the changing scene, moreover, many of the characters felt like the cowboys in the railhead towns—away from home and restrictions and a participant in a new and exciting panorama. The easy wealth, easily gained and more easily lost, made the miner a gul-

lible victim of the multitude of institutions quickly erected to "mine the miner."

Historians have been unkind to the Victorian Age for a number of years, because of its double standards and phony facades, and until recent years Victorians have been the object of scorn and ridicule. However, one question continues to loom and disturb critics, throwing loopholes in their condemnations—if the Victorian age was so far "out of it," why does life still seem to fall just as far short, or more, than the rosy promises of the "gay nineties?" Could it be that there is some phoniness in all people and the Victorian Age provided safety valves and escapes that made it possible for most people to live up to the Victorian code in their own way and assume respectability? Certainly, on the surface, most mid-American towns had an aura of respectability that was easily discernable, but they all had another side, not so visible, and the saloon, gambling casino, and redlight district were almost always present.

There was no shortage of women in most of America during the "Gilded Age," but it was a man's world, therefore, many of the institutions of this age were men's while only disreputable women would frequent the saloon or casino; the other women present in these institutions were employees. One of the peculiar quirks of the "Gilded Age" was that while most of these institutions, or at least a part of their activities, were against the law, this never seemed to hamper their operation, as the "law" either did not notice their activities or was in on the "rakeoff." In many towns these establishments paid most or all of the city taxes, therefore, as long as they continued, residents did not have to pay city taxes. Telluride is an example of a town where the citizenry did not have to pay taxes, consequently, privileges of this nature were difficult to surrender on the altar of reform. The main attraction remained, however—there was a good profit in all of these establishments, moreover, most of the owners returned a good net on their investment, because drinking, gambling, and prostitution did not suffer from depression, change of weather, or style.

The saloon was one of the most apparent and popular institutions of the "Gilded Age", therefore, many of the small mining towns had as many as twenty or thirty before they had much of anything else. The saloon was a gathering place which also provided a variety of entertainment; food was often served and gambling was generally provided for, or the patrons could simply play poker at one of the tables. Men would gather here during their lunch hour or after work to have a friendly beer or to discuss some business transaction or politics. More business was conducted in the saloon than anywhere else, accordingly, in a day when welfare, employment, and charitable agencies were not the domain of federal government, many of these needs were provided for in the saloons. Collections would be taken up for the poor or unfortunate, frequently more would be collected in the saloons for these purposes than in the churches. If a stranger in town needed to locate a resident, the bartender, who was usually a storehouse of information, could send him in the right direction. When a farmer or a cattleman was short of hands, a word to the bartender would generally result in some men heading in the direction needed. Men looking for work could find jobs frequently listed on a blackboard in the saloon, therefore, did not have to wait in line to see an agent of the employment bureau. Items for sale were also listed, also a request about where a good horse or wagon or buggy could be purchased was easily answered. The saloon was also the safety valve where men could temporarily escape the cares and woes of the world, or respite from their nagging women, and a secluded spot where they could brag about their accomplishments to an appreciative audience.

Gambling was as much a part of life as food and drink, therefore, many people spent their entire pay in a gambling casino on payday. The gambling casinos provided a variety of games of chance to cater to the widest tastes. Some were elegant casinos that catered to the most pretentious clientele; others were a back room card game in a pool hall or hotel. The gambling houses naturally were appropriate to the "get-rich-quick" attitudes of your mining towns, but in many ways the prospectors searching for gold in the mountains, the cattlemen on the plains, or the sodbuster in the valleys were gambling for higher stakes and with greater risks than the patrons of these main street establishments.

The saloons, casinos, brothels and other activities were widely various to capture the most discriminate taste. There were also opium dens, shows of all kinds with freaks and con artists, snake charmers, and dancing girls. In an attempt to describe the atmosphere of the mining towns, it is easy to realize how words are sometimes inadequate and seem incapable of doing justice to the subject as in the case of trying to describe a scenic mountain landscape in the Centennial State.

The shortage of women made prostitution one of the most prevalent and profitable institutions of the mining, cattle, and railroad towns; but this oldes of professions also prevailed in most American communities. Different schools of thought existed as to the justification of such activities—illegal by ordinances in most towns. Defenders insisted that prostitution made it safe for decent and respectable women to walk the streets at night without fear of being molested or attacked. They further alleged many marriages were saved by the "red-light district" because it provided an opportunity for a married man to seek variety without the danger of involvement. A man could step aside and out of the code—only temporarily, of course, and return to respectability without any ostracism or condemnation and suffer no recriminations or guilt frustrations.

The gambling casinos and saloons were the most abundant business concerns on main street, taking up most of the more choice locations. The "red-light district," named after the red signal lights railroaders left on the front porches, usually was located a block from main street and, strange as it may seem, usually south. The girls sat out on the porch and brazenly beckoned prospective clients into their midst. The mining towns of Colorado had a wide assortment of saloons, gambling houses, and brothels, but Denver, during the nineties, had the greatest array of saloons, casinos and prostitutes in the West and was second only to New Orleans in this dubious distinction in the whole United States. The 1900 block on Market Street was the center of

Denver's "tenderloin district," although there were many others in different locations.

Prostitution was a part of the history and lore of the West, moreover, it was handled in a business-like manner, providing a way of escape from the code while suffering no consequences. Most of these institutions prospered, treating their clients in a discrete manner to encourage business. Blackmail occurred, but this was an infrequent practice. Many of the more prominent madams amassed huge fortunes. Names like Jennie Rogers, Mattie Silks, Red Stockings, Poker Alice, Verona Baldwin, Anna Gould, Katie Fulton, Laura Evans, Pearl DeVere, Gussie Blake, Jeanie Harris, Broken Jaw Nell, Silvertip Bess, May Lee, Vestol Lillis, Lois Lovell, Molly May, and a host of others were often the town's wealthiest residents, consequently, their wealth gave them a good deal of political power in their respective communities. They would seldom turn down a good cause or charity, therefore, many of the parks, playgrounds, civic projects, and charitable agencies were aided, or partially constructed, from funds contributed by generous madams. They were expected to carry more than their share of the load on these projects and generally willingly complied.

Prostitution was a varied operation from the one-room, one-bed, one-woman crib to the elegant parlor like "Jennie Rogers Hall of Faces and Mirrors." Many prostitutes followed the railroad construction gangs west then stayed on to go into business in the new towns as they began to form. The army camps were also attractive to the profession and, since most post commanders would not tolerate saloons, gambling or prostitutes, they would usually spring up a few miles from the forts in a handy location—sometimes on the farm that had the pork contract and was forced to set up a few miles downwind. The pig farm would become a combination farm, saloon, gambling casino, and brothel. Some post commanders were more liberal and showed female entertainers or laundresses on their list of post residents.

In the more isolated parts of the West, white women were rare, therefore, some women traveled much like a drummer or circuit rider, providing the same entertainment available on Market Street. Some of the better known of these "soiled doves on horseback" were Cattle Kate and Calamity Jane. The girls of the "row", as it was frequently called, became well-known to many and often were an easy touch for flattery or purported genuine love, becom-

ing easy prey for fast talkers. Many of them were married or had lovers who spent most of their earnings for them. The parlor girls were wealthy enough to afford the best gowns available, were often the most attractive of girls, and had first choice of the new styles in the choice shops. This led to frequent attacks from other women and demands for reform. Parlors and houses were raided and madams were arrested for running illegal establishments or for disturbing the peace. Some of the more illustrious madams like Jennie Rogers or Laura Evans had a penchant for the spectacular and raced horses or chariots down the street in a wild manner and were hauled into court. They were always able to get off with a light sentence or bribe their way out with money, seldom serving any time in jail. Many of the police officers or town leaders were well known and frequent patrons of the parlors, making reform efforts extremely difficult. On one occasion, an ordinance was passed in Denver demanding the girls identify themselves with a yellow ribbon. They were so enraged they staged a protest march dressed in yellow dresses, bonnets, hose and shoes and walked down town in a group and began to call many of the city fathers and leaders by their first names. The yellow ribbon ordinance was immediately repealed.

Reform and the Progressive Movement finally began to make an impression on the saloons, gambling, and prostitution, forcing them to move out of the heart of the city. In Denver they moved to Edgewater and Littleton; in Grand Junction, the brothels shifted their operation from Colorado Avenue to South Avenue, but they continued to opera in the same place and manner in mining towns li Cripple Creek, Leadville, Telluride, and Central Cit Prohibition of the twenties replaced the saloon wi the speakeasy; then, after repeal in 1933, there w a renaissance of these institutions, but they we never the same as during the "Gilded Age." T word "tavern" began to replace "saloon," and mo pressure was put on gambling and prostitution close down. Your author can remember watchi poker games among soily-handed miners in Silvert and Telluride in wide-eyed wonderment in t thirties and forties. With the coming of World W II, a determined effort was made to prevent can followers from flourishing near the many servi installations expected, therefore, prostitution w wiped out in most communities, to be replaced by t call girl or the more modern mobile unit now ope ating in much of America under circumstances a most impossible to control or regulate. The day the "hooker" is no longer present, but many of th trappings remain. The Old Homestead is still stan ing on Myers Avenue in Cripple Creek, and Pea Devere, its madam, left most of the furnishing behind for tourists to see and ponder over. Whe a Victorian prude named Julian Street wrote of th "red-light district" on Myers Avenue in a nation weekly magazine in a derogatory manner, the o fended city fathers voted to change the name c Cripple Creek's row to Julian Street to even th score. The Victorian Age has had its critics and it defenders. There may be more victorianism in mos people than is freely admitted.

27—THE ROCKY MOUNTAIN CANARY

"Why does only an ass eat thistles?" "Because only an ass would!" This cliche is typical of the cross one of man's oldest and noblest servants has to bear. The word "asinine" denotes the specie of the asses or "asslike" and is another barb this valuable quadruped carries unjustly. The ass, donkey or burro, all the same animal, is a native of the old world and was domesticated thousands of years ago. The Syranian Wild Ass, the Onager of Persia and Asia, and the Kiang of the Tibetan Highlands are some of the ancestors of the donkeys and mules of the early mining, wagon trail and agricultural eras of the Centennial State. The Kiang is the most horse-like of the wild asses and is one of the surest footed animals in the world, easily capable of maneuvering among the crags of the Himalayas without any difficulty.

The word "donkey" first appeared in England in the 1700's and no one seems to know exactly how it originated or from where it came. Many speculate it began as a nickname; anyway, the donkey has been called many names and the appellation "donkey" is certainly an improvement over the original nomenclature. Regardless of what he has been called, the donkey has consistently been linked with stupidity, stuborness and lowliness. The creature is frequently mentioned in early history, the Bible, and chronicles, but seldom with distinction. The place of the horse is permanently etched in history; horses were the glamour mounts of all men of rank who would not think of going to war on foot, especially many American Indians. Nevertheless, the persistent mention and continual appearance of the donkey and then, eventually, the mule,

suggested that he carried many burdens on his back other than riders.

There are several breeds of donkeys, also color and size vary almost with each type, their colors range from black to white, and even their performance differs. The light in weight and delicately built donkeys were used by women for mounts, the Virgin was carried to Bethlehem by a donkey of this kind. The stouter and heavier built donkeys were more likely to be used for ploughing and cargo work on the caravans. The Damascas breed is one of the largest of the donkey family, has unusually long ears, is white in color and one of the most durable of all the different breeds. Durability is the nature of this animal.

Mules are hybrids or crosses between the equine and asinine species. The offspring of a male ass, or jack, and a female horse is the mule proper, and the offspring of a stallion and a female ass (Jenny) is called a hinny. To many, the mule is considered far more valuable than the breed of either of its parents. The mule seems to take on the majority of the best qualities of each of its forbearers and omit most of the worst. It has long ears, a short mane, small feet, thin limbs, a thick head, no chestnuts (horny growths inside the hocks), and the endurance of the donkey. Mules are more the size of horses, have the same shaped body, neck and croup, and their teeth are equine. Yet, the mule has neither the voice of the horse or jackass and is plagued with a feeble, hoarse-sounding noise that seems to be unlike any sound found in the realms of the living. The sobriety, patience, endurance and sure-footedness of the donkey blend with the vigor, courage, and strength of the horse to make the mule an improvement over either. Eternally damned by rarely being able to produce its own kind, it surpasses the intelligence and endurance of both its parents by combining intelligence and strength when it is forced to work hard for extended periods, to save on strength to carry it through and not become panicky and over-strain like a horse. Probably the most unusual example of the wisdom of a mule is their uncanny discipline in avoiding over-eating and over-drinking. Horses, cows and sheep will kill themselves by eating or drinking too much, therefore, this self-control of the mule puts him in a lofty and exalted position among the four-legged animals of the world, without mentioning the two-legged variety.

Mules also resist disease well, with some allegations claiming them immune to all diseases, which has been proven to be untrue; however, reports of mules or donkeys living to the unheard of age of 70, or even 80, are heard frequently enough to convince even the dubious that these animals are long-lived. As mentioned above, unfortunately, mules do not have offspring of their own, except in extremely rare cases. All male mules and most female mules are sterile, but a few females have produced young when bred to male asses or stallions. These rare offspring of female mules are either three-fourths donkey or three-fourths horse.

Mules can remain strong under much harsher conditions, poorer food and treatment, and work longer in hot weather without water than horses. This is the reason that the majority of mules in the United States were in the South during the age of horses and mules in agriculture. Their ability to bear up under the roughest work has condemned them to the toughest tasks and, naturally, linked their efforts with the mining industry. For the first seventy years of mining in the Centennial State, most of the supplies and equipment needed in the mines and isolated mining towns were carried in by mules or donkeys. The ore was carried out in heavy leather or canvas pack bags, and, when mills or smelters were built, the mules carried concentrate.

The more rugged and isolated mines were serviced by the donkey or burro. The first uranium used by Madame Curie in the development of radium for x-ray was carried by donkeys from the Colorado Plateau. The prospector was the catalyst of the mining industry. Someone had to locate the lode, therefore, the prospector, alone but for his faithful donkey as his bearer and companion, got most of the mining rushes going. Many of the donkeys were turned loose after mining slowed down in the San

Juans, hence, the hardy little creature had to make it on his own. Unlike the mule, they were able to reproduce and did in large numbers until there were herds of them roaming the San Juans. The cattlemen organized a campaign to kill them off to stop them from overgrazing, and now they are gone. A few wild horses remain, but their days may be numbered.

No animals have been forced to endure more abuse and brutality from the hand of man than the mule and donkey, especially the mule, and yet man is indebted to these two lowly creatures for service rendered above and beyond the call of duty, in many instances more than the horse. Harriet Fish Backus in **Tomboy Bride,** gives a vivid account of the mule trains and the rugged trail they were forced to negotiate winter and summer. Given the opportunity to travel the shelf road from Telluride to Tomboy one with imagination becomes readily convinced of the struggle involved in supplying this "crow's nest" summer and winter. Mrs. Backus' description of life in this town above the clouds is one of the best accounts the author has read, because of its explicit descriptions and her poignant relating of personal experiences.

The pack trains traveled in single file because of the narrow trails, and the mules were tied closely together, with the mule skinner in front on his horse and a bell tied to the mule bringing up the rear. The bell informed the skinner if something was missing, because he frequently could not see the end of his string on the winding mountain trails. Each pack train usually was made up of from fourteen to sixteen mules; each mule carried 200 or more pounds in freight, depending on how strong he was and the urgency of the need for the items he carried. Ore was unwieldy and extremely heavy; since the rate of pay was determined by weight, there was a strong temptation to overload the animals. The wooden cross saddle which was frequently used had a pad under it to protect the mule from rubbing and chafing, but most pack mules had sores on their backs that never were given a chance to heal because of the constant irritation and were always open and running. The cinch around the girth had to be tightened to prevent slippage of the pack and naturally added to the discomfort, but was necessary to prevent slippage, even if it hindered breathing. A loose pack would do more harm to the tender back of the mule than a tight one.[1]

Packs were loaded from the side, one side at a time, and tied in place, forcing the mule to struggle to maintain his balance until the load was equalized on the other side. As the skinner deftly loaded each

mule, his hands effortlessly looped a knot here and there with a mere flip of the hand. When both sides were loaded, another pack was thrown on the middle with ropes again flashing over and under to secure the load, all done with the twinkling of an eye. The skinner's horse seemed to automatically realize when each mule was loaded and would move the string up to the next to be loaded. If the horse was not trained to do this, the skinner would call out to the mules, sometimes calling them by names. The mules had an assortment of colorful names, as imaginative as the names of the mines they served, and the skinner knew the name and character of each from experience.

The toll roads built by Otto Mears were used by the mines and towns to move the necessities until the railroads arrived, but in the San Juans the "Iron Horse" did not make it to many of the operations. Alex Calhoun and Enos Hotchkiss, two names well known in Western Colorado, ran a 100-mule outfit between Lake City and Animas Junction and other points in the vicinity.

The mules carried timber, crates of machinery, ore, food, barrels of oil and kerosene, dynamite and blasting powder, and anything else that had to be moved up or down the mountain. A trip to some of the old mining towns by jeep will reveal the wreckage of mine tipples, whims mills and heavy machinery and, if a cable car operation was not present, then everything there was probably carried to the site, piece by piece, on the backs of mules who made countless trips up and down the trail. When trails were too narrow or non-existent, as in the rougher and more isolated places, the donkey was used.

The clumsiest burdens were the big crates, boxes, and kegs; the bulk on the narrow mountain trails posing more of a problem than the heavier cargo. On the narrow stretches of the trail, the bulkier loads would scrape on the mountain and push the mule closer to the outside of the trail, which at times constituted a serious problem. Probably the greatest test of the mule skinner's ability and his string's temperament was the huge timbers for shoring the mines and frames for buildings that had to be carried, along with everything else. Each mule carried two or more, depending on size, lashed on each side and dragging behind the mule, and reaching high above the mule's head.

To keep a string of pack mules with their assorted cargoes together and moving over the narrow, winding trail was challenging, even for the expert. The mule skinners who loaded and guided these mules were as rugged and cantankerous as their charges and may have gradually assimilated some of their characteristics. Their job certainly was not an easy one, and they represented a breed of man like the true woodsman or mountain man who have become a vanishing breed. Some of the truck drivers have picked up bits of their vocabulary and other characteristics and are plenty rugged, but most of them do not load the trucks they drive.

Meeting a pack train on one of the narrow, precipitous trails could have its exciting moments regardless of whether the traveler was afoot or on horseback. A man on foot could find some place of safety to avoid being compressed by the loaded mules, unless it was a very tight squeeze and then it was best to backtrack until one is found. A man on horseback was considerate enough to let the mules have the outside of the trail, while he threw his feet over his saddle and toward the mountain to avoid having them crushed by a crate or pack as the string passed by. This drama was increased during winter, when trails became narrower and footing was more treacherous.

The same dexterity was demonstrated by the skinner in unloading as in the loading. The pack that were so securely lashed to the backs of the mules came apart with a twist of the rope or the flash of a hand, the requitted animal shook and surged upward a little like a swimmer too long under water. However, his relief was short-lived, as he soon began to retrace his steps after he was quickly loaded and headed back in the direction from which he came. Under normal conditions for a mule, the pack train covered about twenty miles a day, the number of hours required depending on the weather, the trail, and the mules.

The mules seemed to portray dejection and forlorness in their eyes as they trudged along, flapping their over-sized ears to discourage a horsefly or to dislodge sharp particles of ice from around their eyes which had been driven by the harsh winter wind. They plodded onward, accepting their lot without reaction, and ignoring the pack sores, swollen, rheumatic ankles and the abuse heaped on them by the mule skinner.

The stubborn label has been affixed on the mule since his origin, and this mantle has been carefully earned; but the mule is not the only obstinate animal, so, when man and mule come together at their worst, both somewhat alike, the mule is at a disadvantage unless his "business end" is within reach of his adversary. Because of their endurance and strength, they are called on to do the impossible day in and day out. If a mule in a train staggered and went down—he may have just decided to rest awhile—the skinner would do his best to cajole him

to rise, but this was not easy. The string of mules was closely tied together, therefore, when one went down, it would add to the weight of the other already heavily loaded string, causing the most discomfort to the two mules closest to their prone companion. The downed mule, depending on the location, presented a problem of considerable magnitude to the skinner, because if he stayed down, the skinner would have to unload him. If the trail was narrow, as it frequently was, it was almost impossible; some mules would rise to their feet when they were unloaded and sag back to their haunches after the skinner had a laboriously reloaded him. Needless to say, this was a trial for the disposition of even the most patient skinner. More than likely the skinner would apply some physical encouragement before he took the desperate measure of unloading.

When one mule went down, it often caused the whole string to become knotted because of the pull on the short connecting ropes. This made the pack uneasy, and they frequently began to mill around, twisting away to try to ease the unwanted additional burden. If they became too tangled from the twisting and turning, it would pull them all down, so from then on the skinner had his work cut out for him. Sometimes they would go down like a row of dominoes. Another cunning strategy was to lie down deliberately while the skinner was hassling with one of the others in the string. If these problems occurred in a hazardous location, the skinner was not inclined to be too sympathetic or compassionate.

When pleading and coaxing were of no avail, the skinner resorted to other tactics, which started with the most eloquent profanity imaginable and deteriorated to vicious brutality. There are those who solemnly allege that many mule skinners could raise a fallen mule to his feet with the thrust of his words. The thin mountain air would become thicker as he unleashed his massive repertoire, garnered by spending years working with animals capable of expanding the vocabulary of a preacher. This highly developed and perfected eloquence was considered a prerequisite for the job, and it is doubtful success could be achieved by those who were deficient in this category. The mule skinner put the best to shame.

If the beast did not respond to the abusive profanity, then the skinner resorted to brutality. For a mule to rise with two or three hundred pounds strapped to his back, required a superasinine effort, as he had to lunge to get up; in heavy snow with difficult footing, or on steep trails with loose rocks, it was nearly an impossibility. The skinner would kick the mule, beat him with a heavy strap or stick and supplement his physical efforts by continuing

with the verbal onslaught. Sometimes the hapless animal would lunge to his feet, while other times he would serenely remain seated. This flaunting of human effort would bring out the worst in the skinner, therefore, he would begin to pound on the mule's head with his iron shovel, with the sound echoing with each blow. It was hard for him to accept the fact that some mules would simply do what they wanted to do, when they wanted to do it, and practically nothing could change this determination.

Many accidents had to be expected in the rugged terrain and breathtaking trails of the Colorado Rockies. The mules were tied together, therefore when one slipped over the edge of the trail, the others were pulled with him. Dynamite, blasting powder and caps were some of the materials carried by the mule trains, and this made the life of the skinner more interesting. Sometimes mules would fall over the cliffs into deep snowdrifts, heavily loaded and tied together. Because of the snow, it was impossible to rescue them, therefore, the only humane thing that could be done was to shoot them. Snowslides and rockslides were a constant menace to the unwary packtrain.

Al Look in **Utes Last Stand**, pays tribute to the mule for his dedication under fire, while serving in time of war and in the thin mountain air of the higher altitudes. In time of need, pack mules served as food to keep a marooned or starving expedition from death, as was the case during the Battle of Milk Creek near Meeker, or the beleagured Fourth Fremont expedition. Many claim the mule has a better memory than an elephant and he mentally records all the abuse he has received, waiting for the opportunity to respond with his two hind legs when his antagonist is within range. The wise mule skinner or prudent farmer never walked around the hind quarters of a mule, because the kick of a mule would surpass the swipe of a grizzly's paw.

The mule skinner seemed to be able to cope with all the challenges that came his way, regardless of weather or terrain and nothing stumped him.[2] If a piece of equipment had to be carried that could not be loaded on the back of one mule because of its shape, size or weight, the ingenious skinner would hang it on poles hung between two mules. Heavy or long pieces of equipment were pulled up the narrow, winding trail on a sled behind a tandem string of the number needed to get the load to its destination. In ingenuity, brawn and daring, the plain brute courage in all the tricks of dealing with the evil nature of rebellious livestock, the mountain mule skinners had no equal.[3]

One of the more unusual and challenging tasks assigned to the skinner and his pack of mules was the transporting of cable to the various eagles' nests where it was used in the Colorado Rockies. The cable was used for a variety of purposes in mining operations and frequently for the cable-car tramways that honeycombed the hillsides; often the cable had to be taken to places not serviced by even the crudest of roads or trails and sometimes before adequate trails were broken. These cable car anchors—built in the most spectacular places imaginable—required timber, heavy iron braces and bolts, as well as pulleys. The job of taking this equipment to its future location was another of the more difficult of the mules' or donkeys' arduous duties.

The large coils of cable proved to be one of the most difficult items to transport, and called for all the acumen the skinner could muster. To avoid cutting or splicing, a large roll of cable would be parcelled among the mules by hanging as much of the loop—maybe 70 or 80 pounds—as each mule could bear over the wooden cross pack saddle. The skinner would start with the lead mule and go down the line, disbursing portions of the massive loop as he went, and then he would balance the load by continuing back on the other side after he had come to the tail-end of the pack. When he was finished, equal portions of the same coil of cable would be looped from one mule to another on the sides of fourteen or fifteen mules, or however many were needed. Each mule was connected to the original coil along each side of the continuous loop. The skinner carefully

picked his mules for this job, because if they became unmanageable and twisted around in the cable, he had a problem akin to Gen. George Armstrong Custer's last dilemma.

The mule skinners were a hard lot and their jobs were most demanding, so they had to let off steam occasionally. One of their favorite diversions, as one might guess, was mule racing. These races were packed with excitement and action, attracting considerable interest in the towns where they were held. These races were almost as exciting and spectacular as the horse races of the White River Utes, and attracted a comparable amount of betting. The skinners and miners would bet almost anything on these "asinine" contests. Sometimes valuable mining properties changed hands with the "flash of a mule." The races were very serious affairs and were a combination of races, pulling contests, and anything else that struck the fancy or which provided enough competition to merit a wager.

The use of mules and donkeys was not limited to the mountain trails, because many spent almost their entire lives in a mine shaft, moving ore carts or pulling the hoists. Some of these mules were gentle and responsive, therefore, because they were about the only outlet for affection the miners had, they were treated like pets. The miners would save bits of food or bring green grass down to them when it was available. Some were so cantankerous it was not safe to go near them, as mules, like people, greatly varied in their personalities. It was very important to be aware of the eccentricities of of the critter

PACK TRAIN IN SAN JUANS   DIORAMA STATE HISTORICAL SOCIETY

when it was necessary to work in his presence, to protect life and limb from the explosive hind quarters or the teeth on the front end. Besides the mules that were ornery and mean, that would bite and kick on every opportunity, there were also the stubborn varieties. This category would regally refuse to perform certain tasks as if they were beneath their dignity, while they would willingly tackle a seemingly more arduous project. They were not easy to predict or comprehend, therefore, when all the bad qualities were in the personality of one mule, the most accomplished mule skinner had his hands full.

Occasionally mules would become trapped in mines because of cave-ins and because of their size, they were more difficult to rescue than a miner. Sometimes they had to be permanently abandoned or brought food and water temporarily until they could be dug out.

Many mules lived most of their lives in a mine shaft and never returned to daylight until they were dead, dying while pursuing their work. When they were brought out after a long period of service in the mine shaft, precautions were taken to avoid abrupt exposure of their eyes to the rays of the sun in order to protect their vision. Blinders were placed over the eyes of a mule that had not seen daylight for a long time, allowing the mournful eyes a chance to make a gradual adjustment.

The mules used in the mining industry, until they were replaced by mechanization, did the jobs that otherwise could not have been done. Many are still in use in the more isolated or difficult operations. It would be impossible to find a more valuable contributor to the mining industry during its infancy in the Centennial State than these mules or donkeys, who moved men to their mountains and then moved parts of the same mountains.

> "On mules we find two legs behind
> And two we find before.
> We stand behind before we find
> What the two behind be for."

S. Grover

28—LABOR STRIFE AND SILVER POLITICS

The questions of silver and unions provided heated issues for Coloradans to ponder from the 1890's to World War I. The difficult nature of mining and ore processing in Colorado resulted in a merging of interests and advanced technology that made the whole process a large-scale operation. Only prospecting remained a one-man operation after the first mining rush. Mining, milling and smeltering, for the most part, were expensive operations, requiring huge investments and capable direction. Beginning with the silver rush in the 1870s, mining in Colorado underwent an industrial revolution much like the same transition factories in England experienced in the 18th century and plants of the United States underwent immediately after the Civil War. This produced a drastic change in the whole mining industry that was keenly felt by all who participated. To the miner or the mill-hand it was not a popular alteration. Gone was the day when miners owned part of the mine they worked in, moreover, they no

longer were working close to management. They found themselves at a disadvantage because they could not locate their employer, let alone converse or try to bring their problems to him; they were victims of mass production in industry, much like their colleagues in the factories back east, also, they were equally unhappy.

In the beginning the miners had depended on their own capital and labor. With skill and hard work, along with a little luck, they might make their mine pay. They lived in the crudest of conditions in a dream world. What they soon became aware of was the scale of investment required for hoists, trams, steam engines, railroads, smelters and equipment. The capital necessary for these operations soon came to the Centennial State, consequently, the mining industry became highly industrialized. Large companies opened mines then built small scale communities to meet the needs of their employees to sufficiently attract the needed number of laborers.

These company towns were controlled by the mining company almost completely. The houses, schools, churches and store were company property. The preacher and teachers were hired by the company, then directed in their undertakings. Some company towns, principally coal mining towns, paid their miners in company script which was redeemable only at the company store. The workers in these communities benefitted economically by the security offered, but suffered spiritually and philosophically. Frequently, they were informed how they should vote in elections. Although these practices may seem somewhat abusive, they were not too different from policies of contemporary industries all over the world. Of course, the main goal of such an arrangement was to avoid contact by the union with their employees.

By 1890 miners and millhands were making from $2.50 to $3.00 for a ten-hour day—this was for hardrock miners, the coal miners did not make that much. They all worked six days a week with Sunday as a day of rest. The hours worked, the pay and working conditions, were all issues unions could take advantage of in their attempts to organize the workers. Another issue that stirred miners was the practice of paying by the fathom (six feet); in other words, for the amount of ore mined in the shift either by measure or weight. Miners were expected to take care of shoring as they worked as it was highly important for their safety to timber as they moved forward, however, this meant they were not getting paid for this additional responsibility. They might make more money if they skimped on shoring, but they might pay with their lives if they were too careless. These issues were frequently intensified by racial overtones. Cornish miners were imported from Cornwall, Wales, while Finns, Swedes, Germans and Italians added to what was resented as foreign competition by miners already employed. The immigrants were willing to work for lower wages. The most scorn was saved for the Chinese, who were resented most of all. The mining camps attracted people from all walks of life and included representatives of all races and religions.

It would be pleasant to assume that inequality and persecution did not exist in these mining towns, but to do so would mean to gloss over the truth. Towns were segregated by nationalities with each nationality living in its own section or ghetto. Even the cemeteries were segregated by race and social or economic position. When one national group was largely responsible for labor trouble, company policy would frequently call for a ban on hiring any members of that nationality because they were branded as troublemakers. It could be Italians, Finns, Cornish or whatever. Miners were no better. When member of a national group not represented wa hired, they generally protested. When a Mexica was hired at the Tomboy mine, all the miners wer on strike. Labor organizers were not without issue as they moved into the mining industry of Colorad Mill and mine workers were aware of the threat an carefully worked and planned together. The resu was twenty years of conflict and violence.

Violence is not an unknown to Americans; was the credo of the West. Application of violen solutions to problems was a respected methodolog of the American Frontier. Compromise or appeas ment were considered debasing. The theme of vi lence is undoubtedly the most popular basis for mos of the literature written about the West, moreove this violence can not be dismissed. It is interestin to note that the violent nature of the West may b overplayed. Statistics do not support the tales, bu indicate more people are killed per capita in Detro or Chicago of today than a Telluride or Dodge Cit of the 1890s. Statistics also reveal that more peopl were killed in the strikes and labor difficulty in th mining camps than at any other time. Rodman Pau one of America's foremost mining historians, ha done considerable research on this topic and con cludes that the most violent period in the minin camps was during these prolonged strikes. Th typical mining town had its shootings, brawls an hangings, but these activities simply did not accoun for nearly as many deaths as the labor wars.

As labor and management geared for the strug gle for control of the miners and millhands in Colo rado, they had the experience and expertise of out side people who had gone through the same turmo earlier at their disposal. Perhaps this is the reaso the contest was so bitter. Also, many of the mine and smelters were controlled by eastern capitalist that had already lost battles to unions; so, conse quently, they were more determined to win in Colo rado.

The Knights of Labor was the first union t come to Colorado and by 1880 they had a chapte organized in Erie, a coal town. The first sizabl strike was called in Leadville in 1880. Eight thou sand miners were soon on strike over wages an hours. As tension increased, Governor Pikin de clared martial law and called out the state militia The three weeks' strike ended when the miners re turned to work. The men deemed to be the leader of the strike were forced to leave Leadville.

The Western Federation of Miners, a hard-roc miners' union, was formed in 1893. This union wa

DAVIS
H.
WAITE

more ambitious and less susceptible to intimidation by the owners. It also was not conservative in its tactics. By the end of 1893 the W.F. of M. had 42 branch unions in Colorado. Their Colorado headquarters was Cripple Creek, the most active mining area at the time. Trouble was just around the corner.

The silver crash created a horde of unemployed miners that naturally headed in the direction of Cripple Creek. This situation was too tempting to the owners, who were anxious to implement the principle of the law of supply and demand. Some owners cut wages, while others increased the working day and informed their miners to leave if they did not like the new standards. The strike in Cripple Creek began in 1903 and lasted almost eighteen months. On January 17, 1894, a notice at the Pharmacist mine stated that miners would be required to work ten hours a day and lunch on their own time for $3.00 a day or work eight hours for $2.50. Several notices of a similar nature followed. The union scale called for a minimum wage of $3.00 for eight hours work. The mine owners justified their decrease by claiming the production at their mines did not warrant the wages formerly paid. Mass meetings of miners followed. John Calderwood, the leader of the W.F. of M., spoke to the gathered throng. At that time the unions of Colorado were organized on the local level and were not affiliated with each other. Consequently, strikes occurred only at one place at a time.

Governor Waite, the populist governor of Colorado, was somewhat sympathetic with the striking miners. The people of Colorado Springs were unsympathetic with the miners and detested Waite. Each side pushed the other to the limit. Miners branded as troublemakers were loaded in cattle cars and hauled to the Kansas line where they were pushed out of the car and instructed to "start walking in an easterly direction." "Big Bill" Haywood, a union organizer, used coercive means to increase the union membership. Harry Orchard dynamited the Independence railroad station June 6, 1904. The blast killed 13 non-union miners and seriously injured many others. In this prolonged strike, both antagonists raised militias and drilled. There were actual battles fought and positions attacked and defended. Most of the violence that occurred was blamed on the W.F. of M. In the end the union lost the battle and the mines were re-opened with non-union miners. Damage to property went into the millions of dollars and, although the W.F. of L. never regained its power, labor trouble continued to plague Cripple Creek and kept production limited. 1900, the

biggest year the region ever had, was never again approached.

President Charles E. Moyer of the W.F. of L. was jailed in Ouray March 26, 1904 for desecration of the American Flag, for having copies of the flag painted with inscriptions. This was not an uncommon practice at the time, but was considered sufficient to limit union activities in the San Juans. A series of strikes followed. Much of the difficulty centered around the Tomboy Mine, where trouble started before the arrest of Moyer. The mine had been reopened with non-union miners; also, in the ensuing struggle members of both sides were captured and transported out of town. The superintendent of the Tomboy Mine was murdered and Fort Peabody, high atop Imogene Pass, was constructed by the mineowners to keep union organizers from coming over the pass. A delegation of union miners was escorted over the pass with orders to "start walking." Instead, they occupied a deserted mining camp and regrouped, then successfully stormed Fort Peabody. Finally, Governor Peabody suspended martial law and the union settled for the eight-hour day for $3.00 pay. The union had been more successful in this strike.

The series of strikes in the hardrock mines of Colorado were followed by similar activities in the coal fields. Many of the coal towns were owned by Colorado Fuel and Iron, owned by John C. Osgood since its inception in 1892. While Osgood owned what was then Colorado's largest state-owned corporation, miners were treated more equitable. However, Osgood lost out in his effort to maintain control of his company by seeking the help of John D. Rockefeller. Rockefeller aided Osgood in his struggle, but characteristically ended up controlling C. F. and I. After that the miners were not treated as well and trouble followed. There were many strikes however, the most famous occurred at Trinidad. The coal mines belonged to the United Mine Workers Union which was headed by John Lawson. Mary Harris, known as "Mother Jones" by the miners was an eighty-two year old socialist who proved to be a helpful union organizer. The events in Trinidad were not dissimilar to other incidents, only more heated. Trinidad was a company town, consequently when the strike began in 1914 the union miners moved to tents provided by union funds. The tent colony was named Ludlow and housed 900 people. The union miners tried to keep the mines closed while management tried to keep them operating with non-union miners. During a skirmish five miners and one militiaman was killed. While the battle ensued a fire broke out in Ludlow and two women and eleven children died. Murders, dynamitings and burnings followed the "Ludlow Massacre."

Governor Elias Ammons asked President Woodrow Wilson to intervene, so a contingent of troops was dispatched to Trinidad. With the arrival of the army, conditions improved and the strike was settled. The miners did not get union recognition, moreover, their union was replaced by a company union. However, they did gain better working conditions, along with improved pay and shorter hours. Evidence revealed a large number of the militia was on the payroll of C. F. and I., also that some of them had fired directly into the tent colony. This time public opinion was more on the side of the union, so the Rockefeller interests were forced to give in to save face. This did not end the struggle. Both sides gathered momentum for a continuation, but the 1904 Cripple Creek and 1914 Trinidad strikes were the worst Colorado was forced to endure.

The silver issue in the United States began with the advent of the first administration. Alexander Hamilton, first Secretary of the Treasury, favored a monometal system, but feared gold was not sufficiently abundant in quantity, so finally accepted a bimetallic standard. The Coinage Act of 1792 established the silver dollar as the basic unit of currency with a ratio of 15 to 1 between silver and gold. This ratio was raised to 16 to 1 by congress in 1834. From 1834 to the Civil War the ratio gravitated and kept American currency in chaos. Finally, to improve the situation, a new law was passed in 1873. Gold production by this time convinced economists that gold could be made available as a universal medium of exchange throughout the world. Most of the world was moving in this direction. So, at this time the United States switched to monometalism and a new gold dollar replaced the silver one, which was no longer coined. This action restricted currency by including the retirement of war-issue greenbacks. The political and economic ramifications of the "Crime of 73" are well known. Deflation followed, along with the panic of 1873. The battle of the standards now began.

Finally, in 1878 the Bland-Allison act provided for coinage of two to four million dollars worth of silver each month. The arguments supporting monometalism and bimetalism are lengthy. It devolves to those that have money and those who do not. In

ROTTINGHAUS
'75

the silver-producing states, it was something much different. It was life or death. When the newly formed populist party supported free and unlimited coinage of silver, it gained strong support from silver producing states. David H. Waite of Aspen became the populist candidate for governor of Colorado in 1891; his campaign resulted in his election. Coloradans placed loyalty to their party below their interest in silver.

Nationally, the amount of money in circulation was based on the amount of government bonds representing the national debt. Because of a decrease in the national debt, the amount of currency was cut in half by 1900. In 1890 the Sherman Silver Purchase Act increased the amount of silver purchased by the government to 4.5 million ounces of silver monthly; however, production still outstripped the demand, and the price of silver continued downward to a 26 to 1 ratio to gold by 1893. The panic of 1893 prompted President Grover Cleveland, a gold democrat, to push for the repeal of the Sherman Act which he felt was largely responsible for the panic. With the repeal of the act, the price of silver plummeted downward, therefore, most silver miners were ruined. The silver-producing states united in an effort to return to the double standard, hoping to revive their lost fortunes. Finally, in 1896 the silverites found their champion in William Jennings Bryan, the "silver tongued orator" from Nebraska. The Populist party backed Bryan, so the Democrats and Populists merged. The campaign was one of the most controversial ever held. William McKinley, Bryan's Republican opponent, stayed at home while Bryan stumped the country. Winfield Scott Stratton, the Cripple Creek "Midas of the Rockies", bet $100,000 on Bryan. He was fortunate that there were no takers, because Bryan lost and the silver issue was put aside. Gold in Cripple Creek, Leadville and the San Juans helped keep mining going and new industries began to assume some of the attention formerly given to mining. By 1900, Colorado could claim 500,000 residents, while the industrial mining nature of the Centennial State began to shift more toward farming and ranching.

S GROVER

29—THE CENTURY TURNS

The 1890s were a transition period in Colorado as elsewhere. The age of the machine and convenience was moving in to take the place of hand labor and life without luxury. These changes were accompanied by the luster of the return of prosperity after the panic of 1893 and high anticipation for the promises of the 20th Century. It seemed nothing was beyond the realm of possibility. Science and technology had advanced beyond the fondest dreams and beckoned mankind to enter a world without sickness or discomfort and free from social ills, the rosy world of the 20th Century yet to be.

The election of 1896 and the return to prosperity had put aside the silver question, while other industries were competing with agriculture and mining for their fair share of the Colorado economy. The United States was now a world power to be reckoned with. It was difficult to be anything but optimistic about the future of the State of Colorado or the Union. Several of the chronic problems remained to challenge growth and optimism, however, not the least of these ailments was transportation. The age of the automobile resulted in a general overhaul and improvement of the network of roads

in the Centennial State and, again, the mountainous terrain added to expense of road extensions and improvements. This problem was compounded because of the rapidly increasing tourist industry. Most of the places tourists wished to see were in the most rugged and isolated parts of the state. Building roads in the Rocky Mountains would be expensive and maintenance of such a network would continue to place a burden on the small number of taxpayers in Colorado. Something had to be done, however, because tourists were no longer satisfied with the limits of touring by train. National Parks opened and National Forests beckoned. People realized the flexibility and privacy of the automobile. This machine completely revolutionized transportation and the American way of life. The question was not whether roads would be built or not, but how they would be built and financed. Coloradans began to put their heads together—the Good Roads Association was one of the results of this concern.

Demands for better roads came from a variety of places. The automobile clubs, tourist industry, chambers of commerce, automobile dealers and people in general all saw the need. What was required was a state highway commission funded to deal with the demand for construction and maintenance of a state network of highways. This commission was created in 1908, but the needs grew so rapidly it was almost impossible to keep up with. The population of the state went from 25,000 in 1861 to 100,000 in 1876 and soared to 500,000 by 1900. As the automobile increased in popularity, it intensified the demand for roads. The dilemma was partially alleviated by resorting to the use of convict labor for construction. Good effort on roadbuilding and good behavior could win a commuted sentence for a convict, while at the same time help the progress of the Good Roads Campaign. The road from Pueblo to Leadville, the Skyline Drive near Canon City, the road to the Royal Gorge Bridge, the Glenwood Springs Canyon and Plateau Canyon roads were all built with convict labor and would have been postponed for a considerable time if this economical labor force had not been available. The discerning eye can locate some of the old campsites used by the convicts at the turn of the century by old cement ovens or firepits in poor condition in isolated flats that have not been used for anything else since they were occupied by the construction gangs.

The increasing use of the automobile was painfully felt by the railroads, at least in loss of passenger traffic, along with the arrival of trucks to haul freight. Decline in mining and the arrival of the automobile ended the existence of most of the narrow-gauge railroads. They were so marginal in their operation they simply could not continue. Some of them hung on until the 1920s, only to be finished by the depression that followed in the 1930s. The Rio Grande, The Rio Grande Southern and the Uintah were some of the few that lasted a little longer. Today, the Cripple Creek to Victor, the Durango to Silverton and Toltec are lonely survivors of the narrow gauge era. These are tourist trains that operate in the summer. The other lines are gone, some of their rolling stock still rolls and some is retired in railroad museums in Golden or elsewhere. The age of steam has gone into oblivion with these narrow gauges. "All aboard" or the whistle of a steam engine have faded into memory like the once present wail of the coyote and their "all's well" message they proclaimed is gone with them.

The Denver Pacific and the Kansas Pacific gave Denver connections with the continental railroad by going directly north from Denver to Cheyenne. Talk of a coast-to-coast railroad through Colorado started before the Civil War and the discussion of a tunnel under the Continental Divide began shortly after that war, when a tunnel seemed

the only way such a railroad could be built. The turn of the century had witnessed the demise of several narrow gauges, some because of the silver crash in 1893, others when the hoped for development of the area they served did not take place. The two decades of the 1880s and 1890s saw an overbuilding of railroads when they were built with the profit of construction in mind. Some were started and never finished. Gradually, after the turn of the century most of the narrow gauges disappeared or were replaced by standard gauge or the automobile. The topic of a railroad through the heartland of Colorado continued, however.

The names of William J. Palmer and Otto Mears have already been mentioned in the history of Colorado railroading. Another should be added, that name is David H. Moffatt. Moffatt arrived in Denver in 1860 and opened a stationery store. During the ensuing years he became involved in the mining business and also went into banking. It was not the need of wealth or livelihood that led Moffatt to railroading, it was the lure of the road. It seemed that railroading was his real love and where his best talents were utilized. The Denver merchant and banker helped in the construction of the Denver Pacific, was an associate in the Boulder Valley Railroad, the Denver Utah and Pacific, the Rio Grande, the Florence and Cripple Creek and about every other railroad that was of any size in Colorado.

The dream of a tunnel through the Continental Divide was a scheme that caught the imagination of David Moffat. The first effort to proceed in this undertaking was the Denver, Utah and Pacific Railroad that was incorporated in 1880. The railroad got only as far as Louisville, but did start a tunnel which is still visible on the west shore of Yankee Doodle Lake. The Atlantic and Pacific Tunnel Company was another venture with a tunnel through the Continental Divide in mind—this company was not successful. Finally, the Denver, Northwestern and Pacific Railroad (Moffat Road) was incorporated in 1902. Moffatt was a big man in Colorado, for at the time he owned three-fourths of the stock of the First National Bank of Denver, about half of the Denver Tramway Stock, as well as the banks of Cripple Creek, Victor, and Hot Sulphur Springs. It would take all the resources he could muster to complete his transcontinental railroad, this time through Colorado and not around the Centennial State. The existing transcontinental railroads were backed by some of the largest capital interests in the east, consequently, they resorted to every means they could conceive to fight the plans of Moffat.

Despite his opposition and competition, Moffatt persevered in his struggle, although it broke him

financially. His first road went over the Continental Divide at Rollins Pass near Corona and passed through Gore Canyon to Yarmony. This part of the road was finished in 1904. The Moffat Road experienced the ravages of winter in the high altitude, so well known by other railroads and the mining industry. It was virtually impossible to keep the road open over the divide during the winter. A tunnel seemed the only plausible answer, but Moffat had already invested his entire fortune, about $9,000,000, in the venture. The railroad builder died in 1911 without seeing his railroad reach Routt County. In 1912, the line was forced into receivership and reorganized as the Denver and Salt Lake Railroad Company. In 1915, the general assembly named the western half of Routt County after the great railroad builder.

With the death of Moffatt the effort to build the tunnel with private funds ended, meanwhile, the subscription for public funds began. It would be an expensive project with tremendous benefit to the Western Slope. In the typical fashion it did not enchant residents of the eastern half of the state, so it was voted down in a referendum in 1912. Several efforts were made to associate the tunnel project on some bill that would include a project beneficial to the Eastern Slope. The results of this attempt proved unfruitful until the flood of the Arkansas in 1921. Lower Pueblo was inundated and nearly 1,000 buildings were destroyed. Immediately, a Moffatt Tunnel and Pueblo Flood Conservancy bill was tied together by a special session of the General Assembly called by Governor Shoup to deal with the problems. The bill passed with a Moffatt Tunnel Improvement District included. Four issues of bonds were sold which raised over $15,000,000. Construction of the tunnel began.

The Moffatt Tunnel under the Continental Divide was completed in 1927 and is six miles long. The construction was an immense task, requiring skill and imagination much like the Alpine Tunnel on the Denver and South Park Railroad. The tunnel itself only cut the distance from Denver to Salt Lake by twenty-three miles, hardly sufficient to justify such an effort and expenditure. Plans called for a 1926 completion to assist in the observance of the 50th anniversary of statehood, but this was too optimistic. The tunnel proved to be more of a challenge than was anticipated. The problem of unstable earth and water seepage continually plagued the operation. The need for expensive shoring materials and the drainage of Lower Crater Lake through the tunnel added to the cost and delay. Finally, after a cost of $18,000,000, almost $11,000,000 more than

was first planned, and twenty-nine fatalities, th tunnel was finished. Traffic through the tunnel be gan to move in 1928.

The pioneer bore was used to explore the te rain and provide several access entrances to th main tunnel. It was driven parallel to the mai bore, was about eight foot high and nine feet wid and was lined with concrete. In 1936 it was con verted and lined with concrete to transfer wate from the Fraser River to the Eastern Slope. Th railroad tunnel is twenty-four feet high and sixtee feet wide. When traffic began to roll through th tunnel in early 1928, as previously mentioned, onl twenty-three miles were saved from the trip be tween Denver and Salt Lake City. The line wa only forty miles away from the Denver and Ri Grande's main line to Grand Junction. A connectio with the main line from the Moffat Tunnel woul cut off 175 miles from the route to Denver from Salt Lake City. Therefore, the Dotsero cut-off wa built in short order and the dream of a continenta railroad route through the center of Colorado be came a reality. What was started by David Moffat was now finished. The day of the railroad was al ready declining with the completion of the tunnel Several hundred miles of defunct tracks were tor up and used for scrap during World War II. Onl the main line routes or nostalgic tourist attraction now remain.

Other means of transportation that were rapidl becoming obsolete were the horses, mules, oxen an donkeys that had served the state so well during it early days. The automobile began to make its ap pearance in the first part of the twentieth century and residents began to gradually abandon the bugg for the more exciting, if less reliable automobile Bicycles were becoming a popular item. The two wheeled bicycle did not require feed and did not hav a stubborn nature. By the 1920s the airplane adde another dimension to transportation in the Centen nial State. No means of transportation, including the mule, was better suited to solve the problems o rugged terrain than this airborne method. No roads tracks, bridges or tunnels to build and it could fl over much of the worst terrain and weather. The airplane moved into the passenger and freight area while the helicopter finally outdid the mule.

World War I did not alter the course of the Cen tennial State nearly as much as World War II. The goods shipped to the European Theatre were loaded in eastern ports for the most part, then shipped to Europe from those points, so there was only a one-way movement of goods through Colorado. World War II was fought in Asia and Europe, so there were goods shipped in both directions. It was a bigger war and during its duration defense plants, military installations and government offices were located in Colorado because of the state's isolated central location. This started a trend that now makes Colorado the second highest in federal employees behind Washington, D. C. in the United States. President Dwight D. Eisenhower started a trend of using Denver for a second White House and vacation area. President Gerald Ford continues in this practice.

Several state young men "shipped over" to Europe during World War I, moreover, a good part of these did not return. They were sorely missed by their relatives and friends. In a state that saw its beginning because of mining, it would not seem strange to guess that World War I might produce a mining boom in Colorado. This time it was different; moreover, it was not gold or silver—these precious metals help pay for wars—but in the new technology of the times new materials and metals with high tolerances were needed. Consequently, a tungsten and uranium boom came to the Centennial State at this time. The category used to refer to these meals is "rare metals". Other rare metals, so named because of their scarcity, found in the Centennial State are molybdenum, vanadium, and cadmium.

Uranium was used by the Indians to provide yellow color. Finally, in 1898 samples of the ore that had been hauled on mules out of the Paradox Valley of Western Colorado were analyzed by Madame Curie and radium was discovered. As the purposes for the new material became better known, demands increased. The medical profession saw the possibilities of the use of radium for x-ray and treatment of ailments; industry used it for luminous dials for watches and clocks. Vanadium, a by-product of uranium, was used to toughen steel. Be-

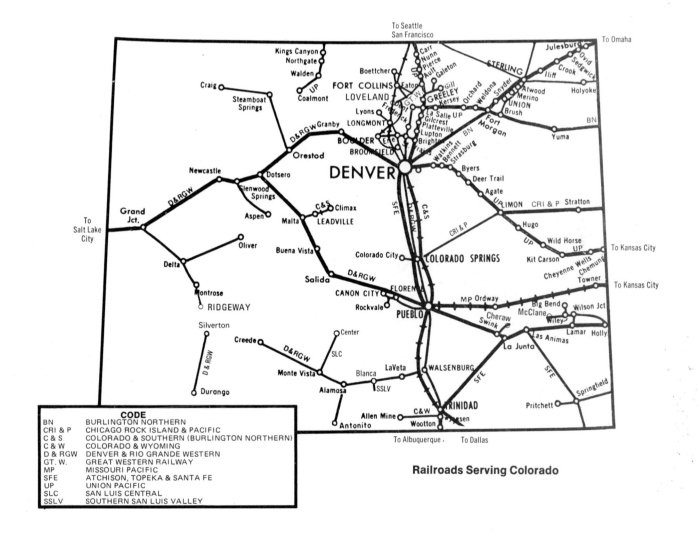

CODE

BN	BURLINGTON NORTHERN
CRI & P	CHICAGO ROCK ISLAND & PACIFIC
C & S	COLORADO & SOUTHERN (BURLINGTON NORTHERN)
C & W	COLORADO & WYOMING
D & RGW	DENVER & RIO GRANDE WESTERN
GT. W.	GREAT WESTERN RAILWAY
MP	MISSOURI PACIFIC
SFE	ATCHISON, TOPEKA & SANTA FE
UP	UNION PACIFIC
SLC	SAN LUIS CENTRAL
SSLV	SOUTHERN SAN LUIS VALLEY

Railroads Serving Colorado

fore another supply of uranium was discovered in the Belgian Congo, Colorado and Utah had virtually a monopoly on the material for almost twenty years. Agents needed to harden and toughen steel were in great demand during wartime. Tungsten was such an element.

The discovery of tungsten in Boulder County resembles other mining periods in the history of the Centennial State. The miners of the Nederland region considered it a nuisance in the way of their efforts to find silver or gold. Again, men after riches did not realize they were walking over millions. John H. Knight of Ward was the first to recognize tungsten in Boulder County in 1899. Stevens Camp and the Conger were two of Colorado's richest tungsten mines. Now that the presence of tungsten was known, all that was needed was a demand and World War I supplied the market.

Besides making steel tougher and more heat resistant, tungsten is also used for electric light filament. During World War I Colorado was producing and marketing $5,000,000 worth of tungsten a year. The unusual demand for the metal because of the war dissipated with the end of the conflict. Colorado's "rare metals boom" slipped soon afterward and went into rapid decline. The depression that soon followed, along with cheaper Chinese tungsten, finished the industry. Since World War I, molybdenum has been proven to be a better source of the same qualities found in tungsten; more important, molybdenum is easier to process, moreover, a recovery of a higher percentage of minerals from the ore is possible. Climax Molybdenum continues to mine the important mineral near Leadville. Another uranium boom occurred in Western Colorado in the 1950s.

30—THE HECTIC TWENTIES

The pervading mood of the nation after World War I did not improve as it swept westward. The same undercurrents present in eastern states had their manifestations in Colorado. People will rise to make sacrifices for lofty causes perhaps once in a generation, it is claimed. By the 1920s Coloradans were "caused out" and wished to return to their normal lives, forever to forget Europe and its hornet's nests. This feeling was widely shared by Americans across the country. No matter how hard they tried, however, they could not escape the lingering feeling that they had been exploited or used. One of the strongest indications of this mood was the return of the Republicans to most of the high offices in Colorado. Although a scramble for office marked the political climate in Colorado during the twenties, the Republicans, for the most part, prevailed.

The economics of the Centennial State did not improve on the dour nature of national trends. Colorado did not profit from the war-time boom in the degree that other states did. The rare metals boom was about the only big boost. Agriculture did not prosper to the extent it did in midwestern states; there were few war industries in the Centennial State and mining was declining so rapidly it offset much of the boom in rare metals. Isolation and lack of transportation still was a disadvantage industrially.

The Progressive Movement brought reform and prohibition to all states. The Progressive Movement resulted in the closing or moving of some of the centers of prostitution, but also contributed to the increase in crime with the Volstead Act of 1919. Most of Colorado, except some of the larger towns and mining camps, was already practically dry in

1919. The United States was about 75% dry when the Volstead Act was passed. It would appear that the act would not be too earth shattering with these circumstances in mind, however, such was not the case. The bootlegger and the racketeer crusaded along side of the Progressive politician and reformer for prohibition. Once it was passed, it seems more liquor was manufactured and consumed than ever before—maybe it was. It did not take long for the bootleggers to get into operation. The devil-may-care attitude rampant in the twenties added to the desire to circumvent the detested Volstead Act. Bootleg liquor was not hard to locate, only expensive to buy and dangerous to consume. The twenties found a number of the old, isolated mining camps about to turn into ghost towns. The prohibition era benevolently provided them with an opportunity to keep afloat. They went into the bootleg business in earnest. Their location was a big advantage, but not their only long-suit. Some of these mining towns were located at the end of the line and could be approached from only one direction; consequently, it was not difficult to have a lookout keeping watch for the revenue agents passing by. The lookout was far enough away that a telephone call would give the town plenty of advance warning, in time to hide the incriminating evidence before the agents arrived.

The informants were sometimes telephone operators, a handy arrangement, indeed. Postmasters of the small post offices, store keepers or filling station operators, and even local law enforcement officials frequently served in this important capacity. The old mine diggings above these towns were ideal locations for stills or what have you. There is a multitude of abandoned mining shafts in the Centennial State that were available when the need was urgent for a hide-away. Vertical shafts that seem to go to the bowels of the earth are dangerous if not covered. A casual passer-by or tourist can fruitlessly gaze down these bottomless pits or drop a stone, never to hear its contact with solid ground after listening for an interminable length of time. Occasionally, people disappear in these old mining locations and are never seen or heard of again. They could be at the bottom of one of these chasms, either victim of foulplay or accident.

In the larger mining towns the national origins were often segregated by ghettos in different sections. Each section would produce its specialty in bootleg, according to their nationality. The Italian section made fine wine, the Germans produced good beer, the Irish whiskey and so it went. Each Friday these mountain distilleries would distribute their "spirits" for weekend consumption in the larger towns in their vicinities. This deprived the ghosts of some more of Colorado's mining camps until mining revivals, tourism or winter sports appeared and helped many residents to weather the demands of their age.

The nativism and xenophobia of the twenties resulted in a resurgence of the Ku Klux Klan on a level that the post-Civil War South could not have matched. The Klan claimed more than 5,000,000 members by the mid-twenties and spread west and north until there were strong units in states like Oregon and Indiana. The Klan became so strong in Colorado that its roster included the names of the prominent people in the larger cities of the state. As it rapidly grew in numbers, its strength increased in state politics until it gained control of the state Republican Party, the office of governor and many of the local governments, including Denver. In 1924 Clarence J. Morley was elected governor of Colorado with Klan support. Under "Grand Dragon" Dr. John Galen Locke, the Klan gained control of the state House of Representatives. They were anti-foreigner, anti-Jew, anti-Catholic, anti-Black and purported to have the goal of returning 100% Americanism. The anti-Catholic bill which forbade the use of sacramental wine during the prohibition passed in Oregon. The proposal to close parochial schools by preventing attendance was the other measure they sponsored. These measures did not become law in Colorado when six Republicans who were not Klan members joined with the Democrats to prevent enactment.

All the trappings of the Klan appeared—parades of hooded members, burning crosses, oppression of minorities and strong-arm tactics. Fortunately, the Klan declined as rapidly as it appeared on the scene. National loss of faith because of scandals in the hierarchy, plus quarrels over the use of the huge sums the Klan solicited, led to the undoing of the Invisible Horde. **The Denver Express**, a small Denver tabloid, led in the fight against the Klan's so-called 100% Americanism. The **Express** blasted the Klan in a series entitled "Invisible Government". The paper was too small to succeed in its campaigns. There were threats, intimidations against the paper and business men that used it for advertising. Eventually, the **Express** was forced out of business, but during its reign it was the most important weapon against the Klan. It informed the public about the workings of the Klan and the unusual activities of "Grand Dragon" Locke. The paper accomplished its purpose as far as the Klan was concerned, but paid a high price for its admirable service.

After 1925 the Klan declined so rapidly in Denver that state headquarters were relocated in Grand

Junction for a brief period in 1927. The Western Colorado town had organized a large number of its citizens into a local chapter. The national disgrace and loss of popularity of the Klan eventually resulted in the end of its activities in the state by 1930. The twenties were beginning to reveal that new inroads in transportation and communication were starting to break down the old barriers of isolation and distance and resulted in the manifestation of more national forces and undercurrents affecting the Centennial State.

Some of the old settlers of the Centennial State made adjustments to the changing scene; the cattle industry was no exception. An earlier chapter deals with the open range cattle industry on the plains and its demise by 1900. The cattlemen simply began to look for newer and more isolated regions to continue their "free-government-hay-bonanza." Wyoming, Montana, the Dakotas and Western Colorado provided them with the open range they were seeking. Time had passed over some of the isolated pockets of the Western Slope, besides the Utes had not been relocated until 1881. Railroads did not add the other needed ingredient of this business until the Moffatt Road arrived after 1908. Towns like Steamboat Springs, Craig and DeBeque became lively cattle shipping points when they shipped the largest number of cattle in the United States during the next two or three decades. The open range cattle business had its renaissance in these places.

The story of the cattle business and all the characters involved in northwestern Colorado, respectable and otherwise, is vividly portrayed in John Rolfe Burroughs', **Where the Old West Stayed Young.** The history of Brown's Park, its cattle barons, sheepmen, and the inevitable conflict; long riders, paid killers, outlaws, rustlers and other bad men cover the gamet of the industry as it unravelled. It appears that when the cattlemen found their new promised land they were even more determined to safeguard it. This made their opponents more resolute, and the isolation provided a haven for the outlaws of the age. What results is some colorful history. Butch Cassidy was not the only bad man, moreover, many cattlemen got into the business by being skillful with a running iron. World War I provided sheepmen with the respite they needed to become established, likewise, the efforts to keep them out were no more successful in Northwestern Colorado than they had been elsewhere. Today, Moffatt County is one of the largest sheep producing counties in the West.

The serious water conflict that began when the first settlers came to Colorado remained to challenge the best legal minds for a solution. Who does the water of the rivers belong to, the state where the river originates or the states it flows through, or does it belong to the state where the river empties into the ocean? This question was a most difficult one, because all involved religiously believed in the paramountcy of their interests. In the case of the Colorado River, the dispute transcended interstate jurisdictions. Mexico has a legitimate claim on the river and, therefore, involves Colorado in this issue. The water problem in the West is a very simple one—there is not enough water to go around. At the onset of the development of the west, there was no large use of water, and irrigation did not alter the flow of rivers appreciably. Once water was diverted from one area to another, shortages or conflicts rapidly resulted, with litigation following. These court battles over water proved to be complex and not always successful in reaching settlements or agreements. The problem of how to divide the water or who it belonged to remained.

The interstate nature of water conflicts was brought to the attention of Coloradans when Kansas and other states began to sue to gain water rights on rivers that have their sources in the Centennial State. Kansas sued the State of Colorado and sixteen corporations on the Arkansas River for consuming all of the late summer flow of the river, hence, preventing Kansas from using the river's water at that time. Colorado attempted to employ the doctrine of prior appropriation that gave all people along the river the use of the water for as long as it lasted. This worked well in regions where ample water was available. The law went on to say that users could divert the flow of the stream; the first user was endowed with a permanent right.

The English common law or riparian rights law regarding water use gave ownership of water to the owner of the land it was flowing over or standing on, but the landowner could not prevent or divert the natural course of the stream. The different circumstances that occur with the runoff or distribution of water made it impossible to find any doctrine acceptable to all water users, moreover, the application of these principles for interstate use proved unworkable. Something else would have to be developed. Kansas would not accept the doctrine of prior application pushed by Colorado on the use of the Arkansas. This suit was followed by similar litigation involving Colorado with Wyoming, Nebraska, Utah, Arizona, California and New Mexico. As the issue became more heated, efforts increased to find some suitable solution. The interstate compacts emerged. The only solution that was acceptable to all states seeking water was to equally divide the water between the states along the river. This is what the compacts attempted. The seven states of the Colorado River Basin met in 1922 in Santa Fe, New Mexico with Secretary of Commerce Herbert Hoover; these states included Colorado, Nevada, Utah, California, Arizona, New Mexico, and Wyoming.

The basin was naturally divided into upper and lower basins by the Grand Canyon which ran through the middle. The Upper Basin became the area above Lee Ferry and the Lower Basin the area below the Ferry. It was estimated that the average flow of the Colorado River was 20,500,000 acre feet of water a year. Of this run-off, 7,500,000 acre feet were reserved for the use of each basin. The Upper Basin states agreed to allow 7,500,000 acre feet of water to flow past Lee Ferry annually and the Lower Basin States agreed not to use more than that amount unless the Upper Basin States were given the same opportunity. Similar compacts were negotiated with Nebraska on the South Platte, with more to follow on the North Platte, Rio Grande and others. The negotiator for Colorado at this meeting was Delph E. Carpenter, who was largely responsible for the logical settlement of these conflicts.

Continued population pressure increases the water shortage and adds to the scramble for water. The Moffatt Tunnel Diversion was soon followed by the Twin Lakes Tunnel and the Green Mountain Dam, with others already on the drawing board. Such diversion projects upset the natural balance of watersheds and deprived Western Colorado of water resources to develop the potential of the Western Slope. The surplus of population on the Colorado Piedmont compounds all the problems associated with large cities. The most desirable growth in the future in Colorado would be in the rural areas, where the increase would be an asset rather than a detriment. The last word is yet to be spoken on the cru-

cial water issue.

New sources of water are constantly being sought. Water created by conservation is frequently the most desirable and economical. Water scientists and ecologists are experimenting with various ideas to save or locate more usable water and prevent waste of this precious resource. In Colorado water waste is being prevented by lining ditches and canals with cement, using chemicals to create a film on the surface of large reservoirs to prevent evaporation and the attempt to limit loss of water to plants along streams that consume enormous amounts of water. Cattails, willows, tamarack and grass are examples of these "waterhogs." So much can be done in other areas. Salinity is another problem that results from irrigation by constantly running water through soil until it contains a damaging amount of salt. Pollution is a topic that needs special consideration. The watersheds are threatened as use of high mountain regions increases in number and penetration. Each year new ski runs are added. Do these ski areas damage the watershed or do they mechanically store water better and longer than mother nature, as claimed? The snowmobile and the backpacker have broken the soliloquy of winter in the mountains. There are very few places that wildlife and forest plants can live the winter through without being abruptly interrupted when they are most vulnerable.

Water priorities have already been set in this order: First comes domestic use, then irrigation followed by industrial consumption. Water for recreational use is given last consideration in the event of serious shortage. Hopefully, new sources of water along with improvements in water conservation, will be developed before these priorities are implemented. The water compacts did not settle the water crisis; they only postponed the deluge.

31—THE DEPRESSION AND WORLD WAR II

The Centennial State had experienced the pains of economic calamity in 1873 and 1893; therefore, when the worst depression ever began in 1929, it did not catch the state completely unaware of its morbid possibilities. The old barrier of isolation proved to be somewhat of a blessing, because it required a longer time for the depression to run its course in the Centennial State. There are those that wryly commented, "Most Coloradans never knew what prosperity was anyway, therefore, the depression was not that much of a change." The panic of 1893 was so disastrous in Colorado because of the damage it wrought on the silver industry, consequently, the state suffered in this case more than other states. In most instances citizens of the Centennial State were not hit as hard by the depression as the larger cities and metropolitan areas of the East. The plains of Colorado were not as lucky. Mother Nature dealt the "dust bowl" from the bottom of her deck and deposited several tons of good Colorado top-soil in the Gulf of Mexico, where it was of questionable service.

The agricultural nature of Colorado did not present the problem of great hordes of unemployed that plagued the larger industrial areas. The farmers whose farms were not blown away stayed on their farms and tried to make the best of the situation. Prices were so low that it did not pay to farm, but at least, the farmer ate much better than his urban fellow sufferers. Some foreclosures occurred, however, the price of real estate sagged to such a dismal low that farmers were told by their bankers to pay on the mortgage when they could and keep the farm, because the mortgage was worth more than the farm. Most of these hard-pressed ranchers hung on, gradually paying off these debts, and were grateful for being able to keep their land.

Gradually the depression began to bring its victims westward. The unemployed and the dust bowl's uprooted headed west, many bound for California, the land of "milk and honey." The migrants chugged through Colorado in their overloaded Model A's or hopped the freights. During the depression the freight trains were covered with the derelicts from the East who traveled around the country hoping to find something a little better, or simply because they took to the life of the "open road." Hobo jungles were erected near the railroad tracks in every town. "Shanty towns" sprang up along the rivers or anywhere vacant land could be found— vagrants were everywhere. A knock on the door frequently resulted in "Ma'm, can I chop some wood for something to eat," or "do you have anything I can do for a sandwich?" It was difficult to say no.

One of the solutions to the "dust bowl" was an attempt to relocate the farmers who had been forced to abandon their land. The Farm Security Administration built houses and farm buildings for former ranchers from the Eastern Slope who were relocated in the San Luis Valley, near Delta, and in the Grand Valley near Grand Junction. Meanwhile, the job of trying to undo the work of Mother Nature began. The Department of Agriculture began a program of recovery and restoration. Farm practices were re-examined to determine how the farmer had contributed to Mother Nature's devious plans. Strip farming, terracing, contour listing and summer fallowing were instituted. Crop rotation was encouraged to prevent the problem of all the land being open and plowed at the same time. New methods of working the soil to prevent it from being subject to wind erosion were started. Wind breaks, and new kinds of wheat and other crops that could withstand dryness, were tested by the government and eventually adopted.

Over-grazing was another reason for the dust bowl, consequently, the Taylor Grazing Act was passed in 1934, providing for a closer scrutiny of public lands to determine their usefulness for grazing. The division of grazing was added to the Department of Interior for the purpose of establishing and controlling grazing districts.

The New Deal was a program of experimentation, constantly probing for ideas to alleviate the economic distress. The WPA, Works Progress Administration, was one of the most successful of the programs instituted by the Federal Government. The two-fold purpose of this plan was to provide jobs and at the same time add needed public improvements such as schools, local town buildings, bridges, parks and whatever fulfilled the requirement. Several of the projects of these efforts still stand in the Centennial State. The unemployed from all occupations were included in this farsighted program. Artists painted, actors acted, musicians, teachers, white collar and blue collar workers as well, were all given work opportunities that were not otherwise available. The results were equally impressive. Historical records were accumulated and classified; Old Fort Vasquez was rebuilt near Platteville, diorama and displays were built in the State Historical Museum in Denver. Without this worthwhile program, thousands of people would have been out of work and food, also, the many worthy projects they undertook would not have been completed.

The CCC, or Civilian Conservation Corps, was another of the worthwhile and interesting results of New Deal planning. The purpose of this program was to give young men an opportunity to work in the out-of-doors away from the cities many of them came from and, at the same time, work at conservation of natural resources. Reclamation was another goal of the CCC. Several CCC camps were built in Colorado. The young men wore uniforms and lived in a semi-military environment. Part of their pay went home to their families, where it was most welcome. Most of the work of the CCC was done in the mountains, consequently, they were a welcome sight in Western Colorado. They worked in the national forests, building picnic areas and trails; they worked on irrigation projects like lining canals with concrete, or they built roads. The Rimrock Drive through the Colorado National Monument near Grand Junction was partly a CCC project. The CCC was one of the most innovative and successful of the New Deal programs and was the forerunner of the present Job Corps. Ample evidence is still present in the Centennial State of the projects that were undertaken and completed during the depression. When World War II came along the CCC was disbanded because the young men were needed for another purpose. More than 2,000,000 men served in the CCC before Congress abolished it in 1942.

The western migration of the homeless and uprooted kept a steady stream of humanity going westward on the highways or freight trains through Colorado. The small fry along the railroad tracks would count the number of traveling transits on each freight as it passed. Occassionally, the number seen from one side would be over 300 and sometime 400. The more devilish of these young spectators tried their hand at hurling tomatoes, apples or anything handy at the passing targets. The uprooted from the dust bowl came in their broken down and overloaded automobiles; most of them were headed for California. Some were not sure where they were going, only sure they had to find some other home as nothing was left for them in their former land. Their destination was sometimes determined by where their car broke down. As they moved westward they wrote friends and relatives back home to follow, then they helped one another to make in

vest. It was natural after their discouraging experience with the dust bowl that areas where irrigation water was available were more attractive to them. The whims of Mother Nature's "water cycle" they knew only too well. For these reasons and others, several of the dust bowl victims found a new home in Colorado.

The resettlement of farmers initiated by the Farm Security Administration assisted in finding new lands to farm. Some formerly abandoned farms were reclaimed and irrigation water made available to bring new lands under cultivation. Almost none of these people had any money, so they had a difficult time. Frequently they bought food from farmers by working it out. Sometimes they bought enough land to farm or build a house on by working it out over a period of years. It was not an easy time, but it was ameliorated somewhat by the fact that times were tough for the majority, so there existed a comrade spirit of togetherness; people tried to help each other when they could.

The depression was not a complete loss, for there were some mixed blessings. It resulted in a re-examination of the financial and banking structure of the country which led to the Federal Reserve Act and prevented a recurrence of the crash of 1929. The fact that the rapid industrialization of the American productive scene had its shortcomings, the depression impressively revealed. The job market could be a fickle and temporary entity. The American Dream showed it had some nightmares. A thoughtful and more mature populace gratefully said goodbye to these depression years, maybe somewhat sadder, but at least wiser.

Lessons learned in agriculture were as beneficial as those in the factories and cities. Some of the methods used by the farmers were questionable, therefore, Mother Nature in her characteristic eloquence demonstrated the folly of too much tilling and plowing. The depression forced many who had moved to the city back to the farm and also forced the farmer, with the help of the Department of Ag-

riculture, to take a new look at what he was doing. The result was marked improvement in productivity. American agriculture suffered during the depression because of overproduction, as well as other problems. The overproduction has been helped by finding new markets. Several agricultural commodities are now shipped to foreign markets. Over half of the wheat, rice and leather produced in the United States is shipped abroad. This increased productivity has been accomplished, along with a steady number of young people forsaking the farm for some other vocation; a trend of decrease in the percentage of Americans in agriculture still persists.

World War II

Going from depression to war is not the change Coloradans hoped for, however, they would agree that anything was better than the depression. As the costly war took its toll, they began to change their minds; the Centennial State changed along with them. World War II brought drastic changes to Colorado which turned the state toward new directions. World War II was a much larger and total war than World War I. It was fought in the Atlantic and the Pacific. This two-ocean war resulted in a traffic of war goods being transported from coast to coast, and not only from the eastern coast of the United States as in World War I.

At the same time, new weapons and techniques of the war threatened the cities of the country. Those large and important cities close to the east or west coast were particularly vulnerable to bombing attacks from airplanes or balloons drifting over from Japan in the jet stream. New atomic weapons that appeared during the war added to this fear. The result was that inland and isolated locations were sought for important government installations, defense or otherwise. The war offered such great challenges no one could accurately foresee the extent of the combat or destruction that might occur. The possibility of an aerial attack on Washington, D. C., was real. It might be necessary to temporarily move the capital to a safer, more isolated, centrally located place. Federal offices and strategic materials were relocated in Colorado; this began a new trend in the Centennial State. The practice of locating federal offices and employees in Colorado in large numbers continued until eventually more federal employees were located in the Centennial State than any other.

During the war Lowry Air Force Base, Buckley Field and Camp Carson were built to train men in the military and aviation. Fort Logan became an inductee center where many Coloradans left for service in the Army. Camp Hale, near Leadville, be-

came a training base for mountain troops. After the war Cooper Hill, used to train these mountain and ski troops, became a recreation area. Petersen Field was added near Colorado Springs, La Junta Army Air Field, along with its 521,000-acre bombing range, trained air force bomber pilots. Camp Carson was the largest military base in Colorado.

The industrial efforts to produce war goods increased manufacturing in the Rocky Mountain area. The isolation appealed to critical industries, consequently, many defense plants began to produce war goods in the shadow of the Rockies. The enclave nature of Colorado also began to become a blessing. Now, with new methods of transportation, Colorado was located on the main routes and accessible to both coasts. This has been one of the factors prompting industries to locate in the Centennial State more recently. This accessibility to markets and raw materials is responsible for manufacturing now surpassing agriculture as Colorado's top industry.

During World War II several prisoner of war camps were located in Colorado; also, the Japanese or Nisei were uprooted from their homes, mostly in California, to be relocated in safer places. The term "Issei" refers to those Japanese born in Japan but residing in the United States. People born in the United States of the Issei were called Nisei by their people. When World War II began it was not considered safe to leave these Issei and Nisei in the western states of California, Washington or Oregon where they had settled. Because of the Alien Act of 1913, the Issei were not allowed to attain citizenship. In 1921 the State of California, where most of the Japanese-Americans were located, took action to prevent land ownership. General John DeWitt, commander of the Western Defense Area, ordered the evacuation of all people with Japanese ancestry. This order applied to 110,000 of the 126,000 Japanese in the United States, two-thirds of whom were Nisei or American Citizens. Some place away from the coasts was needed to relocate these unfortunate people; the evacuation was carried out by the United States Army. Governor Ralph Carr of Colorado was one of the governors compassionate and broadminded enough to allow entry into his state.

The Nisei were forced to abandon most of their possessions at a considerable loss and move to the camps set up for them. One of these camps was located in Colorado near Granada; the camp was called Amachi, after an Indian chief killed at Sand Creek. The 8,500 residents worked in agriculture wherever the could. The camp offered meager housing and sanitation facilities, but in their characteristic way the Nisei organized a government, maintained order

nd made the camp as livable as possible. The os-
racism faced by these people did not include exclu-
ion from the draft, consequently, many of them
erved. The 442nd Regimental Combat Team, the
amous Go-For-Broke all-Nisei regiment, was one
of the most decorated outfits in the European The-
tre. The Nisei camps ended along with the war in
945, an example of misguided caution and short-
ightedness that will not soon be forgotten by the
Jise; however, they recovered rapidly and have
ecently placed an award in the State Capitol, com-
nemorating the kindness and compassion of Gov-
rnor Ralph Carr.

In less than five years after World War II some
f Colorado's young men were called to arms again
o engage in the Korean conflict. A good number
f those selected had served in World War II. The
ontinued threat of war preserved the importance
f Colorado as an important defense location. In
957 the North American Air Defense Command
vas located under Cheyenne Mountain near Colorado
Springs; soon to follow was the Air Force Academy.
The choice of the Colorado Springs area for this
restigious—maybe most prestigious of all—mili-

tary base was a real "feather in the cap" for Colorado.

The atomic age arrived during World War II
and soon after the search for uranium led to a new
mining boom in Colorado, this time in Western
Colorado, mostly on the Uncompahgre Plateau. The
boom brought many eager prospectors to Western
Colorado and Eastern Utah. This time the prospectors were somewhat different than the previous argonauts who wandered the mountains alone but for
a burro. The uranium prospector generally had a
geiger counter as his most important tool, along
with his gear. Some of the more prosperous looked
for uranium with a geiger counter from a helicopter
or airplane. Many fortunes were made and many
were lost and, like all mining rushes, most people
that participated lost money Nevertheless, it
brought new prosperity and a more swinging life
style to Western Colorado. Most of the participants
in the rush were from other locales and, like the
participants of previous rushes, were the more restless and carefree. The Grand Junction area had
never really experienced a mining rush this close
before, so it was a new and exciting time. The excitement was a most welcome change.

32—LOOKING AHEAD

Colorado can now look back on its first hundred years. One hundred years that started with gold and silver as the glittering attraction responsible for luring thousands from their hum-drum life. After the lustre rubbed off, agriculture provided a more reliable, if not as colorful, livelihood. The railroads crossed the continent to resolve the problem of transportation to a promising, but isolated region. Manufacturing and tourism have assumed the place of mining when it began to lag after 1920. If the first hundred years are any indication as to what is yet to come, it would appear that change would be something to expect for the future. The direction taken by this change is not inevitable. Expansion and growth are to be expected. Hopefully, this growth can be directed to areas that would profit most by expansion. The distortion of Colorado's growth rate is evident when it is noted that almost 60% of the population of the Centennial State is located in the Denver metropolitan area

One of the fastest growing industries in the Centennial State is tourism or outdoor recreation. This significant industry attracted 8,000,000 visitors last year and turned $630,000,000 in income for dif-

ferent concerns. In many Western Colorado communities tourism is the number one industry. The thirty ski areas attract 5,000,000 people annually and the number is increasing rapidly. In the last five years it has increased four-fold. Ghost towns and mining camps attract a host of visitors to the mountains in the summer to view the relics of the past, so they can use their imagination to recreate the remainder of the picture. In the setting of most old ghost towns or mining camps this reconstruction is not difficult. With eight national parks and monuments, plus numerous national forests covering over 13,700,000 acres, there is ample opportunity to back pack or travel by horseback. Lakes and large reservoirs are convenient to boaters, fishermen or water skiers. In addition, 400,000 hunters—one quarter out-of-state—flock to the hills each fall to hunt.

One of the most useful considerations for the purpose of planning is population statistics. When Colorado became a territory in 1861 the population totalled about 30,000, while by 1876 when statehood occurred the number had grown to 100,000. At the turn of the century the Centennial State could count

500,000 in its census, and by 1960 the number had appreciated to 1,753,900. Just ten years later, in 1970 population growth showed almost a half million increase when it reached 2,209,500. The projected population figure for 1980 is 2,905,000, almost 3,-000,000. In most instances this growth is not alarming; however, one of the more sobering concerns is the growth of the Denver metropolitan area. It is growing at a much faster rate than the rest of the state. In 1960 the Denver area accounted for 53.5% of the population of Colorado; in 1970 the figure rose to 56.4% and projections have it at 58.2% in 1980. The realization that this percentage is increasing, while the population of the rest of the state is also increasing, reveals the more critical nature of the growth in the Denver metropolitan region. With almost 60% of the populace of the state at a continued present rate of growth, the state could be blessed with a "Los Angeles of Colorado" from one end of the Colorado Piedmont to the other by the turn of the millenium.

Colorado's population grew at a rate of about double the national average during the decade of the sixties. The seventies showed promises of bettering the record of the previous decade. Population density figures are of little use and reveal the same limitations as temperature averages. The density of Colorado's population remains 40% below the national average. With a median age 26.2 years, the Centennial State has one of the more youthful populations in the United States. Even if projected growth rates of 40 to 60% materialize, it would cause no serious problem in Colorado. However, if a rate of a more astronomical nature should suddenly appear in the more crowded areas, it would pose grave problems for planners.

Added to mining, agriculture, manufacturing and outdoor recreation as a new occupational opportunity in Colorado, is the increasing number of government workers. The South Platte Valley, which is mostly agricultural, shows 14.5% of its people in government work; the Northern Front Range has 22.9%; the Pikes Peak area 21.1%; Spanish Peaks area 22.5%; and the Denver Metro region a surprisingly low 15.8%. The state average is close to 20% for government-oriented occupations. The regions that have the largest percentage employed in agriculture are the South Platte Valley with 28.3%, the High Plains with 36.7%, the lower Arkansas Valley with 20.8%, and the Black Canyon region with 17.8%. The only region that shows any sizable mining activity in its employed is the upper Arkansas Valley with 14.9%. This is a far cry from the 1870s and 1880s. The Black Canyon region only

employs 7.3% in mining. If Lake County was separated from the Upper Arkansas region and Oura County from the Black Canyon group, the percentage would increase, but the fact would still remain that mining is not what it once was in the Centennial State. The state ranks ninth in mining in the nation.

With a work force of about 7,00,000 the Denver Metro Area surpasses the labor force of all the other regions of Colorado combined. It has 14.5% engaged in manufacturing, 21.8% in a trade, 16.3% in services and 15.8% in government work. There is smattering involved in other pursuits on a small scale, but none of these categories exceed 7%.

It is interesting to note that of the three industries, manufacturing, agriculture and mining, it manufacturing that is growing the most rapidly. Today manufacturing is the major employer in the Centennial State. Historically, mining paced the Colorado economy during the late 19th century, however, agriculture rose to dominate the economy by the turn of the milleniem. In the mining days the largest manufacturing concerns in the state were CF&I Steel Corporation, Gates Rubber and the Samsonite Corporation. The shift to central locations prompted by World War II brought such industries as Dow Chemical, Martin Marietta and Shell Chemical Company to the Centennial State and started the trend toward manufacturing. Consequently, in 1951 the number employed in manufacturing finally surpassed employment in agriculture. More manufacturers were lured by the opportunities of a central location when Ampex, Hewlett-Packard, Honeywell, IBM, and Eastman Kodak followed. Today, manufacturing accounts for twice as many job opportunities as mining and agriculture combined. In the state's non-metropolitan areas, food processing is the largest manufacturing employer, along with the manufacture of farm implements. The growth rate of manufacturing in Colorado is ahead of the national growth rate.

The centralized location of Colorado's population adds to the attractiveness of the state in considerations of possible plant sites. Availability of labor because of the concentration of the population is an inducement for industry to locate on the Colorado Piedmont. Also, the median number of years of education is higher for Coloradans than the national average. Coloradans have completed 12. years, while the national average is 12.2. With 75% of the labor force centered in the Colorado Piedmont availability is improved. This core of population is surrounded by the next largest population areas which add another 150,000 and are not too far away

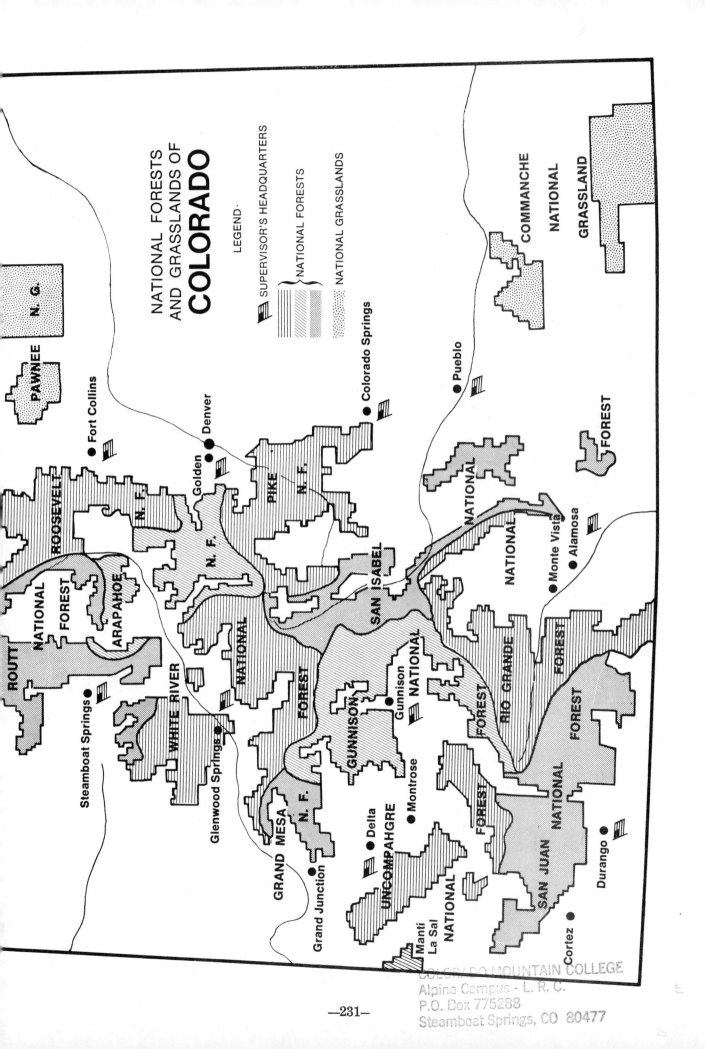

NATIONAL FORESTS
AND GRASSLANDS OF
COLORADO

LEGEND:

SUPERVISOR'S HEADQUARTERS

NATIONAL FORESTS

NATIONAL GRASSLANDS

PAWNEE N. G.

● Fort Collins

● Denver

Golden

● Colorado Springs

● Pueblo

COMMANCHE NATIONAL GRASSLAND

ROUTT NATIONAL FOREST

ARAPAHOE

WHITE RIVER N. F.

PIKE N. F.

N. F.

SAN ISABEL

NATIONAL FOREST

● Steamboat Springs

Glenwood Springs ●

GRAND MESA N. F.

GUNNISON NATIONAL FOREST

Gunnison ●

UNCOMPAHGRE NATIONAL FOREST

● Delta

● Montrose

Grand Junction ●

Manti La Sal NATIONAL FOREST

SAN JUAN NATIONAL FOREST

● Cortez

Durango ●

RIO GRANDE NATIONAL FOREST

● Monte Vista

Alamosa ●

COLORADO MOUNTAIN COLLEGE
Alpine Campus - L. R. C.
P.O. Box 775288
Steamboat Springs, CO 80477

DISTRIBUTION OF COLORADO POPULATION BY ECONOMIC REGIONS, 1960 to 1980

Region	1960	% of Colo.	1970	% of Colo.	1975	% of Colo.	1980	% of Colo.
1 South Platte Valley	65,700	3.7	60,600	2.8	62,200	2.5	67,100	2.3
2 Northern Front Range	125,700	7.2	179,200	8.1	219,800	8.7	242,700	8.4
3 Denver Metropolitan	937,700	53.5	1,244,300	56.4	1,425,700	56.4	1,691,000	58.2
4 Pikes Peak	148,100	8.4	241,500	10.9	298,500	11.8	334,900	11.5
5 High Plains	18,800	1.1	18,700	0.8	19,700	0.8	20,200	0.7
6 Lower Arkansas Valley	57,600	3.3	54,100	2.4	55,100	2.2	61,000	2.1
7 Spanish Peaks	146,600	8.4	140,600	6.4	148,500	5.9	154,300	5.3
8 San Luis Valley	38,700	2.2	37,500	1.7	38,300	1.5	41,100	1.4
9 San Juan Basin	38,900	2.2	37,400	1.7	40,400	1.6	43,400	1.5
10 Black Canyon	44,100	2.5	44,900	2.0	47,600	1.9	51,900	1.8
11 Plateau	74,900	4.3	80,600	3.6	86,700	3.4	99,100	3.4
12 Northern Mountain	20,300	1.1	28,900	1.3	40,100	1.6	52,300	1.8
13. Upper Arkansas Valley	36,900	2.1	41,500	1.9	45,500	1.8	46,300	1.6
STATE TOTAL	1,753,900	100.0	2,209,500	100.0	2,528,000	100.0	2,905,000	100.0

SOURCES: 1960 Census of the Population
1970 Census of the Population
1974 Division of Planning Estimates for 1975 and 1980, adjusted.

NOTE: Regions may not sum to state total due to rounding.

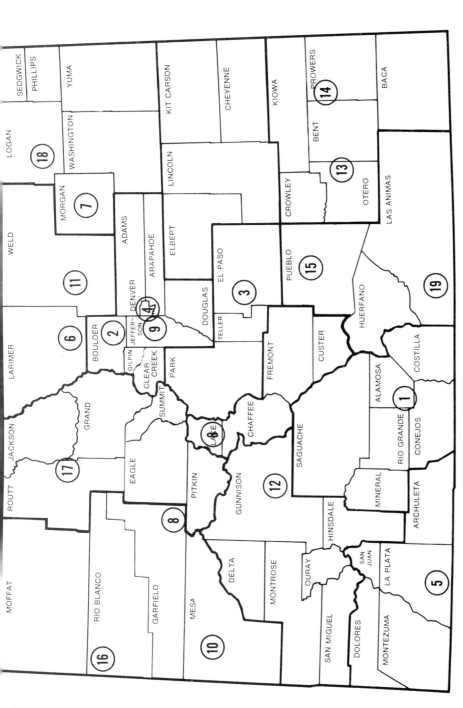

1. Alamosa – ADAMS STATE COLLEGE
2. Boulder – UNIVERSITY OF COLORADO
3. Colorado Springs Area – THE COLORADO COLLEGE
   EL PASO COMMUNITY COLLEGE
   U. S. AIR FORCE ACADEMY
   UNIVERSITY OF COLORADO
4. Denver Area – ARAPAHOE COMMUNITY COLLEGE
   COMMUNITY COLLEGE OF DENVER
   LORETTO HEIGHTS COLLEGE
   METROPOLITAN STATE COLLEGE
   REGIS COLLEGE
   COLORADO WOMEN'S COLLEGE
   UNIVERSITY OF COLORADO
   UNIVERSITY OF DENVER
5. Durango – FORT LEWIS COLLEGE
6. Fort Collins – COLORADO STATE UNIVERSITY

7. Fort Morgan – MORGAN COMMUNITY COLLEGE
8. Glenwood Springs & Leadville – COLORADO
   MOUNTAIN COLLEGE
9. Golden – COLORADO SCHOOL OF MINES
10. Grand Junction – MESA COLLEGE
11. Greeley – AIMS COLLEGE
    UNIVERSITY OF NORTHERN COLORADO
12. Gunnison – WESTERN STATE COLLEGE
13. La Junta – OTERO JUNIOR COLLEGE
14. Lamar – LAMAR COMMUNITY COLLEGE
15. Pueblo – SOUTHERN COLORADO STATE COLLEGE
16. Rangely – COLORADO NORTHWESTERN
    COMMUNITY COLLEGE
17. Steamboat Springs – COLORADO ALPINE COLLEGE
18. Sterling – NORTHEASTERN JUNIOR COLLEGE
19. Trinidad – TRINIDAD STATE JUNIOR COLLEGE

Economic Regions in Colorado

Economic Regions in Colorado

County	City
SEDGWICK	Julesburg
PHILLIPS	Holyoke
YUMA	Yuma, Wray
LOGAN	Sterling
WASHINGTON	Akron
MORGAN	Brush, Ft. Morgan
KIT CARSON	Burlington
CHEYENNE	Cheyenne Wells
KIOWA	Eads
PROWERS	Lamar
BACA	Springfield
BENT	Las Animas
LINCOLN	Limon, Hugo
CROWLEY	Ordway
OTERO	Rocky Ford, La Junta
WELD	Greeley
ADAMS	Brighton
DENVER	
ARAPAHOE	Littleton
ELBERT	Kiowa
EL PASO	Colorado Springs
PUEBLO	Pueblo
LAS ANIMAS	Trinidad
LARIMER	Ft. Collins
BOULDER	Boulder
JEFFERSON	Golden
GILPIN	Central City
CLEAR CREEK	Georgetown
DOUGLAS	Castle Rock
TELLER	Cripple Creek
FREMONT	Canon City, Florence
CUSTER	Westcliffe
HUERFANO	Walsenburg
COSTILLA	San Luis
JACKSON	Walden
GRAND	Hot Sulphur Springs
SUMMIT	Breckenridge
PARK	Fairplay
LAKE	Leadville
CHAFFEE	Buena Vista, Salida
SAGUACHE	Saguache
ALAMOSA	Alamosa
RIO GRANDE	Del Norte, Monte Vista
CONEJOS	Conejos
ROUTT	Steamboat Springs
EAGLE	Eagle
PITKIN	Aspen
GUNNISON	Gunnison
MINERAL	Creede
ARCHULETA	Pagosa Springs
MOFFAT	Craig
RIO BLANCO	Meeker, Rangely
GARFIELD	Glenwood Springs, Rifle
MESA	Grand Junction, Fruita
DELTA	Delta
MONTROSE	Montrose
OURAY	Ouray
HINSDALE	Lake City
SAN JUAN	Silverton
SAN MIGUEL	Telluride
DOLORES	Dove Creek
MONTEZUMA	Cortez
LA PLATA	Durango

CITIES WITH A POPULATION OF 10,000 – 50,000

Region	City	Population (1970)	Region	City	Population (1970)
2	Fort Collins	43,337	2	Loveland	16,220
2	Greeley	38,902	13	Canon City/East Canon	11,011
11	Grand Junction	20,170	1	Sterling	10,636
			9	Durango	10,333

CITIES AND COMMUNITIES WITH A POPULATION OF 5,000 – 10,000

Region	City	Population	Region	City	Population
8	Alamosa	6,985	6	La Junta	7,983
9	Cortez	6,032	6	Lamar	7,797
1	Fort Morgan	7,594	10	Montrose	6,496
			7	Trinidad	9,901

CITIES AND COMMUNITIES WITH A POPULATION OF 1,000 – 5,000

Region	City	Pop.	Region	City	Pop.	Region	City	Pop.
NORTHEASTERN COLORADO			**SOUTHERN COLORADO**			**COLORADO WEST**		
1	Akron	1,775	8	Antonito	1,113	12	Aspen	2,437
2	Berthoud	1,446	13	Buena Vista	1,962	10	Austin	1,163
1	Brush	3,377	8	Center	1,470	11	Craig	4,205
5	Burlington	2,828	8	Del Norte	1,569	10	Delta	3,694
2	Eaton	1,389	13	Florence	2,846	11	Fruita	1,822
2	Erie	1,090	6	Fowler	1,242	11	Glenwood Springs	4,106
2	Estes Park	1,616	6	Las Animas	3,148	10	Gunnison	4,613
2	Evans	2,570	13	Leadville	4,314	11	Meeker	1,597
2	Fort Lupton	2,489	8	Monte Vista	3,909	9	Pagosa Springs	1,360
1	Holyoke	1,640	6	Ordway	1,017	10	Paonia	1,161
2	Johnstown	1,191	6	Rocky Ford	4,859	11	Rangely	1,591
1	Julesburg	1,578	13	Salida	4,355	11	Rifle	2,150
2	La Salle	1,227	6	Springfield	1,660	12	Steamboat Springs	2,340
5	Limon	1,814	7	Walsenburg	4,329			
2	Windsor	1,564				**DENVER-COLORADO SPRINGS METROPOLITAN AREA**		
1	Wray	1,953				3	Castle Rock	1,531
1	Yuma	2,259				3	Idaho Springs	2,003
						4	Woodland Park	1,022

SOURCE: 1970 Census of the Population

NOTE: Many communities have grown substantially since 1970; up-to-date population estimates are available on request from the Division of Commerce and Development.

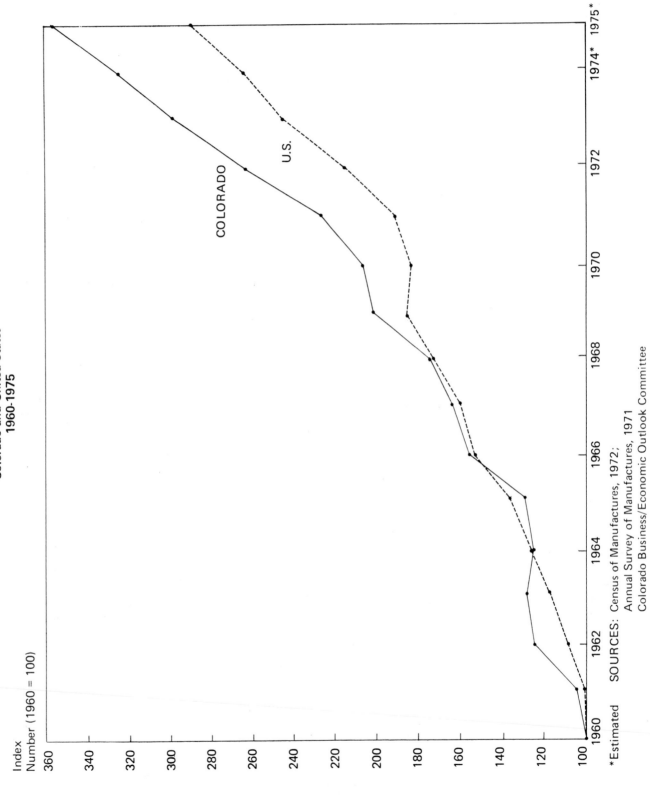

VALUE ADDED BY MANUFACTURING
Colorado and United States
1960-1975

Index
Number (1960 = 100)

360
340
320
300
280
260
240
220
200
180
160
140
120
100

COLORADO

U.S.

1960 1962 1964 1966 1968 1970 1972 1974* 1975*

*Estimated   SOURCES: Census of Manufactures, 1972;
Annual Survey of Manufactures, 1971
Colorado Business/Economic Outlook Committee

ANNUAL AVERAGE EMPLOYMENT BY INDUSTRY GROUP IN COLORADO
1950, 1960, 1965, 1970, and 1975

Percent of Total Labor Force 1950	Percent of Total Labor Force 1975	Industry Group	Employment 1950	1960	1965	1970	1975*	Percent Change (1970-1975)
17.8	20.9	Wholesale and Retail Trade	92,300	123,600	140,300	173,400	232,300	34.0
12.9	18.6	Government	66,800	110,100	136,400	174,700	206,000	17.9
9.3	16.1	Services	48,300	76,200	101,000	130,500	178,700	36.9
11.9	12.5	Manufacturing	61,600	87,700	90,000	117,500	138,800	18.1
8.2	5.2	Transportation, Communication, and Public Utilities	42,400	43,700	44,600	51,300	58,100	13.3
4.3	6.0	Contract Construction	22,100	33,500	37,000	41,100	66,500	61.8
13.4	4.5	Agriculture	69,300	58,600	45,500	51,400	50,000	-2.7
2.8	4.3	Finance, Insurance & Real Estate	14,700	25,200	31,100	39,600	48,100	21.5
1.9	1.5	Mining	10,000	15,400	12,400	14,000	16,900	20.7
13.6	**7.9	Proprietors, Self-Employed & Other	70,300	89,200	90,600	91,600	87,500	-4.5
96.3	95.8	TOTAL EMPLOYMENT	497,800	663,200	728,900	887,800	1,062,900	19.7
3.7	4.2	Unemployed & Labor Disputants	19,300	25,600	26,800	31,000	47,000	51.6
100.0	100.0	TOTAL LABOR FORCE	517,100	688,800	755,700	918,800	1,109,900	20.8

SOURCE: Colorado Division of Employment
Colorado Business/Economic Outlook Committee

*Estimated **1975 Labor Force, Total Employment, Unemployed, and Proprietors categories computed by place of residence; others by place of work. 1975 place-of-work employment for Proprietors, Self-Employed, & Other was about 67,600 (6.1% of labor force)

NOTE: Data for 1970 not directly comparable to 1970 Census of the Population data

More specifically, the Denver-Boulder area has 1,457,000, Colorado Springs 315,000, Pueblo 130,000, Fort Collins 120,000 and the Greeley area numbers 113,000.

The largest minority group included in the population of the Centennial State is the Spanish surnamed which totals about 14%. The non-white group is listed at about 4%. About 78.5% of Colorado's people live in cities and are classified as urban, which accounts for a ranking of 13th in percentage of urban population in the United States. Colorado has five cities with a population in excess of 100,000 and seventeen cities with populations totalling 20,000.

Despite the decline in position of importance as a Colorado industry, agriculture remains a vital part of the economy of the Centennial State. On the state level only about 5% of the working force is engaged in agricultural productivity; however, in some of the farming regions as many as 35% work in agriculture. The decline in agriculture has levelled off some in the last few years, but this good sign is eliminated by the steady decline in the number of farms because of urban sprawl. Agriculture also employs a considerable number of residents in related activities such as sugar beet processing, meat packing and fruit and vegetable canning.

Over three-quarters of the $2.2 billion of agriculture's cash market comes from livestock sales. In 1973 about 2.85 million head of cattle and calves were marketed. Two-thirds of these cattle came from the plains of Eastern Colorado. Colorado also had the largest number of sheep on feed in the nation in 1973 and ranked third in sheep producing states. Texas ranked first and Wyoming second. Total receipts from sheep and wool in 1973 reached $70,000,000. While most of the cattle of the Centennial State are located in the eastern part of the state, the 684,000 sheep are largely located in Western Colorado.

Wheat is Colorado's largest crop, requiring 42% of the state's crop land for its production and yielding over $223,000,000. Corn ranks second and in 1973 the crop was valued at $184,000,000. The charts included with this chapter and provided with the courtesy of State of Colorado Division of Commerce and Development and the State of Colorado Division of Planning, show other industries and their productivity.

Colorado ranks seventh among states in the amount of forested land, with 22,583,000 acres of timber, about one-third of the state's total land area. Of this acreage, 12,275,000 acres is classified as commercial forest land. As yet, Colorado's lumber industry is underdeveloped. Englemen spruce ranks first in lumber production and is followed by the true firs, lodgepole pine, Douglas fir and ponderosa pine. Lumber is one of the resources of Colorado that remains underdeveloped and offers new opportunities.

Water is a resource that directly corresponds to the development of the potential of the Centennial State. To supply the nearly 3,000,000 people, irrigate the land, and supply the needs of industry are severe challenges to this vital resource. In an average year nearly 16,000,000 acre feet originate in Colorado. The inbalance of drainage and population leads to controversy. The majority of this water—about 69%—drains into the Pacific through the Colorado River drainage system. At the same time about 90% of Colorado's people live east of the Continental Divide. The problem is compounded by the existence of interstate water compacts, previously mentioned, that deliver about half of this water to downstream states.

Ground water is another important source of water in the state and adds the advantage of making it difficult to divert to other areas. The shallow aquifiers of Eastern Colorado are particularly productive, where the San Luis Valley draws large amounts of water from the ground for irrigation and domestic use. In most cases ground water is higher in mineral content than surface water and is less contaminated. Both ground and surface waters tend to increase in the level of dissolved solids as the distance from the mountains increases, as a result of irrigation return, and as it flows through natural soluble rock strata. Waters of the Centennial State are administered by the Colorado Division of Water Resources and the Colorado Ground Water Commission.

After being below the value of the state's metallic minerals from 1964 to 1972, increased prices in the non-metallic minerals have altered this circumstance. Leading the way in this change are coal, oil and natural gas. The value of Colorado's oil and gas has tripled and the value of coal increased by two-thirds from 1971 to 1973. Mineral fuel production now exceeds the value of the state's metallic mineral output by 20%. This seems to be a trend that will continue in an upward direction.

Almost one-fourth of Colorado is underlaid by coal deposits and major deposits exist in eight different fields. With an estimated 81 billion tons, Colorado ranks fourth in the nation in proven bituminous and sub-bituminous coal reserves. Total resources are estimated, conservatively, to be about 230 billion tons which go to depths of 6,000 feet

MAJOR COLORADO CROPS BY REGION, 1973
(percent of state total)

1973 Agricultural Employment (% of regional work force)	Region	Wheat	Corn	Hay*	Potatoes*	Dry Beans	Sugar Beets	Sorghum	Barley	Commercial Vegetables**	Fruits**	Total value of crop production
28.3%	1. South Platte Valley	35.9%	34.6%	12.8%	6.3%	25.4%	33.3%	9.9%	7.6%		----	25.7%
11.4	2. North Front Range	7.4	30.8	14.3	8.8	27.6	36.0	0.2	19.4	} 30%		17.2
1.4	3. Denver Metro	9.3	2.9	4.8	----	1.6	2.0	0.2	7.2			5.4
1.6	4. Pikes Peak	0.2	0.2	1.5	----	0.4	----	0.1	0.4			0.4
36.7	5. High Plains	21.0	11.8	5.8	----	2.1	17.0	5.3	1.8			11.5
20.8	6. Lower Arkansas Valley	20.2	13.8	16.3	----	2.9	2.2	81.9	6.8	} 17		16.4
3.6	7. Spanish Peaks	0.7	1.7	2.5	----	2.6	0.2	2.2	0.5			1.6
21.3	8. San Luis Valley	0.4	0.3	9.3	83.1	----	----	----	38.4	33		8.6
10.4	9. San Juan Basin	1.3	0.3	4.3	----	30.3	----	0.1	1.5			2.9
17.8	10. Black Canyon	0.6	2.2	7.5	----	6.8	3.7	0.1	11.4	8	55%	4.2
9.8	11. Plateau	1.8	1.4	9.2	----	0.1	3.3	0.1	3.4		30	3.4
6.7	12. Northern Mountain	1.2	0.1	9.2	----	----	----	----	1.7			2.2
4.8	13. Upper Arkansas Valley	0.1	0.1	2.1	----	----	----	----	0.1		5	0.5
4.9%	STATE TOTAL	100%	100%	100%	100%	100%	100%	100%	100%	100%	100%	100%
	VALUE ($ mil)	$223.4	$183.6	$137.0	$34.0	$33.9	$33.9	$30.4	$26.0	$29.4	$11.7	$741.3

*Regional allocations based on 1972 data.
**Regional allocations estimated by Colorado Crop & Livestock Reporting Service
SOURCE: Colorado Division of Employment; Colorado Agricultural Statistics, 1974 and
Colorado Crop & Livestock Reporting Service.

COLORADO LIVESTOCK BY REGION (January 1, 1974) (% of state)

REGION	CATTLE & CALVES ON FARMS*	CATTLE ON FEED	DAIRY COWS & HEIFERS*	STOCK SHEEP ON FARMS*	HOGS & PIGS ON FARMS*
1. South Platte Valley	21%	34%	13%	3%	32%
2. Northern Front Range	23	42	38	4	16
3. Denver Metro	4	7	14	2	13
4. Pikes Peak	2	---	4	1	2
5. High Plains	10	4	4	1	6
6. Lower Arkansas Valley	13	15	3	2	12
7. Spanish Peaks	5	1	5	1	2
8. San Luis Valley	4	---	2	14	7
9. San Juan Basin	3	---	3	7	1
10. Black Canyon	4	---	5	19	3
11. Plateau	6	---	5	34	3
12. Northern Mountain	4	---	1	13	---
13. Upper Arkansas Valley	1	---	4	1	1
STATE (head)	3,744,000	930,000	75,000	640,000	290,000
Cash Receipts, 1973 ($mil)	$1,364.9		$65.4	$70.2**	$48.4

*Regional allocation based on January 1, 1973 livestock inventory.
**Cash receipts from all sheep, lambs, and wool marketed.
SOURCE: Colorado Agricultural Statistics, 1974.

COLORADO STATE OUTFLOWS AND TRANSMOUNTAIN DIVERSIONS

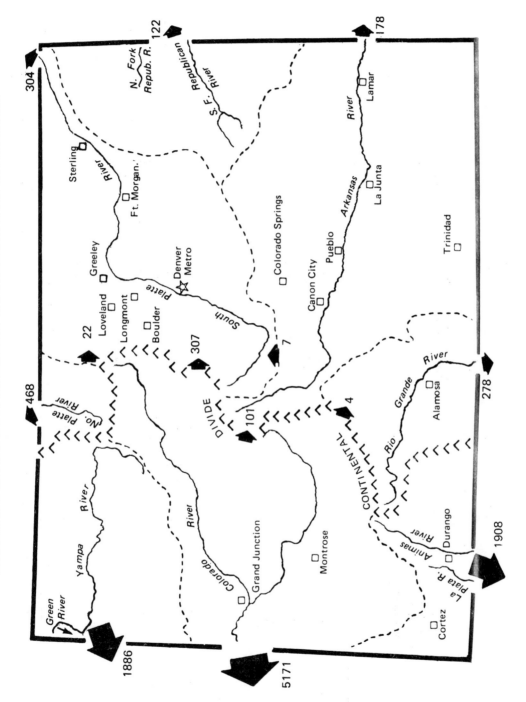

SOURCE: Water for Tomorrow: Colorado State Water Plan, Phase I, Colorado Water Conservation Board and U.S. Bureau of Reclamation, 1974.

-241-

MAJOR MINERAL INDUSTRY PRODUCTION IN COLORADO, 1973 ($ Mil., % of State Total)

REGION	1970 Mining Employment (% of Regional Employment)	Molybdenum	Zinc	Silver	Lead	Uranium	Tungsten	Gold	Vanadium	Copper	Iron	Tin	Cadmium	Total Metallic Minerals
1. South Platte Valley	1.9													
2. Northern Front Range	0.4													
3. Denver Metro	1.2	$9.178 (9.5%)				$4.444 (59.2%)		$ .058 (0.8%)						$13.680 (8.6%)
4. Pikes Peak	0.3							.052 (0.8)						.052 (0.03)
5. High Plains	0.9													
6. Lower Arkansas Valley	0.8													
7. Spanish Peaks	1.3													
8. San Luis Valley	2.6			$4.647 (53.0%)	$ .500 (6.6%)			.052 (0.8)						5.199 (3.3)
9. San Juan Basin	5.0		$2.955 (18.6%)	1.015 (11.6)	1.560 (20.5)			3.595 (58.2)		$ .714 (21.6%)			$ .165 (41.7%)	7.345 (4.6)
10. Black Canyon	8.9		5.742 (36.1)	1.297 (14.8)	3.985 (52.5)	2.667 (35.5)		1.718 (27.8)	$4.438 (91.0%)	2.553 (77.1)			.088 (22.2)	22.488 (14.1)
11. Plateau	4.2					.398 (5.3)			.437 (9.0)					0.835 (0.5)
12. Northern Mountain	6.9		3.902 (24.6)	.276 (3.1)	.397 (5.2)			.029 (0.5)		.022 (0.7)	$ .949 (89.6%)			5.575 (3.5)
13. Upper Arkansas Valley	15.6	87.476 (90.5)	3.291 (20.7)	1.529 (17.4)	1.153 (15.2)		$6.931 (100%)	.665 (10.8)				$ .490 (100%)	.144 (36.4)	101.679 (63.7)
STATE TOTAL	1.7	$96.654	$15.890	$8.765	$7.596	$7.509	$6.931	$6.178	$4.875	$3.313	$1.059	$.490	$.396	$159.656

SOURCE: 1970 Census of Population; Colorado Division of Mines

Coal Regions in Colorado

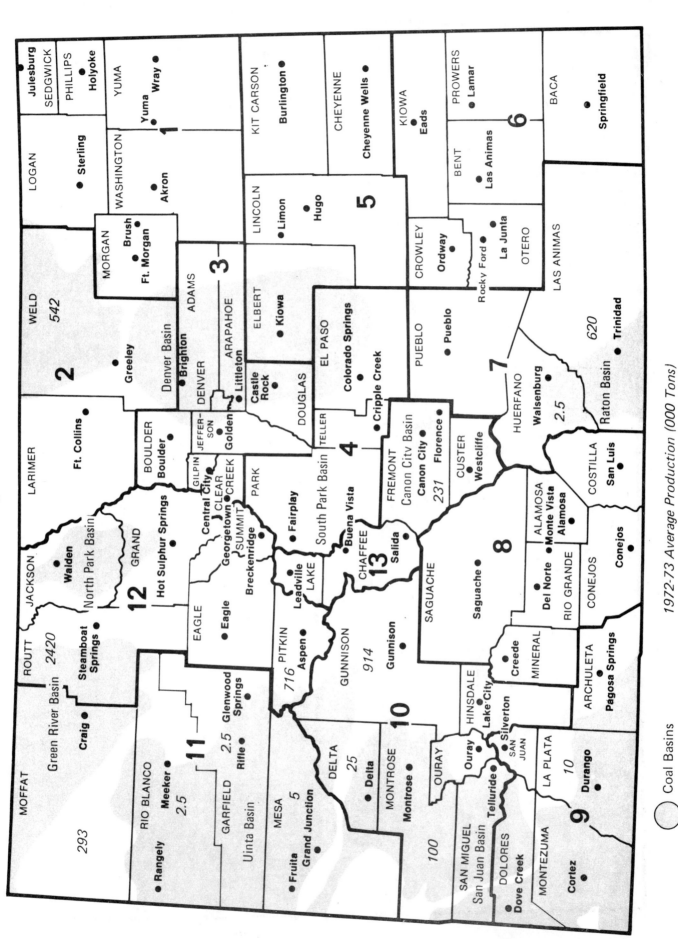

1972-73 Average Production (000 Tons)

Coal Basins

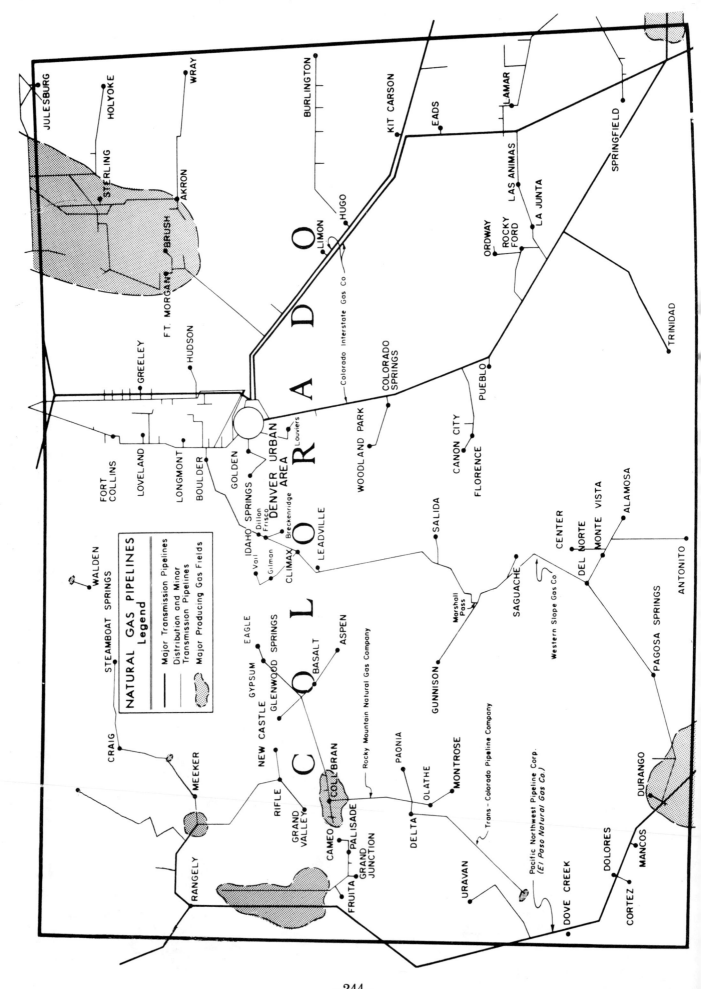

NATURAL GAS PIPELINES

Legend

— Major Transmission Pipelines
— Distribution and Minor Transmission Pipelines
▨ Major Producing Gas Fields

COLORADO

JULESBURG
HOLYOKE
STERLING
WRAY
AKRON
BRUSH
FT. MORGAN
HUDSON
GREELEY
FT. COLLINS
LOVELAND
LONGMONT
BOULDER
GOLDEN
DENVER URBAN AREA
Louviers
IDAHO SPRINGS
Dillon
Frisco
Breckenridge
Vail
Gilman
CLIMAX
LEADVILLE

BURLINGTON
LIMON
HUGO
Colorado Interstate Gas Co
KIT CARSON
EADS
LAMAR
LAS ANIMAS
LA JUNTA
ROCKY FORD
ORDWAY
SPRINGFIELD
TRINIDAD
COLORADO SPRINGS
WOODLAND PARK
CANON CITY
FLORENCE
PUEBLO
SALIDA
Marshall Pass
Western Slope Gas Co
SAGUACHE
CENTER
MONTE VISTA
DEL NORTE
ALAMOSA
ANTONITO
PAGOSA SPRINGS

WALDEN
STEAMBOAT SPRINGS
CRAIG
MEEKER
RANGELY
NEW CASTLE
GYPSUM
EAGLE
GLENWOOD SPRINGS
BASALT
ASPEN
RIFLE
GRAND VALLEY
CAMEO
COLLBRAN
PALISADE
GRAND JUNCTION
FRUITA
Rocky Mountain Natural Gas Company
PAONIA
OLATHE
DELTA
MONTROSE
GUNNISON
URAVAN
Trans-Colorado Pipeline Company
Pacific Northwest Pipeline Corp. (El Paso Natural Gas Co.)
DOVE CREEK
DOLORES
MANCOS
CORTEZ
DURANGO

Scheduled Air Travel Times from Colorado to Selected Cities

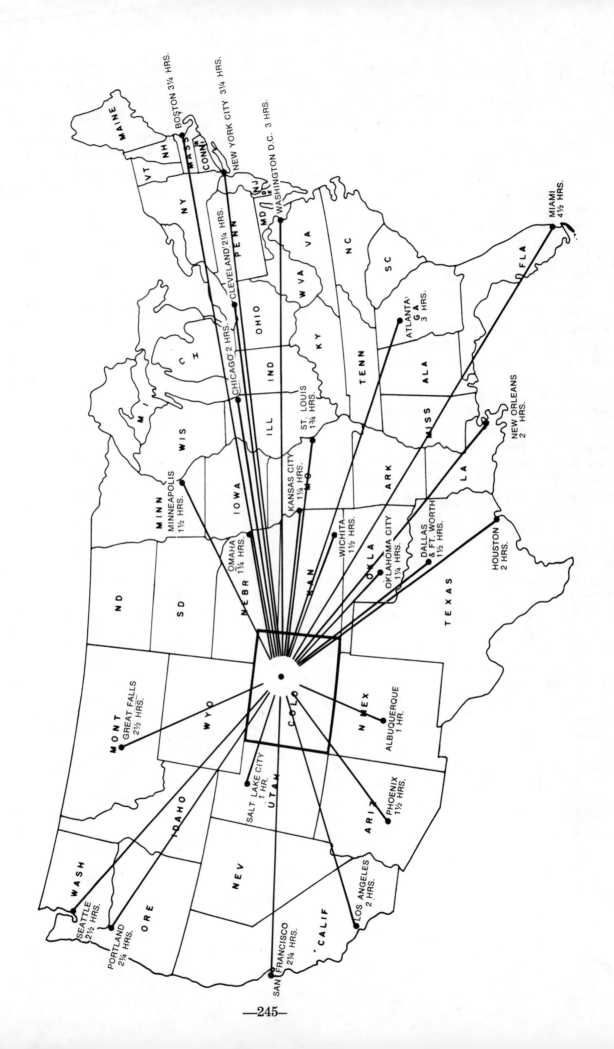

About 77% of this reserve is bituminous, the remainder is sub-bituminous except for some small anthracite deposits. Coal production has been increasing steadily at about 10 to 15% a year the last five years.

Natural gas is enjoyed as a fuel by about 90% of the people of Colorado. The bulk of this gas supply is supplied through the pipelines of Colorado interstate gas company and distributed by the same companies that distribute electricity. Nearly 40% of the state's 1972 consumption was produced from Colorado gas fields. Natural gas is critical throughout the United States because of demands for this practical fuel. The critical nature of this resource will continue to be a problem unless substantial increases in production result from exploration. Residential consumers account for about 30% of this consumption, and supply to this market has not been curtailed. Increases in the state gas supply, and reallocations of gas from non-residential users of the fuel from industries and other non-resident consumers who have switched to other fuels, have provided for growth in residential demand. Increased limitations have been placed on non-resident consumers since 1972 by Public Service Company of Colorado, the state's largest gas distributing utility. New residential customers and those using less than 7,500 cubic feet an hour, are given first priority; larger customers are second and interruptible industrial customers have third priority. An exception to this restriction exists in some of the regions of Western Colorado where captive local wells produce gas on an unlimited basis to users in the Grand Junction, Rangely, and Rifle areas.

Probably the most underdeveloped resource of all in Colorado is oil shale, moreover, it is one of the most promising. The rate of development of this source of energy is influenced by a multitude of complex problems. Land leasing, tax and legal matters, technology, along with economic factors, are some of the questions to be answered. The existence of vast reserves of petroleum in Western Colorado's shale deposits is not a matter of question, however. They are the largest deposits in the world. Lying in Garfield and Rio Blanco Counties, they cover an area of 1,500 square miles with estimates as high as well over a trillion barrels of oil contained in the shale.

Coal, oil shale, timber, water power are all abundant, underdeveloped resources of Colorado. Development will come, this there can be no doubt. Can the development occur with reasonable protection of the environment, fair revenues for the state, and an audible voice for Western Coloradans in their destiny as this scramble takes place? Also, can it be accomplished at a price that is reasonable? Resources belong to all the people in the United States. They are not the private domain of the state where they are located, nor are they the chattel of energy companies to develop as they please, at the same time circumventing severance and property taxes and avoiding the principles of competitive enterprise. In the coming struggle, the energy companies, with their vast financial resources available to commandeer the best legal minds in the country, have all the advantages. They seek the best of all worlds, pleading for the freedom and benefits of the free enterprise system to alleviate unneeded controls; they complain that the costs of development and exploration are beyond their ability. They can not enjoy both. If they want to be free from such scrutiny, it will be necessary to make the investments and take the risks in the same manner that any businessman must. They can not lose anyway, because the consumer will pick up the tab, either in increased cost of the energy or in increased taxes. Hopefully, it will not be too excessive whichever course is taken.

Challenges and opportunities, nothing new to the Centennial State. Are the challenges of today more insurmountable than those of the 1850s and 1860s? Hardly, ingenuity and work can again get the job done. It appears the mineral phase of Colorado may again have another rebirth. Again, it will not be the first. Non-metallic minerals or not, "thar is still gold in them thar hills". Excitement and restless feet, another heritage of the pioneer period; there should be a good measure of this to go along. Let it come. Who knows, the best and most exciting century in the Centennial State may be yet down the road. Whether the road is travelled or not is not the question, Coloradan, only how well.

THE
END

CENTENNIAL VIPS

TERRITORIAL GOVERNORS

Governor	Appointing President	Term
William Gilpin	Abraham Lincoln	July 8, 1861
John Evans	Abraham Lincoln	April 19, 1862
Alexander Cummings	Andrew Johnson	Oct. 17, 1865
A. C. Hunt	Andrew Johnson	May 27, 1867
Edward M. McCook	U. S. Grant	June 15, 1869
Samuel H. Elbert	U. S. Grant	March 9, 1873
Edward M. McCook	U. S. Grant	Aug. 10, 1874
John H. Routt	U. S. Grant	March 29, 1875

GOVERNORS OF COLORADO

John L. Routt (R), 1876-79
Frederick W. Pitkin (R), 1879-83
James B. Grant (D), 1883-85
Benjamin H. Eaton (R), 1885-87
Alva Adams (D), 1887-89
Job A. Cooper (R), 1889-91
John L. Routt (R), 1891-93
Davis H. Waite (P), 1893-95
Albert W. McIntire (R), 1895-97
Alva Adams (D), 1897-99
Charles S. Thomas (D), 1899-1901
James B. Orman (D), 1901-03
James H. Peabody (R), 1903-05

Alvah Adams (D), 1905
James H. Peabody (R), 1905
Jesse F. McDonald (R), 1905-07
Henry A. Buchtel (R), 1907-09
John F. Shaforth (D), 1909-13
Elias M. Ammons (D), 1913-15
George A. Carlson (R), 1915-17
Julius C. Gunter (D), 1917-19
Oliver H. Shoup (R), 1919-23
William E. Sweet (D), 1923-25
Clarence J. Morley (R), 1925-27
William H. Adams (D), 1927-33
Edwin C. Johnson (D), 1933-37

Ray H. Talbot (D), 1937
Teller Ammons (D), 1937-39
Ralph L. Carr (R), 1939-43
John C. Vivian (R), 1943-47
W. Lee Knous (D), 1947-50
Walter W. Johnson (D), 1950-51
Dan Thornton (R) 1951-55
Edwin C. Johnson (D), 1955-57
Stephen L. R. McNichols (D), 1957-63
John A. Love (R), 1963-1973
John L. Vanderhoof (R), 1973-75
Richard D. Lamm (D), 1975-

UNITED STATES REPRESENTATIVES

James B. Belford (R), 1876-77
Thos. M. Patterson (D), 1877-79
James B. Belford (R), 1879-85
George G. Symes (R), 1885-89
Hosea Townsend (R), 1889-93
John C. Bell (P&D), 1893-1903
Lafe Pence (P), 1893-95
John F. Shafroth (R&D), 1895-1903
Robert W. Bonynge (R), 1903-09
Herschel M. Hogg (R), 1903-07
Franklin E. Brooks (R), 1903-07
George W. Cook (R), 1907-09
Warren H. Haggott (R), 1907-09
Edward T. Taylor (D), 1909-41
Atterson W. Rucker (D), 1909-13

John A. Martin (D), 1909-13
Edward Keating (D), 1913-19
George J. Kindel (D), 1913-15
H. H. Seldomridge (D), 1913-15
B. C. Hilliard (D), 1915-19
Chas. B. Timberlake (R), 1915-33
William N. Vaile (R), 1919-27
Guy U. Hardy (R), 1919-33
S. Harrison White (D), 1927-28
William R. Eaton (R), 1928-33
Lawrence Lewis (D), 1933-43
John A. Martin (D), 1933-40
Fred Cummings (D), 1933-41
William S. Hill (R), 1941-59
J.Edgar Chenoweth (R), 41-49, 51-65

Robert F. Rockwell (R), 1941-49
Dean M. Gillespie (R), 1944-47
John A. Carroll (D), 1947-51
Wayne N. Aspinall (D), 1949-72
John H. Marsalis (D), 1949-51
Byron G. Rogers (D), 1951-70
Byron L. Johnson (D), 1959-61
Peter H. Dominick (R), 1961-63
Donald Brotzman (R), 1963-65
Roy H. McVicker (D), 1965-67
Frank E. Evans (D), 1965-
James P. Johnson (R), 1973-
Patricia Schroeder (D), 1973-
William L. Armstrong (R), 1973-
Timothy E. Wirth (D), 1975-

UNITED STATES SENATORS

Henry M. Teller (R), 1876-82
Jerome B. Chaffee (R), 1876-79
Nathan P. Hill (R), 1879-85
George M. Chilcott (R), 1882
Horace A. W. Tabor (R), 1883
Thomas M. Bowen (R), 1883-89
Henry M. Teller (R&D), 1885-1909
Edw. O. Wolcott (R), 1889-1901
Thos. M. Patterson (D), 1901-07
Simon Guggenheim (R), 1907-13

Chas. J. Hughes, Jr. (D), 1909-11
Charles S. Thomas (D), 1913-21
John F. Shafroth (D), 1913-19
Lawrence C. Phipps (R), 1919-31
S. D. Nicholson (R) 1921-23
Alvah B. Adams (D), 1923-25
Rice W. Means (R) 1925-27
Chas. W. Waterman (R), 1927-32
Edw. P. Costigan (D) 1931-37
Walter Walker (D), 1932

Karl C. Schuyler (R), 1932-33
Alvah B. Adams (D), 1933-41
Edwin C. Johnson (D), 1937-55
Elgene D. Millikin (R), 1941-57
Gordon Allott (R), 1955-72
John A. Carroll (D), 1957-1963
Floyd K. Haskell (D), 1973-
Peter H. Dominick (R), 1963-1975
Gary Hart (D), 1975-

Where The Columbines Grow

ADOPTED, 1915, BY THE COLORADO LEGISLATURE AS THE OFFICIAL STATE SONG.

A. J. FYNN

Valse Moderato

Where the snow - y peaks gleam in the moon -
The bi - son is gone from the up -
Let the vi - o - let bright - en the brook -

Piu Lento   *Tempo*

light, A - bove the dark for - ests of pine,_____ And the
land, The deer from the can - yon has fled,_____ The
side, In sun - light of ear - li - er spring,_____ Let the

Piu lento   *rit.*

pur - ple robed West, the land that is best, The
nymphs of the grove in their lone - li - ness rove, But the
fair West - ern home, may the col - um - bine bloom Till our

pi - o - neer land that we love._____
col - um - bine blooms just the same._____
great moun - tain riv - ers run dry._____

CHORUS *a tempo*   *accel.*   *accel.*

'Tis the land where the col - um - bines grow,_____ O - ver-looking the plains far be - low,_____ While the

cool sum-mer breeze in the ev-er-green trees Soft -ly sings where the colum-bines grow._____

wild foam-ing wa - ters dash on - ward To - ward lands where the
home of the wolf is de - sert - ed, The an - te - lope
clo - ver be - deck the green mead - ow, In days when the

a tempo

trop - ic stars shine;_____ Where the scream of the bold moun - tain
moans for his dead,_____ The war - whoop re - ech - oes no
o - ri - oles sing,_____ Let the gold - en - rod her - ald the

Piu mosso

ea - gle Re - sponds to the notes of the dove_____ Is the
lon - ger, The In - di - an's on - ly a name,_____ And the
au - tumn, But, un - der the mid - sum - mer sky,_____ In its

SOPRANO *a tempo*   *accel.*

'Tis the land where the columbines grow,_____ Over looking the plains far below;_____ While the

ALTO *a tempo*

'Tis the land where the columbines grow,_____ Over looking the plains far below;_____ While the

TENOR *a tempo*

'Tis the land where the columbines, columbines grow, Over looking the plains far below, far below, While the

BASS *a tempo*

'Tis the land where the columbines grow,_____ Over looking the plains far below,_____ While the

cool summer breeze in the ev-er-green trees Soft -ly sings where the col-um-bines grow._____

cool summer breeze in the ev-er-green trees Soft -ly sings where the col-um-bines grow._____

cool summer breeze in the ev-er-green trees Soft -ly sings where the col-um-bines grow._____

COLORADO: PERSPECTIVE

COLORADO EMBLEMS

ORIGIN OF NAME: Spanish for "Colored Red"

INHABITANT: Coloradan

STATE MOTTO: Nil Sine Numine (Nothing Without Providence)

FLAG: A red letter "C" encloses gold ball and
                           rests against blue, white, and blue bars.

SEAL: A triangular figure, representing "All
                           Seeing" eye of God, bound rods, three
                           mountains, and pick and hammer.

ANIMAL: Rocky Mountain Big Horn Sheep

BIRD: Lark Bunting

FLOWER: Rocky Mountain Columbine

TREE: Blue Spruce

SONG: "Where the Columbines Grow"

NICKNAME: Centennial State

ENTERED UNION: 1876 (38th state)

PRESENT CONSTITUTION ADOPTED: 1876

COLORADO GEOGRAPHY

LOCATION AND BOUNDARIES: Rocky Mountain state; bounded on the
                           north by Wyoming and Nebraska; on the
                           east by Nebraska and Kansas; on the
                           south by Oklahoma and New Mexico; and
                           on the west by Utah.

TOTAL AREA: 104,247 square miles (8th state)

EXTREME LENGTH AND BREADTH: 387 miles long; 276 miles wide

HIGHEST ELEVATION: 14,433 feet above sea level (Mt. Elbert);
                           54 mountain peaks over 14,000 feet

LOWEST ELEVATION: 3,350 feet (Arkansas River E. of Holly)

RIVER BASINS:	Colorado, Arkansas, South Platte, Rio Grande, North Platte, Republican
MAJOR LAKES:	Blue Mesa, John Martin, Granby, Pueblo
CAPITAL:	Denver
NUMBER OF COUNTIES:	63

COLORADO GOVERNMENT

GOVERNOR, 1975-1979:	Richard D. Lamm (D)
ANNUAL SALARY:	$40,000
GENERAL ASSEMBLY, 1975-1976:	Senate - 16 (D); 19 (R)
	House - 39 (D); 26 (R)
U.S. CONGRESSIONAL DELEGATION:	Senator Floyd Haskell (D; 1973-79)
	Senator Gary Hart (D; 1975-81)
	Rep. William L. Armstrong (R)
	Rep. Frank E. Evans (D)
	Rep. James P. Johnson (R)
	Rep. Patricia Schroeder (D)
	Rep. Timothy E. Wirth (D)
VOTER PARTICIPATION, 1972:	61.2% of voting age population
VOTING REQUIREMENTS:	18 years old and U.S. citizen; resident of state and county 90 days; precinct 15 days; no literacy test.

STATE TAXES, 1974-1975:	$856.3 million
PERSONAL INCOME (2½-8%):	32% of total
SALES AND USE (3%)	31%
HIGHWAY FUEL (7¢/gal.) & FEES:	16%
CORPORATE INCOME (5%):	7%
OTHER TAXES:	8%
MISCELLANEOUS INCOME:	6%

STATE & LOCAL TAXES PER CAPITA, 1972-73:	$543 (19th state)
PER $1000 OF PERSONAL INCOME:	$207 (25th state)
FEDERAL AID PER CAPITA, 1972-73:	$169 (18th state)

STATE EXPENDITURES, 1974-1975:	$887 million
EDUCATION & HIGHER EDUCATION:	$478 million
SOCIAL SERVICES:	$ 98 million
INSTITUTIONS:	$ 69 million
HIGHWAYS:	$ 67 million
OTHER GENERAL FUND:	$108 million
OTHER HIGHWAY FUND:	$ 67 million

POPULATION:
  1960 CENSUS: 1,753,947
  1970 CENSUS: 2,209,528 (30th state)
  1975 ESTIMATE: 2,590,000
  1980 PROJECTION: 2,800,000 - 2,950,000

POPULATION INCREASE,
  1960-1970:   26.0% (7th state)
  1970-1973:   11.7% (4th state)
  1970-1980 (PROJ.):   27% - 34%

ETHNIC COMPOSITION, 1970:

  WHITE (ANGLO):   82.7%
  HISPANIC: 13.0% (9th state)
  NON-WHITE: 4.3% (36th state)

METROPOLITAN AREAS, 1975   Denver-Boulder: 1,457,000
  ESTIMATED POPULATIONS :   Colorado Springs: 315,000
                                   Pueblo: 130,000
                                   Fort Collins: 120,000
                                   Greeley: 113,000

PLACES OVER 100,000 POPULATION,   Denver, Colorado Springs, Lakewood,
  1974:   Aurora, Pueblo

NUMBER OF PLACES OVER 20,000
  POPULATION, 1974:   17

POPULATION DENSITY, 1970:   21.2 per square mile (39th state)

URBAN POPULATION, 1970:   78.5% (13th state)

MEDIAN AGE, 1974 EST.:   26.7 years

BIRTH RATE, 1974:   15.2 per 1,000 people

DEATH RATE, 1974:   7.0 per 1,000 people

INFANT DEATH RATE, 1974:   15.8 per 1,000 live births

MARRIAGE RATE, 1974:   10.2 per 1,000 people

DIVORCE RATE, 1974:   5.7 per 1,000 people

PHYSICIANS, 1974:   176 per 100,000 people (6th state, 1972)

DENTISTS, 1972:   57 per 100,000 people (12th state)

ACTIVE REGISTERED NURSES, 1972:   520 per 100,000 people (7th state)

HOSPITAL BEDS, 1975:   4.1 per 1,000 people

SOURCES: U.S. Census; Colorado Division of Planning; Colo. Dept. of Health.

STATE AND LOCAL EXPENDITURES FOR
  EDUCATION PER CAPITA, 1972-73: $383 (11th state)

      HIGHER EDUCATION ONLY: $126 (8th state)

NUMBER OF PUPILS ENROLLED IN
  PUBLIC SCHOOLS, FALL 1974:   568,060

PUBLIC SCHOOL EXPENDITURE PER PUPIL
  IN ATTENDANCE, 1974: $1,075 (19th state)

AVERAGE ANNUAL SALARY OF PUBLIC
  SCHOOL TEACHERS, FALL 1974: $10,930

PUPIL-TEACHER RATIO, 1974:   21.3:1

EDUCATIONAL ATTAINMENT OF ADULT
  POPULATION, 1970:

      MEDIAN SCHOOL YEARS COMPLETED: 12.4 years (2nd state)
      LESS THAN 5 YEARS OF EDUCATION: 3.1% (16th state)
      4 OR MORE YEARS OF COLLEGE: 14.9% (1st state)

SCHOOL DROPOUTS, 1973-1974:   4.8% of public school students

INSTITUTIONS OF HIGHER EDUCATION:

  NUMBER: 28, with 19 4-year campuses and 15 2-year

  ENROLLMENT, FALL 1975:
      4-year: 112,029
      2-year: 37,389

SOURCES: U.S. Census of Population, 1970; U.S. Census Bureau, Government
Finances, 1973; Colorado Department of Education; Colorado Department of
Higher Education.

COLORADO ECONOMY

TOTAL INCOME	1960	1970	1974
GROSS STATE PRODUCT:	$5,069 million	$10,339 mil.	$15,750 mil.
TOTAL PERSONAL INCOME:	$4,008 million	$8,569 mil.	$13,765 mil.
PERSONAL INCOME PER CAPITA:	$2,266	$3,855	$5,515 (14th state)
PERSONAL INCOME PER CAPITA AS PERCENT OF U.S. AVERAGE:	102.0%	97.2%	101.2%
MEDIAN HOUSEHOLD EFFECTIVE BUYING INCOME:	$6,600	$9,800	$12,029

PERCENT OF HOUSEHOLDS WITH EFFECTIVE BUYING INCOME (1974)	COLORADO	U.S.
LESS THAN $3,000:	10.7%	11.9%
MORE THAN $25,000:	9.3%	9.6%

AVERAGE WEEKLY EARNINGS FOR MANU- FACTURING PRODUCTION WORKERS, 1974:	$183.22	$176.00
COST OF LIVING, INTERMEDIATE BUDGET FOR FAMILY OF 4, AUTUMN 1974:	$13,606	$14,333
UNEMPLOYMENT RATE, 1974:	3.8%	5.6%
JAN.-AUG., 1975:	5.5%	8.6%

ECONOMIC SECTORS	PERSONAL INCOME, 1974		(U.S.)	EMPLOYMENT, 1974		(U.S.)
TOTAL:	$13,765 mil.	100 %	(100%)	1,096,000	100 %	(100%)
GOVERNMENT:	2,385	17.3	(13.7)	201,900	18.4	(16.6)
FEDERAL:	1,158	8.4	(5.0)	48,900	4.5	(3.2)
STATE & LOCAL:	1,227	8.9	(8.7)	153,000	13.9	(13.4)
TRADE:	1,941	14.1	(12.7)	232,200	21.2	(19.8)
MANUFACTURING:	1,751	12.7	(20.9)	144,000	13.1	(23.3)
SERVICES:	1,633	11.9	(12.1)	180,000	16.4	(15.7)
CONSTRUCTION:	931	6.8	(4.8)	66,000	6.0	(4.6)
TRANSP., COMMUNI- CATIONS, UTIL.:	832	6.0	(5.6)	61,000	5.6	(5.5)
FINANCE, INSUR., REAL ESTATE:	620	4.5	(4.1)	56,500	5.2	(4.8)
AGRICULTURE:	583	4.2	(2.8)	50,100	4.6	(4.1)
MINING:	231	1.7	(0.8)	16,300	1.5	(0.8)
OTHER:	2,828*	20.6	(22.5)	87,900**	8.0	(4.7)

* Property income, transfer payments, less social insurance contributions.
** Self-employed, domestics, unpaid family workers.
SOURCES: Bank of California; Sales Management Magazine; U.S. Department of Commerce; U.S. Bureau of Labor Statistics; Colorado Division of Employment.

MANUFACTURING

	1972		1967	
	Number	% of total Employment	Number	% of total Employment
NUMBER OF ESTABLISHMENTS:	2,842	100%	2,461	100%
WITH LESS THAN 20 EMPLOYEES:	2,007	8.2%	1,797	9.8%
20-99 EMPLOYEES:	609	21.2%	481	20.7%
100-499 EMPLOYEES:	193	27.1%	158	26.5%
MORE THAN 500 EMPLOYEES:	33	43.5%	25	43.0%

	1972	1967
VALUE OF SHIPMENTS:	$5,796.0 mil.	$3,226.6 mil.
VALUE ADDED:	$2,509.6 mil.	$1,509.9 mil.
% IN DENVER METRO AREA:	73.8%	74.3%
EMPLOYMENT:	132,600	104,000
% OF U.S. MFG. EMPLOYMENT:	0.70%	0.54%

MANUFACTURING INDUSTRIES:	Value Added, 1972	Employment, 1974
FOOD AND KINDRED PRODUCTS:	$511.5 mil.	23,600

Major Employers: Adolph Coors (beer, containers), Great Western Sugar, Monfort of Colorado (meat packing, cattle feeding)

MACHINERY, EXCEPT ELECTRICAL:	$302.8 mil.	16,800

Major Employers: I.B.M., Storage Technology Corp. (computer and office equipment); Denver Equipment Division of Joy Manufacturing, Gardner-Denver Co., General Iron Works, Mine & Smelter Supply (mining and industrial eqpt.)

TRANSPORTATION EQUIPMENT:	$259.1 mil.	8,700

Major Employers: Martin Marietta Aerospace, Sundstrand Aviation, Timpte Industries (truck trailers)

FABRICATED METAL PRODUCTS & ORDNANCE:	$210.8 mil.	12,800

Major Employers: Rockwell International Atomics Division, Western Forge (hand tools), C.A. Norgren (valves)

INSTRUMENTS & PHOTOGRAPHIC EQPT.:	$198.2 mil.	12,400

Major Employers: Hewlett-Packard, Eastman Kodak, Honeywell, Ball Brothers Research Corp.

PRINTING & PUBLISHING:	$181.9 mil.	12,000

Major Employers: Denver Post, Rocky Mountain News, Looart Press

RUBBER & PLASTICS PRODUCTS:	$147.1 mil.	7,300

Major Employers: Gates Rubber Co.

MANUFACTURING INDUSTRIES, cont.   Value Added, 1972   Employment, 1974

STONE, CLAY, & GLASS PRODUCTS: $139.6 mil.   9,100
    Major Employers: Coors Porcelain, Ideal Basic Industries,
                                             Prestressed Concrete of Colorado, Johns
                                             Manville

PRIMARY METAL INDUSTRIES: $130.2 mil.   8,500
    Major Employers: CF&I Steel

CHEMICALS & ALLIED PRODUCTS: $ 85.8 mil.   2,600
    Major Employers: Shell Chemical, Arapahoe Chemicals,
                                             Kwal Paints, Kohler-McLister Paint,
                                             Scott's Liquid Gold

ELECTRICAL EQUIPMENT: $ 85.6 mil.   9,800
    Major Employers: Western Electric, Ampex, Dixson

LUMBER & WOOD PRODUCTS: $ 55.8 mil.   3,900
    Major Employers: Kaibab Industries, San Juan Lumber,
                                             Montezuma Plywood, Central Homes

LEATHER & LUGGAGE: $ 51.0 mil.   4,500
    Major Employers: Samsonite Corporation

PAPER PRODUCTS: $ 30.8 mil.   1,700
    Major Employers: Rockmont Envelope, Packaging Corporation
                                             of America

FURNITURE & FIXTURES: $ 27.9 mil.   2,600
    Major Employers: Riviera Products Div. of Evans Products,
                                             Hughes & Co.

APPAREL: $ 27.0 mil.   3,100
    Major Employers: Aspen Skiwear, Bayly Corp., Gerry
                                             Division of Outdoor Sports Industries

PETROLEUM PRODUCTS: $ 24.0 mil.   800
    Major Employers: Continental Oil Co., Gary Western

MISCELLANEOUS MFG.: $ 39.8 mil.   4,100
    Major Employers: Head Ski Div. of AMF, Lange Co. Div.
                                             Garcia, Wright & McGill, Estes Industries

SOURCES: U.S. Census of Manufactures, 1972; U.S. Census Bureau, County
Business Patterns; Colorado Division of Employment; University of
Colorado Business Research Division, Directory of Colorado Manufacturers;
Colorado Division of Commerce & Development.

AGRICULTURE

	1974	1969	1959
NUMBER OF FARMS:	29,500	31,000	33,400
LAND IN FARMS (million acres):	39.9	40.0	38.8
AVERAGE FARM SIZE (acres):	1,353	1,290	1,160
AVERAGE FARM VALUE:	n.a.	$124,180	$61,494
HARVESTED CROP LAND (mil. acres):	5.934	5.226	5.879
IRRIGATED LAND (million acres):	n.a.	2.895	2.685
TOTAL CASH MARKETINGS ($ million):	$2,053	$1,014	$ 580

LEADING PRODUCTS, 1973:	Value of Production ($ mil.)	Production (Livestock Inventory) (millions)	Rank Among States
CATTLE:	$1,364.9	3,013 lbs. (3.74 head)	11
WHEAT:	231.8	59.3 bushels	6
CORN:	196.7	44.7 bushels & 5.55 tons silage	18 8
HAY:	139.7	3.11 tons	20
SHEEP:	61.0	180 lbs. (1.14 head)	3
WOOL:	9.3	11.35 lbs.	4
DAIRY PRODUCTS:	66.9	854 lbs.	32
SUGAR BEETS:	66.4	1.85 tons	5
POTATOES:	49.2	9.67 cwt.	10
HOGS & PIGS:	48.5	129 lbs. (.290 head)	25
DRY BEANS:	39.0	1.45 cwt.	5
ALL POULTRY PRODUCTS:	47.1		
ALL COMMERCIAL VEGETABLES & FRUIT:	42.5		

SOURCES: Colorado Crop and Livestock Reporting Service, Colorado Agricultural Statistics; U.S. Census of Agriculture, 1969.

MINERAL INDUSTRIES

ESTABLISHMENTS, 1972:   665
   WITH MORE THAN 100 EMPLOYEES: 27

VALUE ADDED, 1972: $409 million

TOTAL VALUE OF PRODUCTION, 1972: $406 million
                    1974: $698 million

EMPLOYMENT, 1974:   16,200
   OIL AND GAS: 7,900
   METAL MINING: 6,000
   COAL: 1,500
   NON-METALLIC MINERALS: 900

LEADING PRODUCTS, 1974:

	VALUE	PRODUCTION
CRUDE OIL:	$307.6 mil.	37.5 mil. bbl.
Leading Producers:	Chevron Oil, Amoco Production, Texaco	
MOLYBDENUM:	$124.0 mil.	63.16mil. lbs.
Leading Producer:	Climax Molybdenum Div. of AMAX	
COAL:	$68.6 mil.	6.69 mil. tons
Leading Producers:	Energy Fuels, Pittsburg & Midway Coal, U.S. Steel, Mid-Continent Coal & Coke	
SAND & GRAVEL:	$41.6 mil.	
NATURAL GAS:	$29.9 mil.	144.9 mil. Mcf
Leading Producers:	Mountain Fuel Supply, Amoco Production, El Paso Natural Gas, Mobil Oil, Continental Oil	
ZINC:	$25.4 mil.	65.1 mil. lbs.
Leading Producers:	New Jersey Zinc, Idarado Mining, Standard Metals	
CEMENT & LIMESTONE:	$23.9 mil.	
Leading Producers:	Ideal Basic Industries, CF&I Steel, Martin Marietta Cement	
URANIUM:	$12.2 mil.	1.53 mil. lbs.
Leading Producers:	Cotter Corp., Union Carbide	
VANADIUM:	$11.6 mil.	4.89 mil. lbs.
Leading Producers:	Union Carbide	
SILVER:	$11.6 mil.	2.66 mil. oz.
Leading Producers:	Homestake Mining, Idarado Mining	
LEAD:	$9.4 mil.	38.4 mil. lbs.
Leading Producers:	Idarado Mining, Standard Metals	
TUNGSTEN:	$9.1 mil.	
Leading Producer:	Climax Molybdenum Div. of AMAX	
GOLD:	$7.7 mil.	41,800 oz.
Leading Producers:	Standard Metals, Idarado Mining	

SOURCES: Colorado Division of Mines; U.S. Census of Mineral Industries, 1972.

WHOLESALE TRADE

NUMBER OF ESTABLISHMENTS, 1972:	4,754
WITH MORE THAN 20 EMPLOYEES:	582
% OF TOTAL EMPLOYMENT:	63%
SALES, 1972:	$8,030.3 million
% IN DENVER METRO AREA:	80%
EMPLOYEES, 1972:	49,435

RETAIL TRADE

NUMBER OF ESTABLISHMENTS, 1972:	24,335
WITH NO PAYROLL:	8,537
WITH MORE THAN 20 EMPLOYEES:	1,596
% OF TOTAL EMPLOYMENT:	64%
SALES, 1972:	$5,896.0 million
% IN DENVER METRO AREA:	60%
PAID EMPLOYEES, 1972:	146,202

SERVICES

LODGING, PERSONAL, BUSINESS,
REPAIR, & RECREATION SERVICES:

NUMBER OF ESTABLISHMENTS, 1972:	20,601
WITH NO PAYROLL:	12,068
WITH MORE THAN 20 EMPLOYEES:	678
% OF TOTAL EMPLOYMENT:	65%
RECEIPTS, 1972:	$1,124.6 million
% IN DENVER METRO AREA:	67%
PAID EMPLOYEES, 1972:	67,094

MEDICAL AND OTHER PROFESSIONAL
& NON-PROFIT SERVICES:

ESTABLISHMENTS WITH PAYROLL, 1972:	7,284
EMPLOYEES, 1972:	81,266

SOURCES: U.S. Censuses of Wholesale Trade, Retail Trade, and Selected Services, 1972; U.S. Census Bureau, County Business Patterns, 1972.

FINANCE, INSURANCE, AND REAL ESTATE

ESTABLISHMENTS WITH PAYROLL, 1972:   4,696

EMPLOYMENT, 1972:   47,665

COMMERCIAL BANKS, 1974:   263

   DEPOSITS, Dec. 31, 1974: $6,995.7 million

SAVINGS AND LOAN ASSOCIATIONS, 1974:   47

   DEPOSITS, Dec. 31, 1974: $3,254.0 million

INSURANCE COMPANIES, 1974:   1,131
   COLORADO CORPORATIONS: 115

   LIFE INSURANCE SALES, 1974: $2,864.7 million

SOURCES: County Business Patterns, 1972; U.S. FDIC; Savings League of Colorado; Colorado Commissioner of Insurance.

TOURISM

TOTAL VISITORS, 1974:   7,833,000

SKIER DAYS, 1974-75:   5,194,720

NATIONAL PARKS, MONUMENTS, RECREA-
   TION AREAS, AND HISTORICAL SITES: 11
   VISITORS, 1974:   5,363,903

TOURIST EXPENDITURES, 1974: $630 million

EMPLOYMENT, 1974:   50,000 (4.6% of total) (est.)

PERSONAL INCOME GENERATED, 1974: $200 million (1.5% of total) (est.)

SOURCE: Colorado Division of Commerce and Development. Employment and personal income estimated on 1968 survey benchmark data in Denver Research Institute, A Profile of the Tourist Market in Colorado;(included in retail trade and services totals).

TOP PRIVATE EMPLOYERS, 1974:

   1. Mountain Bell   6. Gates Rubber
   2. Adolph Coors/Coors Porcelain   7. Public Service Co. of Colorado
   3. Safeway Stores   8. IBM
   4. CF & I Steel   9. Martin Marietta
   5. King Soopers Stores   10. Hewlett-Packard

GOVERNMENT

STATE EMPLOYEES, 1974:
    HIGHER EDUCATION: 30,900

    OTHER STATE: 18,400

LOCAL GOVERNMENT EMPLOYEES, 1974:
    EDUCATION: 61,700

    OTHER LOCAL: 42,000

FEDERAL GOVERNMENT, 1974:

    MILITARY PERSONNEL: 52,000

    CIVILIAN EMPLOYMENT, MILITARY
       FACILITIES: 19,000

    MILITARY PAYROLLS: $514 million (3.9% of personal income)

    DEFENSE DEPARTMENT, NASA, AND AEC
       PRIME CONTRACTS, 1973-74: $642 million

    MAJOR MILITARY INSTALLATIONS: Air Force Academy
                                     Air Force Accounting and Finance Center
                                     Ent Air Force Base-Peterson Field
                                     Fitzsimmons Army Medical Center
                                     Fort Carson Army Infantry Base
                                     Lowry Air Force Base
                                     Pueblo Army Depot

    CIVILIAN AGENCY EMPLOYMENT: 30,000

    CIVILIAN AGENCY PAYROLLS: $639 million (4.8% of personal income)

    MAJOR FACILITIES: Bureau of Reclamation
                                       Geological Survey
                                     National Bureau of Standards
                                     National Oceanic and Atmospheric Admin.
                                     Forest Service
                                     Denver Mint
                                     Department of Transportation Test Center
                                     Federal Administrative Region VIII
                                         Offices of many agencies

TRANSPORTATION AND COMMUNICATIONS

HIGHWAYS

PASSENGER CAR REGISTRATIONS, 1974:   1,403,474
          PER 1000 PEOPLE: 561 (6th state, 1973)

TOTAL HIGHWAY MILEAGE, 1974:   84,524 miles

MINIMUM AGE FOR DRIVER'S LICENSE: 16 years

MOTOR VEHICLE ACCIDENTS, 1973:   111,425
              DEATHS: 674
      DEATHS PER 100,000 PEOPLE: 27.6
  DEATHS PER 100,000 VEHICLE-MILES: 4.2

RAILROADS

CARRIER:	MAINLINE AND BRANCH TRACK MILEAGE:
DENVER & RIO GRANDE WESTERN:	1,225
UNION PACIFIC:	593
ATCHESON TOPEKA & SANTA FE:	542
BURLINGTON NORTHERN:	390
COLORADO & SOUTHERN (BURLINGTON):	332
CHICAGO, ROCK ISLAND & PACIFIC:	168
MISSOURI PACIFIC:	138
CLASS I TOTAL:	3,388
GREAT WESTERN:	58
COLORADO & WYOMING:	32
SAN LUIS CENTRAL:	12
SOUTHERN SAN LUIS VALLEY:	1
CLASS II & III TOTAL:	103

AIR

NUMBER OF AIRPORTS, 1972:   74 public, 140 private

NUMBER OF PASSENGERS, STAPLETON
   INTERNATIONAL AIRPORT, 1974:   11,202,799

NUMBER OF COMMERCIAL AIRLINES
   SERVING COLORADO, 1975:   14

COMMUNICATIONS

RADIO STATIONS, 1973:   66 AM, 30 FM

TELEVISION STATIONS, 1973:   11

ENERGY

ELECTRICITY PRODUCED, 1974:   18.3 MWH

NATURAL GAS CONSUMPTION, 1974:   328.8 billion cubic feet

SOURCES OF BASIC ENERGY, 1972:

PETROLEUM:	40%
NATURAL GAS:	39%
COAL:	17%
HYDROELECTRIC:	4%

END USES OF ENERGY, 1972:

TRANSPORTATION:	30%
INDUSTRIAL:	20%
COMMERCIAL:	16%
ELECTRICAL GENERATION (Conversion Losses):	16%
RESIDENTIAL:	15%
OTHER:	3%

SOURCES: Colorado Department of Revenue; Colorado Division of Highways; Colorado Public Utilities Commission; Stapleton International Airport; Colorado School of Mines, "Economic Impact of Alternative Energy Supply Policies in Colorado."

BIBLIOGRAPHY

No book is ever the exclusive product of the genius of its author. This book is the result of years of living in Colorado and teaching Colorado History. The byproduct of experience and experiences of people close to the author. Your author has gathered material from a variety of sources--some not recollectable and others difficult to locate. While wandering through institutions of higher learing in the Centennial State, it has been the author's good fortune to study under many capable and inspiring instructors. Professor Donald MacKendrick of Mesa College presented Colorado History in an inspiring and scholarly manner, moreover, many of the concepts used in this work are the results of his research or teaching. Also, Prof. MacKendrick proofread and added helpful suggestions along the way. Dr. Robert G. Athearn gave your author new insights and inspiration in writing than has anyone else. Dr. Dell Foutz was kind enough to offer suggestion and aid in proofreading.

One of the greatest motivations in learning is to teach a subject. The pressure of presenting material to others forces a teacher to carefully prepare his lessons. When the teacher presents material, his ideas and concepts are tested and examined by his students. In addition, the students frequently add new, fresh ideas to the subject and criticize the teacher's thinking, consequently, he also learns a good deal. An attempt was made to write this book in the same form that was used in lecturing students, rather than the customary textbook style. In teaching Colorado History in the public schools and at Mesa College, your author has used LeRoy and Ann Hafen's The Colorado Story, Carl Ubbelohde's A Colorado History, Percy S. Fritz's Colorado, The Centennial State and his own materials, gathered over several years, as texts and references. Frank Hall's History of the State of Colorado in five volumes, LeRoy Hafen's History of Colorado in three volumes and Wilbur F. Stone's History of Colorado in four volumes have served as valuable references. The Colorado Magazine and the State Historical Museum have made materials available that have been valuable in compiling the information used in this book.

The Denver Public Library has one of the best collections of Colorado History materials in the State. The Empire Magazine of the Denver Post and its special issues were consulted for information, along with similar publications. Your author has rambled· over the Centennial State for years, visiting places of historical interest and talking to oldtimers and residents enthusiastic to share their experiences. Few of the areas described in this text are strange to your author, and this firsthand knowledge has been most helpful in describing the history of the same locations.

Chapter 1--The Setting
    The brief description of the geography and topography of the Centennial State come from Fritz, Colorado, The Centennial State; Bancroft, Colorful Colorado; Hafen, The Colorado Story; Stone, A History of Colorado; Waters, The Colorado, and a graduate course in the Geography of Colorado taken at Colorado University.

Chapter 2--Man in North America
    The story of the early migration of people to North America and their eventual adjustment to the demands of their new environment is only touched on in this volume. Prof. I. J. Nicholson,

Professor of Anthropology at Mesa College, graciously served as a consultant for the preparation of this chapter; also, Jennings' Prehistory of North America, along with Starr's Early Man and Fritz's Colorado, the Centennial State, Colorado Magazine, "Folsom Man in the San Luis Valley," Vol. XVIII, page 226, "Yuma Points in Eastern Colorado," Vol. XXVII, 154-155.

Chapter 3--Mesa Vistas and Canyon Sanctuaries
    The author has visited Mesa Verde and studied the materials made available by the National Park Service, also visited several other cliff dwelling sites not in Mesa Verde. Several museums have good Anasazi collections to study, as well as dioramas. Ubbelohde's A Colorado History; Stone's History of Colorado; The Images of America Series book, Anasazi, the People of the Rock by Donald G. Pike, with photographs by David Muenich, are all fabulous pictoral and written accounts of Mesa Verde. The photography in the book, Anasazi, the People of the Rock, is so well done that it is better than a visit to the park. Articles from the Colorado Magazine that were read were "Folsom Man in the San Luis Valley," Vol. XVIII, page 226; "Yuma Points in Eastern Colorado," Vol. XXVII, 154.155.

Chapter 4--The Sky People
    No complete history of the Utes has been published to date, but many sources are available. In preparing this chapter, Marshall Sprague's Massacre, the Tragedy at White River, is an excellent source for early history of the Utes. The Southern Utes, a Tribal History, published in 1972, is the most up-to-date source and provides good maps of the land and hunting grounds of the early Utes. Wilson Rockwell's The Utes, a Forgotten People, Al Look's Utes Last Stand, the historical museums at Montrose and Meeker provide valuable assistance, along with The Colorado Magazine and newspapers from Western Colorado; Colorado Magazine, "Utes in the San Luis Valley," Vol. XXVIII, 266.

Chapter 5--The Proud Cheyenne
1--Grinnell, George Bird, The Cheyenne Indians, The University
    of Nebraska Press.
    Several authors have written Cheyenne history, but Grinnell has done the most definitive work and is the best source frequently consulted for material on the Cheyenne contained in this book. There are several fine museums on the Plains Indians' culture in general and the Cheyenne. The Colorado State Historical Museum in Denver, the Heard Museum in Phoenix, Arizona and the Nebraska State Museum are good sources for exhibits on Plains Indians' culture; also consulted were Thomas E. Mails' Dog Soldiers, Bear Men and Buffalo Women and The Southern Cheyennes by Donald J. Berthrong.

Chapter 6--Exploring the Windfall
    Several volumes of the history of Western America are available. A good beginning would be Ray Allen Billington's Western Expansion; LeRoy R. Hafen and Carl C. Rister's, Western America; Robert G. Athearn's America Moves West and Huber Howe Bancroft's series on individual states is a must.

Chapter 7--The Mountain Men
     Many personal accounts of the trapper are available and offer
good first-hand information about his way of life. The Personal
Narrative of James Ohio Pattie, edited by Timothy Flint; Kit
Carson's Life and Adventure from Facts Narrated by Himself, by
DeWitt Peters; The Life and Adventures of James Beckwourth as
dictated to T. D. Bonner; Adventures in Mexico and the Rocky
Mountains by George Frederick Ruxton are all good first-hand
accounts, and books like The Big Sky by Guthrie and Mountain Man
by Vardis Fisher have interesting narratives about the life of
the mountain men in the Rockies. Also consulted were Colorado
Magazine, "Old Bill Williams," Hafen, Vol. XXX, Page 16 and "Big
Phil the Cannibal," Hafen, Vol. XIII, 53-58.

Chapter 8--The Pathfinder Gets Lost
1--Riegel, Robert and Athearn, Robert, America Moves West.
2--Ibid.
     The volumes mentioned in connection with Chapter 7 are good
sources for Fremont's expeditions. Fremont's Journals--one printed
by the Library of Congress--are informative. Wilbur Fiske Stone's
History of Colorado has good descriptions of exploration of
Colorado in Chapter 3.

Chapter 9--Spanish Culture Moves North
1--Spicer, Edward H., Cycles of Conquest, University of Arizona
     Press.
     Spicer's Cycles of Conquest is one of the best sources for
early history of the Southwest of which your author is aware,
and this was consulted frequently for material about the early
history of the Southwest. Dr. Spicer is well known for his work
in this field. Material regarding the Penitentes was taken from
the March 22, 1966 Empire Magazine of the Denver Post, Richard
Ahlborn's The Penitente Moradas of Abiquiu, Alex Durley's The
Holy Brotherhood, William Tate's The Penitentes of the Sangre de
Cristos, Charles Lummis' The Land of Poco Tiempo, Alice Hendersons'
Brothers of the Light and Marta Welgle's The Penitentes of the
Southwest and first-hand accounts and interviews.

Chapter 10--Bent's Fort and the Santa Fe Trail
     The author is indebted to Lena Straka for giving her col-
lection of many years on Bent's Fort for use in compiling this
book. David Lavendar's Bent's Fort, C. W. Hurd's Bent's Stockade,
The Colorado Magazine and the State Museum also were helpful to
find material on the stockade.
     For information on the Santa Fe Trail, Josiah Gregg's
Commerce of the Prairies; Athearn and Riegel's America Moves
West; W. Eugene Hollon's The Southwest, Old and New; Ray Billington's
Westward Expansion; Hafen and Rister's Western America, The Colorado
Magazine and The American West Magazine all served as source
material.

Chapter 11--The Pikes Peak Hoax
1--Ubbelohde, Carl, A Colorado History, Pruett Press, Boulder, Colo.
     Rodman Paul's Mining Frontiers of the Far West, 1848-1880
is the best general approach to the total mining rush your author
has read, and it gives a good overlook, also citing the obvious

connections of the various mining rushes. It also has good descriptions of early mining methods. Wilbur Fiske Stone, The History of Colorado, W. Storrs Lee, Colorado, a Literary Chronicle, The Rocky Mountain News, The Colorado Magazine and several local accounts have been most useful. Ovando J. Hollister, The Mines of Colorado, Percy Fritz, Colorado, the Centennial State and the State Historical Museum all added material.

Chapter 12—Colorado Becomes a Territory and Fights the Civil War
1—Stone, Wilbur Fiske, History of Colorado, Vol. I, The S. J.
    Clarke Co., 1918.
2—Ubbelohde, A Colorado History, Pruett Press, Boulder, Colo.
3—Stone
    Stone gives good accounts of the war in the Southwest and valuable related information. Riegel and Athearn's, America Moves West was often consulted, along with Billington's, Western Expansion and Hafen and Rister's Western America.

Chapter 13—Raiding Becomes a Reality
    Stone's The History of Colorado was the principle source consulted for information regarding the Confederate raids into Colorado. The Colorado Magazine, the Rocky Mountain News and military records also were helpful. For further information regarding buried treasure in Colorado, see Caroline Bancroft's Lost Treasures in the Rockies; also, Brown's An Empire of Silver and Athearn and Riegel's America Moves West.

Chapter 14—Goodbye to the Cheyenne and Arapaho
    The Indian wars of the Centennial State are well recorded and, the later the publication, the more likely it will be to condemn most of the actions against the Indians. Reginald Craig's The Fighting Parson is the kindest treatment of a tragic event; Stan Hoig's The Sand Creek Massacre, Wilbur Fiske Stone's History of Colorado are also useful. The Colorado Magazine has several fine articles on the Massacre, including "The Puzzle of Sand Creek," 1964 XII, Raymond Carey; and, for a personal account, "Major Hal Sayr's Diary of the Sand Creek Campaign," March 1938, Vol. XV.

Chapter 15—The 1870's and Greater Prospects
1—Ubbelohde, Carl, A Colorado History, Pruett Press, Boulder, Colo.
    Athearn's Rebel of the Rockies is the best source for information on the Denver and Rio Grande Railroad. Beebe and Clegg's Narrow Gauges of the Rockies is a good source for general information on narrow gauges.

Chapter 16—The Glitter of Silver
    Your author has visited most of the silver camps and has done extensive research in many museums and libraries in these silver-mining cities, talking with many of the oldtimers. Ubbelohde, Hafen, Hall and Stone provided background material on mining.
    Sources used for the Tabor account are: The Saga of H.A.W. Tabor by Rene L. Colquoz and The Colorado Magazine.

Chapter 17—Up and Down Country
    The San Juan mining frontier is the one most familiar to your author. Each summer workshops and symposiums are offered

by Mesa College and directed by your author.
Sources for this chapter include Pioneers of the San Juan Country, Sarah Platte Decker Chapter D.A.R., Durango, Colorado; Early Days on the Western Slope of Colorado, Sidney Jocknick; The San Juan Basin by MacDonald and Arrington; San Juan Silver by Arthur W. Monroe; An Empire of Silver by Robert Brown; The Rio Grande Southern Railroad by Josie Moore Crum; The Telluride Times and the Diamond Jubilee Edition of The Daily Sentinel.

Chapter 18---Politics Begin
Most of the information used in this chapter came from Stone's History of Colorado.

Chapter 19---Narrow Gauges and Broad Visions
1---Beebe, Lucius and Clegg, Charles, Narrow Gauges of the Rockies.
2---Ibid.
3---Ibid.
4---Ormes, Robert, Railroads and the Rockies, Denver, 1963.

Chapter 20---Ouray, the Arrow
1---Southern Utes, A Tribal History, edited by Floyd A. O'Neil.
2---Sprague, Marshall, Massacre, the Tragedy at White River, Little, Brown and Co., 1957.
3---The Southern Utes, A Tribal History.
4---Ibid.
The best source of information regarding Chief Ouray is in Montrose, Colorado at the Historical Museum and the Montrose library. Other sources used have been mentioned in footnotes.

Chapter 21---New Lords of the Prairies
Andy Adams' The Log of a Cowboy is a vivid personal account of the trail drive and Alvin T. Steinel's History of Agriculture in Colorado give good accounts of the open range cattle industry.

Chapter 22---The Puritan Meets the Renegades
Marshall Sprague's Massacre, the Tragedy at White River is the most complete and useful guide to this event. Al Look's Utes Last Stand is a well-illustrated work on the Meeker episode. The Meeker Historical Society sponsored This is What I Remember, compiled and edited by Susan and John Bury, also useful.

Chapter 23---Towns, Farms, Fun and Games
The story of Colorado's festivals and holidays is briefly described and comes from Fritz's Colorado, the Centennial State, The Colorado Magazine, Mountain & Plain History Notes, State Historical Society, and the author's personal experience.

Chapter 24---The Bowl of Gold
Marshall Sprague's Money Mountain, Frank Water's Midas of the Rockies, along with Fred and Jo Mazzulla's pictoral account of Cripple Creek and the Pikes Region were principle aids in this chapter.

Chapter 25---King of the Cannibals
The story of Alferd Packer has been told and retold so many times and it has improved with each telling, making it difficult to separate the facts from the myths. Marshall Sprague

includes mention of Packer in Massacre, the Tragedy at White River; Wilson Rockwell takes a stab at the tale in Sunset Slope; William Blair, The Story of Packer, the Maneater is another account. Sidney Jocknik's Early Days on the Western Slope of Colorado is probably the oldest account, written in 1913; Betty Wallace, in Gunnison Country, also includes this epic tale, along with most of the newspapers in the Centennial State.

Chapter 26--Victorian Days
Fred and Jo Muzzulla have written several accounts of the life styles of the Victorian Age; Holladay Street by Max Miller and Fred Muzzulla, Ballantine Books, 1971, portrays Denver's illustrious past in a forthright manner.

Chapter 27--The Rocky Mountain Canary
Sources mentioned in chapter.

Chapter 28--Labor Strife and Silver Politics
Sources consulted in preparing this chapter were Sprague, Money Mountain; Fritz, Colorado, the Centennial State; Ubbelohde, A Colorado History; United Banks of Colorado, Colorado Headlines and Colorado Magazine.

Chapter 29--The Century Turns
Ubbelohde, A Colorado History; Fritz, Colorado, the Centennial State; Hall, History of the State of Colorado; The Special Centennial Magazine, This is Colorado (Denver Post) were sources for this chapter.

Chapter 30--The Hectic Twenties
Fritz, Colorado, the Centennial State; United Banks of Colorado, Colorado Headlines; Ubbelohde, A Colorado History; Denver Post Special Centennial Magazine, This is Colorado; Burroughs, Where the West Stayed Young; and Bannon, The Spanish Borderlands Frontier, 1513-1821 were helpful in compiling this chapter.

Chapter 31--Depression and World War II
Sources consulted were Ubbelohde, A Colorado History; Fritz, Colorado, the Centennial State; Denver Post Centennial Magazine, This is Colorado; Colorado Magazine for articles on the Nisei and The Denver Post for additional information.

Chapter 32--Looking Ahead
Most helpful for this chapter were Gregg Chancellor and Sherry Pahler of the Division of Commerce and Development of the State of Colorado. They provided Colorado, a Regional Approach, an important summary of Colorado, also, The Denver Post, "Colorado, the Dynamic Present," First of Four Special Denver Post Issues and United States Bank of Colorado, Colorado Headlines, plus additional publications of the Colorado Division of Commerce and Development and the Colorado Division of Planning.

Younger, Cole, 100
Younger, Jim, 100
Yucca, 18
Yuma Indians, 62
Yuma Man, 8, 10, 15

Zink, 124
Zuni, 62